ITHELL COLQUHOUN

ARTIST AND OCCULTIST

Genius of the Fern Loved Gully: The Supersensual Life of Ithell Colquhoun, Artist and Occultist by Amy Hale

FIRST PUBLISHED by Strange Attractor Press in 2020, in a limited hardback and unlimited paperback edition.

DESIGN by Tihana Šare.
TYPESET in Alverata Regular & Irregular.

ISBN: 9781907222863

DISTRIBUTED by The MIT Press, Cambridge, Massachusetts. And London, England.

PRINTED AND BOUND in Estonia by Tallinna Raamatutrükikoda.

STRANGE ATTRACTOR PRESS
BM SAP, London, WC1N 3XX UK,
www.strangeattractor.co.uk

Genius of the
Fern Loved Gully:

THE SUPERSENSUAL LIFE OF

ITHELL COLQUHOUN

ARTIST AND OCCULTIST

AMY HALE

CONTENTS

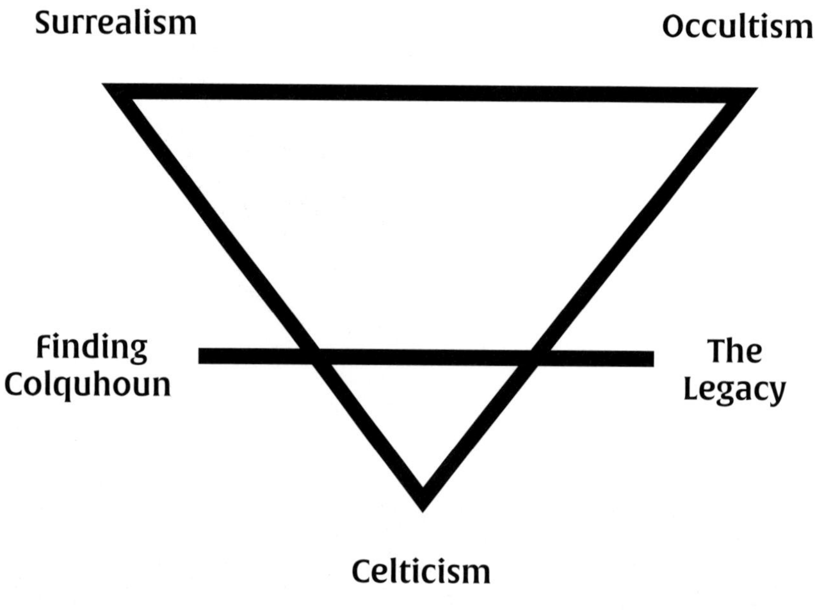
Surrealism
Occultism
Finding Colquhoun
The Legacy
Celticism

TO

all the women magicians,
past, present and future. May
our stories continue to be told.

I – Finding Colquhoun

NEXT PAGE Colquhoun in her garden at Stone Cross Cottage, photographed by Philip Stokes, c. 1977–1984.

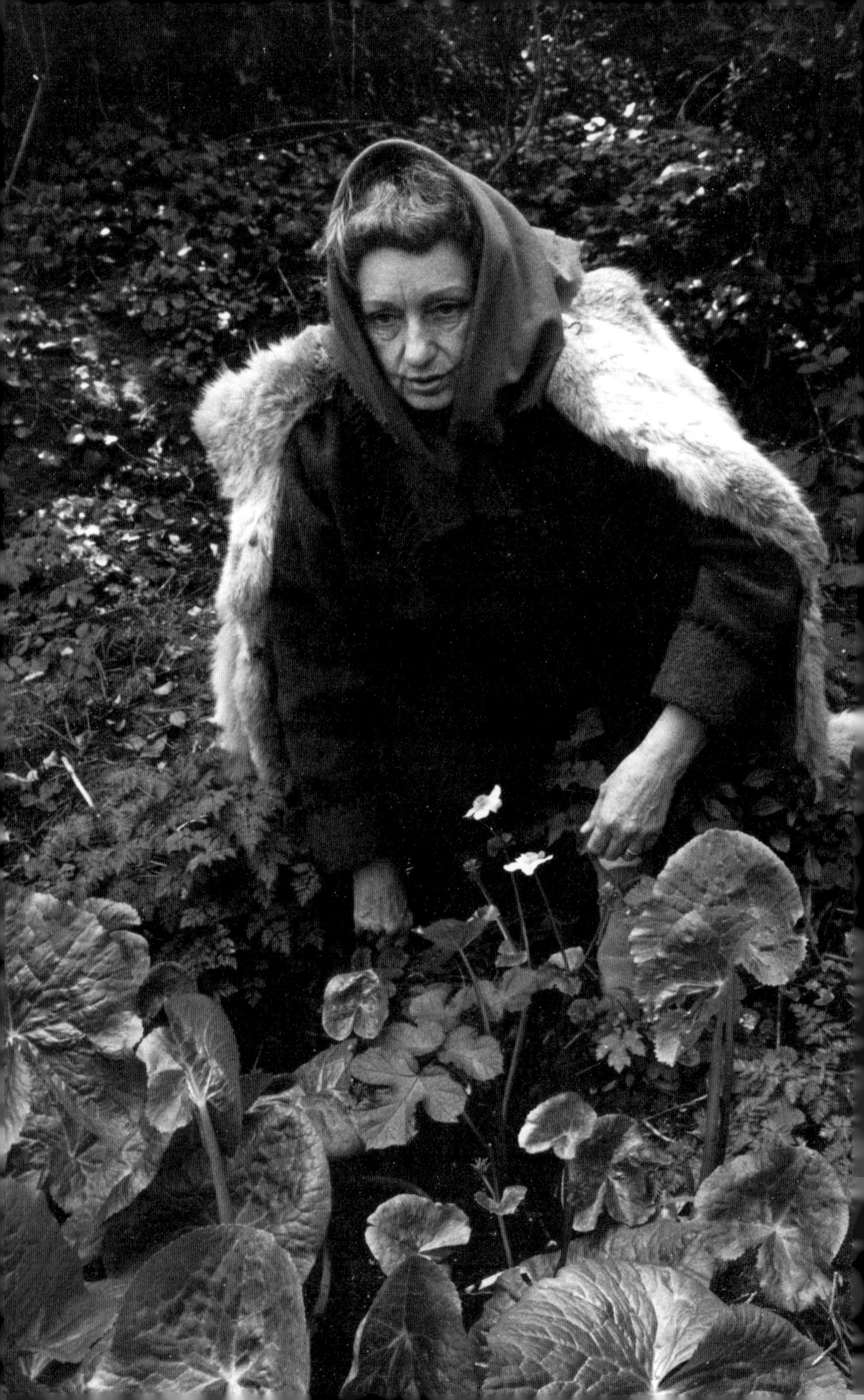

1

It's 'EYE-thell'. It was her middle name. Her given name was Margaret Ithell Colquhoun, and Ithell was also one of her mother's middle names. Perhaps this was a small way of asserting her mother's influence in her line. It is not a form of Ethel. Colquhoun claimed Benedict Ithell, deputy treasurer of Chelsea Hospital in the 17th century, as a maternal ancestor, and at one stage she was working on a biography of him. It never materialised, but the name carries on, perpetually eluding correct pronunciation. Still, Peggy would never have suited her. Ithell Colquhoun was a challenging personality. I have also come to believe that she was the most consequential, creative and committed female occultist of the twentieth century, and occultists don't exactly have a reputation for being easy to deal with.

When I first learned of Colquhoun, it was the year 2000. I had been working in Cornwall as an anthropologist for six years studying everything Celtic: Cornish nationalists, Cornish language fanatics, Pagans, Druids, and King Arthur enthusiasts, frequently in exquisite combinations. I was told of Colquhoun over lunch with a friend in Penzance. 'No one has told you about Ithell Colquhoun?'

> 'Never heard of her. Who is she?'
>
> 'She was a woman Surrealist who died in 1988. Eccentric. Really into the occult and witchcraft. She was a Druid! Lived right up the hill from Newlyn. Some people around here still remember her, but she fell out with most people. The Tate has all her papers. She's right up your alley.'

I was surprised I hadn't heard of her before. Paganism and the occult history of Cornwall was a huge interest of mine; I had done part of my PhD on it but had never heard of Ithell Colquhoun. My friend, another American about 25 years my senior, ran the West Cornwall Art Archive, which documented the art scenes that dominated the cultural history of much of late 19th and early 20th century West Cornwall. She is an incredible human database of artistic activity there. Although Surrealism as a movement has had one or two notable historical moments in Cornwall, such as the 1937 Surrealist gathering in Falmouth, Surrealism was never a significant part of the story of the artists' colonies in St. Ives and Newlyn, so I wondered what caused this particular Surrealist to settle there.

I discovered that in most books on Surrealism addressing women, Ithell Colquhoun was merely a footnote, and that she was kicked out of the British Surrealist movement for being too committed to esoteric research. I also found that she was known in occult circles as the writer of *The Sword of Wisdom*, an idiosyncratic biography of Samuel 'MacGregor' Mathers , a founder of the Hermetic Order of the Golden Dawn, published in 1975. The book was one of the first to look at the members of the Golden Dawn in any real detail, but due to the inclusion of some of Colquhoun's own personal occult history and a lot of seemingly unverified gossip, it was often dismissed as interesting reading but unreliable history. I also learned that, after her marriage fell apart in the late 1940s, she lived in Lamorna and wrote one of the first books about the sacred landscapes of Cornwall. How had I not heard of this woman?

Here was a woman artist and eccentric figure in Cornwall who was in danger of being forgotten. I made a pitch to my boss to send me up to London to poke around in the archives at the Tate, and he agreed to let me see what I could find. Back in 2000, the Tate archives were in a warehouse in an alleyway separate from the museum building, with concrete floors and simple tables. The staff warned me that her papers had not yet been catalogued.

I told them that was fine; I was just eager to see what they had. I was given a small pencil to make notes with. I waited for some time after the archivist walked back through the heavy glass doors into the warehouse, and I had no idea what she was going to bring.

When she returned, she was wheeling a large flat trolley with 25 boxes on it, precariously perched. 'Here you go.' I was stunned by the sheer amount of material in front of me, and I didn't know where to start. Over the next five days, I went through as many of the boxes as I could, trying to get an overview of what was there in the thousands of pages before me, yet wanting to deeply and slowly inhale every piece. There were dozens of manuscripts, poems, weird magical experiments on graph paper, conjurations of angels, love spells, petitions to healers, colourful tesseracts, magical journals and so, so many letters. I had never seen anything like it. It became very clear that she was very well connected in the British magical community of the mid-20th century. She seemed to know everyone, yet no one now knew of her. I returned to Cornwall in an excited frenzy. This felt like a monumental discovery.

By 2001 I had returned to the States, but I still wanted to continue researching the life of this incredible woman of whom I had only had the most tantalising glimpse. I found that many of her papers and art works were dispersed and hard to access. I knew that the Tate was busy cataloguing all her material, which was an exciting development, but it meant that the archive was going to be inaccessible to researchers for quite some time. I also started getting e-mail announcements that some of her papers and letters were being sold by private dealers into private collections. A London colleague explained that while she was still alive, in her vulnerable later years, someone had gained her confidence and told her he would save her most important magical correspondence and artifacts and use them as a basis for an archive dedicated to her life and work. This cache included the famous portrait of 'MacGregor' Mathers, painted by his wife Moina, that had been entrusted to Colquhoun's care. Years after her death, these items started appearing in sale catalogues of occult manuscripts and the remnants of private collections. Colquhoun wasn't exactly a household name, but she was known among occultists, and her letters contained secrets. Secrets people wanted kept secret.

A couple of years later, when I heard that the Tate had finished cataloguing her material and made it available to researchers again, I started going over to London regularly. I'd stay for weeks at a time, visiting the Tate daily. I started to see the more poignant artifacts of her life: a pair of small, white Masonic gloves gifted to her as a token of deep love from her French lover. A love spell written for a woman she had fallen in love with in Greece in the early 1930s. Pictures of her home, and her cat, and Colquhoun herself, thin, blonde, and sexy with unusual, slightly bulging eyes and a love of nude sunbathing. I was starting to understand how she thought, what compelled her, what obsessed her, the lovers she pushed away, the magical systems she rejected and embraced. I wondered if she ever imagined that one day an American woman would be sifting through these papers trying to put her life in order. I suspect she would have loved this attention. I can also imagine her chiding me for every theory about her I get wrong, because for all that is left behind for me to see, there is so much that is missing and so much unexplained.

On one British visit while I was staying in Penzance with my American friend, she mentioned that the contents of Ithell's studio had all gone to the National Trust, and perhaps she could arrange a visit for me to see the works they held there. We drove from Penzance to the National Trust estate, Lanhydrock near Bodmin, a huge old Victorian manor house on many acres of manicured land with forests and gardens. It was winter, so the house was cold and quiet. I was shown to a side room off the main reception area. Again, I had no idea what I was in for.

The curator of the property built a messy pile before me consisting of file folders stuffed with loose papers. They contained thousands of drawings, sketches, mock-ups for larger works, murals, book jackets and illustrations. Again, clear occult content was recognisable: the

Kabbalistic tree of life in various colours and guises, giant blocky heads and torsos in numerous odd magical colour schemes, strange buildings looking like a mating of Le Corbusier and Escher, attempts at generating fourth-dimensional portals through sacred megalithic monuments, granite phalluses thrusting into and out of the earth, and giant gynaecological caves on beaches. It was clear from the dates on the paintings and the Tate archives that she would work on a theme or experiment for many, many years at a time, returning to it over and over again, sometimes for decades. The volume of art placed in front of me, mostly uncatalogued, was staggering. The real shock discovery of this first visit was the literally hundreds of explicit erotic watercolours and drawings. It was clear that she was theorising about sex magic in a way that was unparalleled for women artists at the time, and certainly not by women occultists, at any time. Colquhoun had a reputation for breaking boundaries with her art, which was frequently explicit, but this collection was beyond anything I had imagined.

It was just the tip of the iceberg. In a rather run down, cold, dusty shed out in the back of the property there were even more pieces that had been untouched for many years. This freezing shed contained everything from shining images of Goddesses and angels to less successful found art attempts involving broken egg cartons and spray paint. As a whole, Lanhydrock contained nearly everything she had done that was not already in a collection, from her earliest artistic scrawlings and her brilliantly abstract 'Taro' cards from 1977, to some of her final pieces from the 1980s. When the National Trust had received this collection as part of a bequest from Colquhoun's confusing and Byzantine will, they were unprepared. This was not their area. They couldn't keep it, and yet they couldn't sell it. Researchers could hardly use it or even access it. The importance and enormity of this collection and the strangeness and brilliance that it held made me even more determined to tell her story.

The story I was seeing was something different from that I had found in the books. Although most historical mentions of Ithell Colquhoun focus on her relationship with the Surrealist movement in Britain, her commitment to occultism was more consequential and, in fact, her Surrealism was in service to that obsession, which was the principal driver of most of her life's work. Perhaps she should be recast primarily as a woman occultist with a tremendous output of writing, esoteric art and theory that greatly contributes to our understanding of what occult practice looks like. Like many occultists, she had been sidelined and marginalised. She was brilliant but fractious, didn't know how to promote herself, and died with a tremendous legacy that was in danger of going silent. We now have the opportunity to see, through her writings, art, and esoteric pursuits, the ways in which a woman was making her mark in the traditionally male-dominated world of 20th century occultism and how occultism shaped her body of visual art and writings. We can also look at the impact a number of important cultural moments and movements in post-War Britain had on her life and work, including the rise of interest in Celtic ethno-nationalism, feminism, and the growth of contemporary Paganism. Ultimately, the story is about how this woman, in the quest for enlightenment, made sense of the changing world around her, and how the forces animating that changing world came to shape her spirituality and ultimately her art.

For the next decade, I went back and forth between the US and London, working to understand the various pieces of Colquhoun's life. It may be that because she left so much by way of letters and art that the lacunae in her archives feel like such gaping holes. So many of the letters regarding her life in Surrealism are missing, but there are tantalising clues pointing to them, such as a slip of paper with Man Ray's address. There are some notes from her time in several magical orders in the 1950s and 1960s, but much of the correspondence about that time is in private hands. Several generous people have come forward to share their knowledge and collections with me, for which I am so very grateful.

Over the years, I have come to realise that I have been in contact with a cantankerous spirit who still has a mind of her own. She tried hard to be heard while she was alive. Her archives contain many rejection letters, but she did make some very unusual pitches, such as the one, probably from the 1960s, offering to do a radio commentary for the BBC about her views on women's clothing. What starts as a mild opinion piece ends up as a full-blown rant about how clothing enslaves women. She wasn't wrong, but did she really expect that the BBC would give her a platform for these views? She was so often ahead of her time and unafraid to punch convention square in the face, but she also wanted recognition. She wanted to change the way people thought. She tried. Hard. Yet she was often her own worst enemy, in life and also in death.

Over the years, the secrets of her brilliance started to seep out. In the mid-2000s, there was an emerging buzz about esoteric art. Once again, artists were becoming inspired to communicate with other realms and to help their audiences see other worlds, and this interest has grown since. Women Surrealists are finally coming into their own power, and are now being seen on their own terms instead of as muses or companions reflecting the genius of Surrealist men. A few key exhibitions showed Colquhoun's work, including the *Dark Monarch: Magic and Modernity* show held at the Tate St. Ives in 2009. Young women artists in Britain heard about Ithell, saw her art, and became inspired to use some of her automatic methods. In Cornwall, she became one of the witchy ancestors, as local artists and Pagans started honouring her life, building altars to her memory and recreating her ritualistic and artistic experiments. The doors started to open. Finally, her light started to shine through.

§

This is not a linear biography. It is a book about the enthusiasms and passions that shaped Ithell Colquhoun's life and how they wove together against the backdrop of subcultural, artistic and literary movements in mid-20th century Britain. Colquhoun was not a woman of short-term obsessions. Many of the themes and interests that define her life and work were established in her twenties and rearticulated through her life. Although her interests became refined and took different shapes with different projects, her worldview was remarkably consistent, and she was wedded to it. She believed in a highly structured, idealistic universe with many layers, forms and entities that could be reached by the sensitive and the adept. Most of her artistic and esoteric projects were in support of this vision.

Anyone reading this hoping for a solid art-historical approach will be sorely disappointed. I am an anthropologist and folklorist by training, and this book is in many ways an ethno-history. I will trace the threads of many ideas and movements to explore how they shaped the art and practice of a singular individual. I have chosen three different but interrelated lenses through which to view Colquhoun's work: Surrealism, Occultism and Celticism. Although there is a loose chronology to these sections, these were life-long interconnected themes in her art and magic. She became a Surrealist because she believed she was a Celt and that gave her a natural ability to penetrate and communicate with other realms and her own dreamy subconscious. Her occultism provided the fundamentals for using Surrealist automatic techniques as a form of divination and contemplation of the beyond. Although these themes are foundational to Colquhoun's own personal and idiosyncratic work, they also reflect wider themes in mid-century Britain, as people were trying to heal from the devastation of war in a radically reshaped Europe by searching out that which was constant and sacred.

Colquhoun was in this world but not of it. She was born and lived between things, a condition of which she was keenly aware from her earliest days, and which she ultimately embraced as one who worked to traverse the many planes of existence, opening up portals for herself and others to take otherworldly journeys. In addition to considering the wider arcs of history, this study aims to understand Colquhoun's work within the matrix of a variety of alternative and subcultural discourses in mid-20th century Britain, where there is still very little understanding of women's participation. This is a story of a woman's life, but the focus is as much on what shaped her. Looking at the wider frame of reference for Colquhoun can give us clues to how she navigated the world. Colquhoun's interests and preoccupations arose from her circumstances and the time in which she lived.

First, Colquhoun came from what would have been considered a firmly middle-class background, and one which afforded her a great measure of privilege. Like many middle-class British people, she professed a great spiritual connection to the countryside and a romanticised love of the pastoral and timeless, but her antimodern sensibilities were a measure and feature of her privilege and upbringing. She idealised a life that never entrapped her. She lived modestly on a trust for most of her life. She could travel overseas, and for long periods of time. She was bilingual, speaking French as well as English. She owned property in both London and Cornwall. While she sold art, had some commercial commissions and was interested in the commercial applications of architecture and design, it was only for a short time that she held anything that could be considered to be conventional employment.

Second, her family background was deeply entrenched in British colonialism. She was born in northern India into a military family who had been working in India for many generations. She had a deep connection to the British landscape, but much of her own identity and sense of ethnicity was fractured. Although she moved to England as an infant, one shouldn't assume a confident feeling of Britishness. When she wasn't concerned with navigating the ethers, she spent a lot of time navigating her own place in the world.

Third, Colquhoun's formative years were spent during times of extraordinary social upheaval: the First World War, the Russian Revolution, the Spanish Civil War and the Second World War not only devastated Europe; they also all challenged the traditional order. Changing social roles, the end of monarchies, and the rise of Communism and fascism all formed the historical backdrop against which esoteric subcultures were developing, and directly responding to, in the early twentieth century. It was in this half century, of extreme disorder, that Colquhoun sought the ultimate order which esoteric societies tantalisingly offered.

Fourth, this was a time of changing gender roles for women, and Colquhoun resisted the social expectations for a woman of her class. She took lovers, was married only briefly, and seemed uninterested in having children. She was bisexual, and this may have been uncomfortable for her. She ultimately rejected same-sex relationships, and was openly hostile toward male homosexuality. Nevertheless, she idealised the hermaphrodite as a spiritual ideal.

Colquhoun both reflected and rejected the social currents and contexts in which she worked. This was a singular artist and individual who challenged convention to push her own boundaries and those of her audience. Her feminism does not fit into typically theorised understandings of the term. She may not have ever labelled herself as a feminist, but women's concerns were always at the forefront of her work. She maintained a particular esoteric worldview that, at one stage, the genders were united and the Divine Feminine was a given; the liberation of women is, therefore, an essential component of returning humanity to its divine origins, and we can only move forward to escape our rapidly degrading state through collective enlightenment.

Colquhoun's primary motivation through all her work is the pursuit of her own enlightenment. We may never know if she was happy with her own levels of attainment in that regard, but her journey has left us with a remarkable look into one woman's unique vision.

II – 'Already I knew my own mind'

NEXT PAGE A young Colquhoun looking thoughtful with her sketchbook.

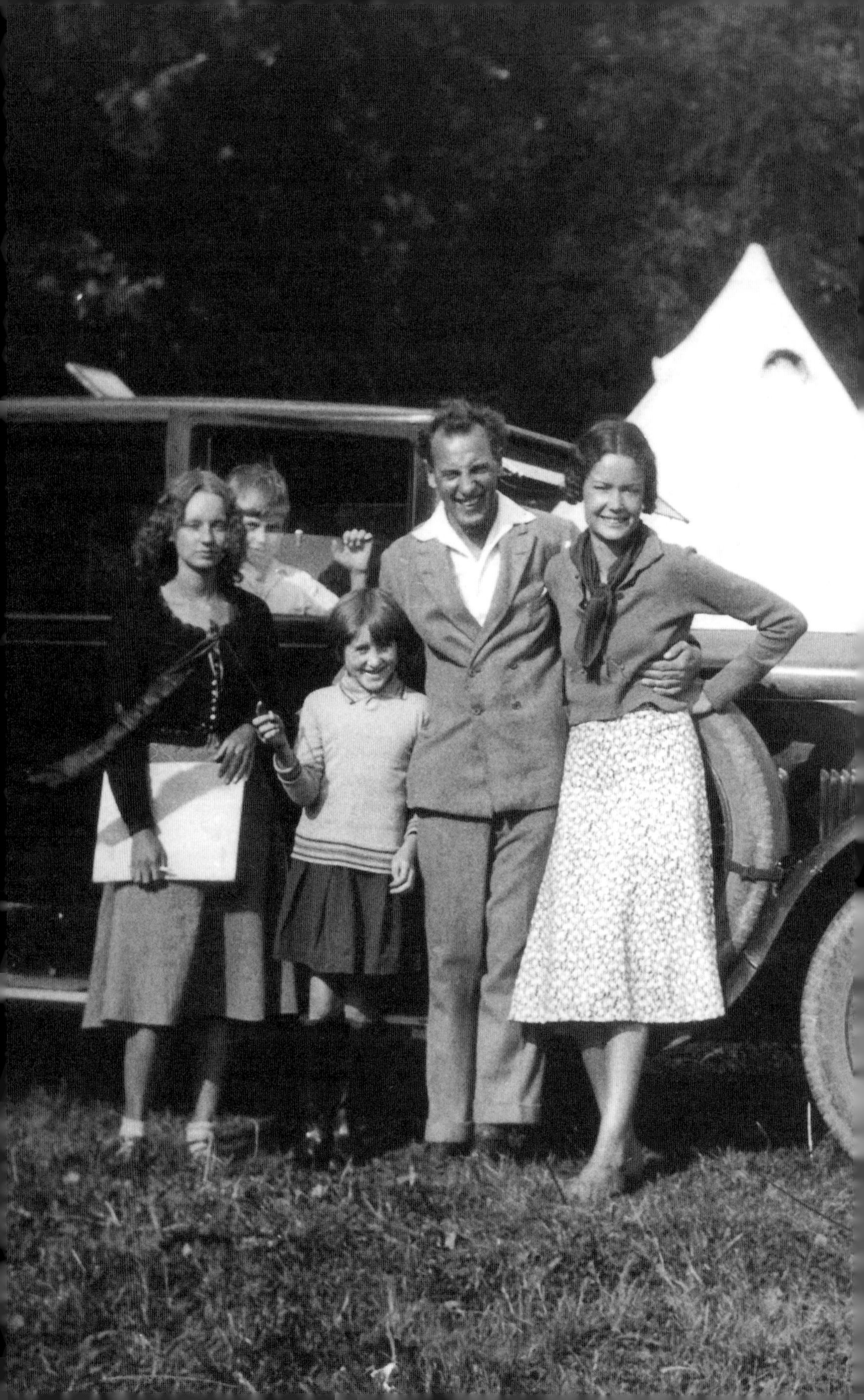

II

> At ten I said that when I grew up I never wanted to do anything but paint, and write and study nature. Already I knew my own mind.
>
> — Ithell Colquhoun
> 'The Future' from *Until Twelve*

It is tempting to construct an image of Ithell Colquhoun as a remote occultist, driven by nature, living in the distant wilds of Cornwall rejecting civilisation and modernity, but we need to keep in mind that Colquhoun's condition, and in many ways her view of the ideal world, was one born of privilege. She didn't really have to work, she came from a well-off family, and her idealization of the pre-modern came with never really having to live without a safety net. If we look at the life and work of Ithell Colquhoun as, partially, a study in the relationship between tradition and innovation, her family is a good starting point. Colquhoun was enmeshed in generations of the military on all sides of her family. Her father, grandfathers, great grandfathers, and uncles were all deeply embedded in the British military, serving in India and elsewhere. We can see a long line of order, discipline and tradition that runs deep in these family lines, reinforced at every turn, until there was resistance. And resist she did.

The circumstances of Colquhoun's birth caused a split sense of identity that she struggled to reconcile. She was born in Assam, northern India, where her father was stationed. Although the British military would inculcate in its soldiers a strong sense of Britishness, especially in a colonial context, there is still the inescapable fact that having your family in one place for several generations will impact your sense of identity. India acted as a reflecting glass for Colquhoun's Britishness, particularly her Englishness, and she chose to define herself in other terms. Ithell Colquhoun had deep roots in Northern India from her family, and she felt separated from them, her entire life because she was never allowed to fully experience the culture.

> I used to claim that I was a Hindou because I was born in India. A strict Hindou must not only be born there but must remain there, never leaving the sub-continent.[1]

But Colquhoun could not meet these requirements. After looking into the history of the birthplace she considered her homeland, she concluded:

> Vedic Hinduism was an intrusive system which gradually imposed itself on the age-long animism of the population. This explains and underlies my support of the animist viewpoint.[2]

This is how she made sense of her condition. Although her parents returned to India frequently, she left as a very young child and never returned. Although it is common for people to think of ethnicity and heritage as a thing of the blood, and Colquhoun certainly believed that as well, culture is also inherited by people through lived experience in places. Even though Colquhoun never really lived in India, she felt its impact, and struggled with the liminality of having been born in a place, with genuine cultural roots set down by generations of her family working there, and then being torn away to move to a new, ostensibly ancestral homeland. She felt, having been born in India, that she was tied to the land, the people and the spirituality of the place, and that she had been cheated out of her birthright.

Colquhoun's family had been in India for at least two generations, as both her father and her grandfather had served there. Her father, Henry Archibald Colebrooke Colquhoun, was born in India, as was his father, and he did his early schooling in the northern state of Assam, before returning to England to earn a degree at Oxford. In 1895 he returned to Assam and served as Deputy Commissioner. Assam is a state in the northeast of India adjacent to Tibet, primarily Hindu with a large Muslim minority. It is easy to imagine how her family circumstance might have stoked Colquhoun's own interest in Tantra and her lifelong description of herself as an animist. Colquhoun's father was deeply invested in the people he was working with, and took an interest in Manipuri culture. In 1902 he was working on a manuscript about traditional Manipuri folksongs that he had collected and translated. Later Colquhoun worked on an introduction to the manuscript, but it was never published.

Her deep attachment to her Celtic roots was come by honestly. Her family on her father's side was from Scotland, and her mother was of Irish descent. Colquhoun's mother was Georgia Francis Ithell Manley, and she was in India when she met Colquhoun's father. She, too, came from a military family and had seven siblings. Georgia's father, William George Nicholas Manley, was born in Dublin, evidently of the Anglo-Irish caste, which may partially explain the ambivalence Colquhoun later shows toward the Catholic Irish in *Crying of the Wind*. He was a fierce army surgeon who survived many battles and must have witnessed unspeakable things. He was a heavily decorated warrior, with ten awards including the Victoria Cross.[3] He served with the British Ambulance Corps bringing aid in conflicts worldwide, including the Crimean War, the New Zealand 'Maori' Wars, and the Franco-Prussian War. Manley seemed like a quite unpleasant man, which given his experiences might come as no surprise. Colquhoun once described him as distinguished in battle, angry and impulsive. He appeared to have no respect for women, and treated his daughter poorly. Georgia Francis had an ability with the violin and although she was a music teacher, her father forbade her to play the violin in public. In fact she was not allowed to marry until his death, which occurred in 1901.

> Gnawing nervousness – should we ever be ready? A cab, a train, a boat, a train a cab. Diarrhoea and travel-sickness next day –

> surely we would never arrive. Where were we going? Was everything happening at the same time everywhere? My fifth birthday at our destination.
>
> — 'First Anxiety' from *Until Twelve*

Colquhoun's childhood was unsettled in many ways. In accord with common beliefs that English children should not remain in India due to health concerns, Colquhoun was relocated in 1907 at the age of one, celebrating her first birthday on an ocean liner back to England. She lived as an infant in London and Devon, sometimes with her mother and mostly without her father, who she did not see again until she was six. Colquhoun and her younger brother Robin were sent to the Isle of Wight to stay with her mother's aunt while her mother returned to India to be with her father. Colquhoun and Robin were shuttled around to family members until 1919, when they returned to the family home in Cheltenham. Her father only returned to England in 1921. Colquhoun's early relationships with her parents were marked by absence, but nature rushed in to fill the emotional void left by a lack of parental nurturing.

> Someone was employed to teach me to read, but I did not want to learn this, or anything (except perhaps how to paint) since I already knew more than any book could tell me.
>
> — 'Education' from *Until Twelve*

Most of Colquhoun's early education was conducted by tutors and nannies. Perhaps as a response to the rigid atmosphere in which her mother Georgia was raised, her remote parenting style seems very unrestrictive. According to sections of Colquhoun's unpublished autobiography, *Until Twelve*, her mother had some rather unconventional child-rearing practices. Georgia believed that learning to read too early would harm the development of eyesight and memory, so Colquhoun could not read until she was eight, and even then only simple things with illustrations. She was also not made to wear confining shoes as a child, so she was never forced to wear 'ladies' shoes that would force her feet to develop unnaturally. This may well have shaped Colquhoun's own views on high heels and confining dress for women, with which she disagreed all her life.

It is evident that Colquhoun's childhood condition instilled in her a life-long love of nature and the idea of 'the natural'. Her childhood almost sounds too idyllic, having been completely unfettered by academic expectation. She describes running around in fields, catching butterflies and enjoying the quiet of her pastoral surroundings. Given Colquhoun's lack of teaching in her childhood, that she was able to excel in the way that she eventually did is testament to the raw horsepower of her intellect. It also helps explain her highly developed visual sensibility. She wasn't restricted by words.

Her grandmother on her mother's side was from Cheltenham, and this unique town played a very important role in Colquhoun's development and early life. Cheltenham, near the Cotswolds, was a very early example of a spa resort town, having developed in the early eighteenth century around mineral springs. Growing up in an area where ideas of nature and health were so intertwined may have influenced Colquhoun's own sensibilities regarding alternative health care. Cheltenham seemed to have a progressive streak in several areas, including the education of women.

Although Colquhoun had no formal schooling as a young child, her later education supported her talents in very direct ways. It is likely that Colquhoun's feminist orientation was at least partially stoked by her education at Cheltenham Ladies College, which Colquhoun attended from 1919 when she was 13 years old until 1925. Despite the traditional sounding name, this was no finishing school. Cheltenham Ladies College was founded as a school for women in 1853, and had a radical agenda for educating young women. Very early on it promoted education in maths and sciences, participation in sports, and careers, at a time when many thought this degree of professional education for women was unacceptable. Undoubtedly, her early schooling would have affected Colquhoun's developing sense of equity for women, as the school was actively addressing the ways in which women's roles were changing. Perhaps her parents not only sought for their daughter a good, solid education, but one which would prepare her for being a woman in a modern world.

> My first painting was an oval rose on a triple stem, with a bud at each side; my second was a purple sun with orange rays setting behind a green slope.
>
> — 'Flowers and Light' from *Until Twelve*

Yet even in a school that emphasised practicalities, Colquhoun nevertheless gravitated towards the dreamy side and a love of the pastoral. Many of her early notebooks from her time at Cheltenham Ladies College show fine-lined, beautifully delicate drawings of fairies, elves and goblins. By the age of 14 she already showed exceptional figurative skill. Clearly attracted to natural forms and botanical subjects even at a young age, as a young teen she completed an early series of still-life watercolour studies of flowers in vases. Beyond representation, however, we also see her facility with illustration in ethereal watercolours of young girls being showered with leaves or feeding peacocks by hand. As a young girl she also visited Donegal in Ireland, possibly to visit family, where she completed a number of landscape studies; another theme she returned to later in life.

From 1925 to 1927, Colquhoun pursued a more focused arts education at Cheltenham School of Art, as it was known then, where she studied under E.A. Sallis Benney before he became Principal of the Brighton School of Art. The curriculum was well grounded in a variety of artistic pursuits. Although Colquhoun leaned toward the fine arts, she was also well trained vocationally. During this time she undertook her first formal studies in architectural drawing, another theme to which she returns at several stages in the first half of her artistic career. We also see forays into theatre design, costuming and performance. She had already started her occult pursuits at this stage, and Cheltenham School of Art is where she staged her first alchemically themed work, *Bird of Hermes*, indicating her first graspings with the Philosopher's Stone. She

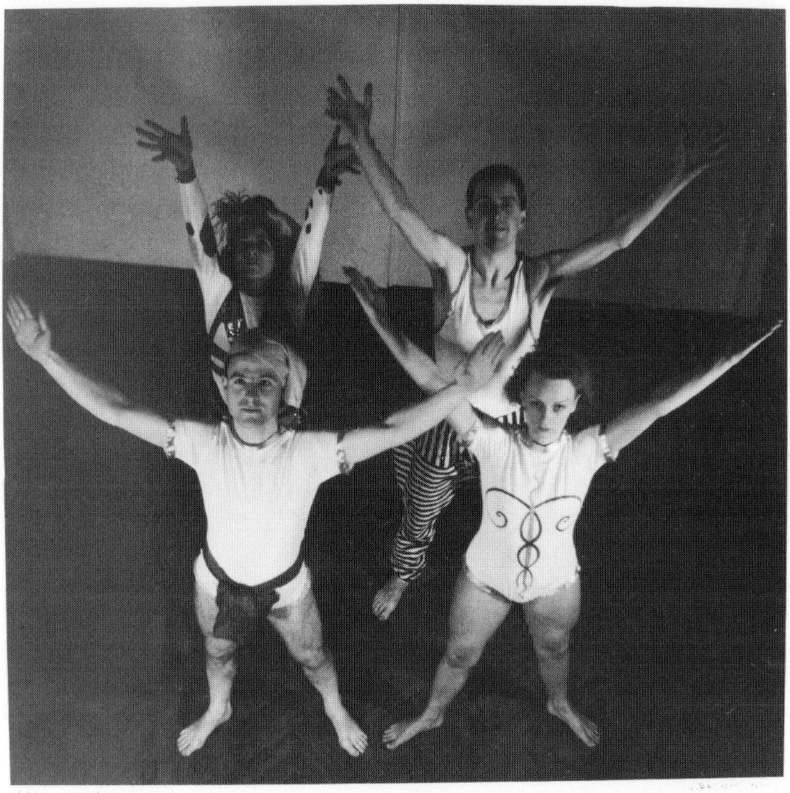

ABOVE Colquhoun in a dance performance at Cheltenham School of Art, 1925–1927. Photographed by Hugo van Wadenoyen.

also designed sets and costumes for the plays of other students and took roles in them. Yet despite her evident interest in dance at the time, the theatrical sensibility does not seem to have stuck with her. In fact, aside from poetry readings and one collaboration with a composer, Colquhoun ultimately seemed little attracted to performance.

The Slade

With a solid arts foundation from Cheltenham, in 1927 Colquhoun moved to London to continue her formal art training at the Slade School of Fine Arts. Here she immersed herself in the technical aspects of art, while also jumping feet first into the heady occult culture of early twentieth-century London. Her notebooks show evidence of her work in perspective, colour, and proportion, in addition to architectural and figurative studies.

But even within the traditional curriculum of a fine art school, Colquhoun was integrating the weird, occult and imaginative. Her archives show that within a fairly short time she took the foundations of her architectural interests and moved them into the realm of the fantastic, with Escher-like studies of structures in the sky, using odd angles and strange perspectives. She also played with occult themes and, on a number of occasions, instead of relegating occult material to private contemplative studies, she created pieces that were to be used as set design or that would otherwise have to be in some way confronted, such as tarot card studies for party decorations, or a party mural with alchemical themes. Although these choices may well not have been particularly controversial in that cultural moment in an art school, as with her earlier play *The Bird of Hermes*, Colquhoun was already forcing public engagement and dialogue with occult material, and was even exploring how occult themes might impact public spaces.

Although many of the themes that Colquhoun explored in her student work were standard subjects of the time for art students, she frequently selected stories that had a strong and challenging woman's point of view.[4] In 1929, Colquhoun tied for first place in the Slade Summer Composition with *Judith Showing the Head of Holofernes*, which was restored in the 1970s and which remains in the University College London collection. Colquhoun's Judith looks modern and triumphant in a flowing gown as she presents her trophy. Even in this painting we can see Colquhoun's evident interest in architecture. Towering buildings, again looking almost contemporary, fill the background space. Although they were representational, these still have the feel of the work of an illustrator, with figures and images feeling almost cartoonish at times.

Unsurprisingly, she continued her explorations of vocational aspects of design and public art, very likely as a required part of the diploma curriculum. Colquhoun took an early interest in mural painting, and made several attempts at becoming a commercial mural painter in her early and even mid-career. Three times she submitted entries to the Rome Scholarship in Mural Painting, yet was not successful. Nevertheless, Colquhoun kept occasionally returning to commercial applications for her art, in mural, architecture and design. Did she feel as though she needed to be prepared to make money from artistic endeavours, or did she have a genuine interest in public engagement and playing with the ways in which art, shape and colour can impact space?

Colquhoun received a Diploma in Arts in 1930 and her years after the Slade were, perhaps, unusual for a woman in her late twenties. No beau, no vocation; she was a woman of at least some means setting out on her own, but seemingly without much direction. Colquhoun had a family trust set aside to support her, and it seems it was at least enough to fund travel for several years, and perhaps to cultivate some eccentricities. She continued reading occult works, and sketching and painting. After she left the Slade in 1931, Colquhoun enjoyed several years of travel abroad, staying in a well-placed private studio in Paris, centrally located at 7 Rue de la Grande Chaumière. She was certainly enjoying the heady Paris art scene of the time, attending exhibitions and sketching, and also taking time to travel to various places in the Mediterranean. It is clear that this was a creatively formative period for her, and we can see the impact of the landscapes she encountered in her art and writing for decades to come, although she noted much later that this was not a period where she completed large scale projects, for which she would have required a personal studio. She continued her art training, occasionally picking up life drawing classes at the Académie Colarossi, known for its liberal approaches to allowing female students to draw male nude life models. During this period, she began her various interactions with the art world as an art professional and also started to develop her uncompromising position toward a number of social conventions.

Colquhoun was a single woman in her mid-twenties during her travels, and while many women of her age during this period may have been in search of a husband, this did not seem to be a primary concern for her. She played the field, which would have been expected, but she also found herself in some rather unconventional relationships. From 1933 to 1935 she spent time with the married archaeologist Humfry Payne, who had been appointed at a young age to the lofty position of Director of the British School in Athens. Colquhoun had visited Payne's excavations with her close friend from the Slade, Elektra Magnoletsi, who was based in Greece. Colquhoun and Payne had started a correspondence and spent what was clearly intimate time together, despite the fact that he was married to the writer Dilys Powell. In the end, however, Payne did not seem to share Colquhoun's aspirations for the relationship to become more serious, and she called it off shortly before he died tragically of septicaemia. Colquhoun's legacy of the relationship remains in the portrait she completed of him in 1935, now in the National Portrait Gallery.

In 1933, during her stay in Greece, the twenty-seven-year-old Colquhoun became deeply infatuated with a woman. She wrote about her obsession in a manuscript, 'Lesbian Shore', which was never published but exists in a number of hand-written drafts. It contains some of Colquhoun's most passionate writing, and the number of drafts perhaps suggest that she was working through a new-found set of emotional responses.

> And then my mind wandered into a Kabbalistic reverie and how each type of beauty has its own place on the tree of life and how the signs of the Zodiac and the planets that are at home in them can influence the forms of the body. Her beauty must be lunar, I thought, her morbid charm

> derives from the pallid spell weaving of Hecate. It has a piercing loveliness, it pierces the breast bone like light from the horns of the new moon. The architecture of her face is so proportioned the forms follow one another in so subtle a sequence that they seem to chime audibly and shine visibly with that 'claritas' or 'radiance' which the Seraphic Doctor calls essential lustre perceived.[5]

The woman in question was 'Kyria' or Andromache Kazou, about whom little is known. Colquhoun first came across her while staying in Mykonos, and her attraction was immediate and intense. The reverse of one page of a draft even entreats the Gods to bring the object of affection closer to her. The tale is one of longing and plotting to be closer, hoping that one day she might convince Kyria to model for her. Eventually she does, and we can see her beloved in several sketches and paintings from 1933 and 1934, titled *Kyria Kazou*. While 'Lesbian Shore' ends there, her story with Kyria does not.

A series of letters between them, in French, survives, but the story is not clear. They seem to have had a relationship of some sort, and Kazou seems to visited Colquhoun in Paris. Were they living as a couple among artistic lesbians in Paris, even briefly? It is hard to know, but Colquhoun in 'Lesbian Shore' seems unruffled by her affections. Interestingly, when Colquhoun finds that she is being pulled to 'the lesbian shore' she does not seem to experience much upset, confusion or reservation. Colquhoun appears to have made an offer for Kazou, who was a little older and divorced, to come and live with her in London. Ultimately, Kazou declined to do so. Was Colquhoun's intention that they live as a lesbian couple there? Perhaps. In any case, this would have still been a radical proposition for the early 1930s. Colquhoun had encountered lesbians and masculine women in her artistic circles and she would continue to cultivate friendships with lesbians throughout her artistic life, the socialite Dorothy Wellesley and the Lamorna-based painter Gluck being two examples. This seems to have been Colquhoun's only documented flirtation with an actual lesbian relationship, although one cannot discount the possibility of other same-sex encounters. Without a doubt, her interest in intimate, if not necessarily sexual, relationships between women was expressed in a number of contexts throughout her life, perhaps most intently in her novel *I Saw Water*, set on an other-worldly island of unconventional nuns. While Colquhoun eventually realised that committing to lesbian relationships was not going to suit her, there is no doubt that her attraction to women is a feature of her art and work which can't be ignored.

During the early to mid-1930s, Colquhoun's artistic subjects were somewhat quotidian and more than competently figurative, focusing on close studies of flowers and vegetation, images from her stay in the Mediterranean, portraits and figure studies, all of which seem like rather natural extensions of an art school curriculum. There is some occult content in her early work – her 1934 'Designs for A Painting on Silk' was a study of symbolism around Malkuth – but this is certainly not the focus of the bulk of her work. Mostly, during the period of her travels we see Colquhoun catching images in time: a laundry basket full of clothes, windows, a doorway. There are images of those she loved, Kazou, Payne and others who sat for her, in addition to studies of archaeological remains. This time abroad was clearly very fruitful, personally and professionally, as she prepared for life as an artist, and as with all things she was driven, passionate and went all out.

She exhibited in a 1933 Salon in Paris with three paintings. In May 1934 she had a floral study exhibited at the Royal Society of Art in Scotland, and correspondence with the British composer Rutland Boughton from 1935 suggests that Colquhoun may have been engaged in doing set design for him. Boughton composed operas on Celtic mythological, Arthurian and magical themes, which would have been in line with Colquhoun's emerging interests. In some senses she appeared to be drifting, yet her artistic output was nevertheless staggering and was soon to be revealed. By 1936, her thirtieth year, Colquhoun was ready to move forward.

1936 turned out to be an explosive year. After several years of creating and working towards a career as a showing artist, this was the year that she was truly ready to bloom. She maintained an apartment in London for several years after returning to Britain, but professionally she was working toward building a reputation as a local artist in the areas around Cheltenham where her parents still lived, possibly helped by their reputation. She won a commercial bid to decorate a hospital ward in the Moreton-in-Marsh hospital in Gloucestershire, not far from their home. In February of that year she had her first ever solo show at the Cheltenham Public Art Gallery, at which she showed 91 pieces, a major showing and a testament to the intensity of her production. In many ways this was an artistic coming out for her. Already, Colquhoun was making her mark with an unconventional artistic identity. The head of the Cheltenham School of Art, Mr. Seaton-White, opened the show and noted that her strong personality was the key principle that tied together the wide variety of subjects on display. He commented, with seeming affection, that 'I can quite realise that a large section of the public would fail to understand what Miss Colquhoun is driving at in a lot of cases.'[6]

This debut exhibition was wide-ranging and included not only some of her flower paintings and studies from her Mediterranean trip, but also her earlier large canvas works including *Death of the Virgin* (1931) and *Judgment of Paris* (1930). A local paper commented on her artistic industry, saying that the show was large and yet comprised under half of the art she had produced in the preceding five years. A few months later, in July, she had three pieces in an exhibition at Cheltenham Ladies College. But many of these pieces were years old by now, and she was still in the process of finding herself artistically.

Also in 1936, Colquhoun staged a show at the Fine Art Society focusing entirely on her botanical studies. Her pictures of flowers were detailed, intimate and sensual, and from her subject matter you can see where she was headed. She chose botanical studies that were already rich with the possibility of double entendre; lilies, gloxinia, bananas and cacti, with their metaphorical nature eager to be revealed. She found her subjects in the warmer climates of her travels, and also in the hothouses of Kew Gardens. It would ultimately be her passion for the natural world and all the mysteries it contains that provided her initial vehicle for the expressions of the mythic, the deeply sexual and the surreal. And Surrealism was about to find her.

‘OBJECTIVE HAZARD’:

III – Surrealism

NEXT PAGE The chateau at Chemilieu, 1939, L–R: Colquhoun, Elizabeth Onslow Ford, Ann Matta, Esteban Francés, Gordon Onslow Ford.

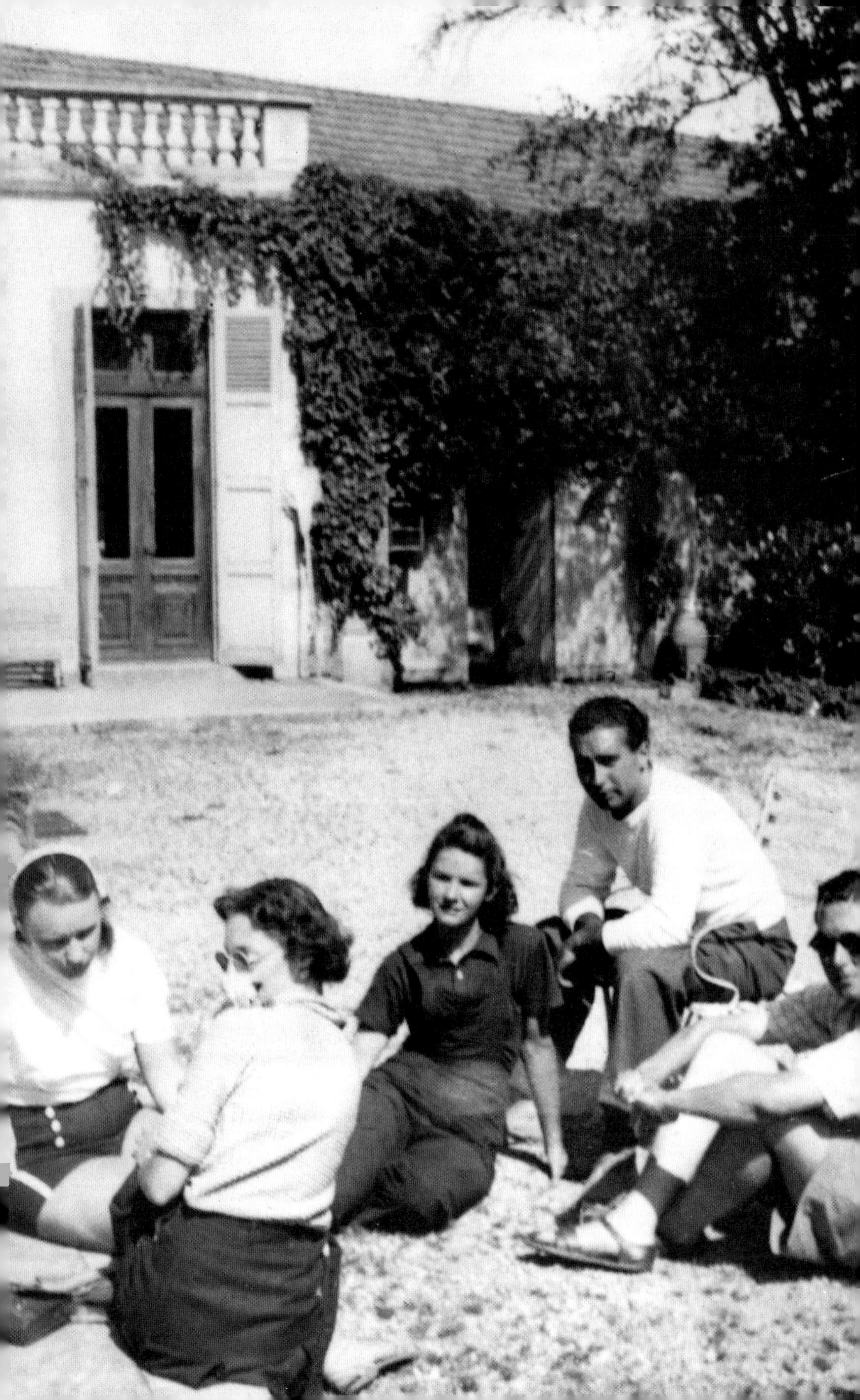

III

In looking at the big picture of Colquhoun's life-long commitment to Surrealist methods, the body of work she created is visually very different from other widely recognised women Surrealists. Throughout her life most of her output was automatic in nature, and even her representational work lacks the tight yet dreamy and witchy quality of a Leonora Carrington or Leonor Fini. Most of her Surrealist work after the early 1940s is not highly representational, nor is it based upon jarring juxtapositions of imagery. Colquhoun's work is full of codes and symbolic power, but it does not always provide a visual narrative, real or imaginary, that is easily accessible to the viewer. Yet thematically Colquhoun does have a lot in common with other Surrealist counterparts, particularly Carrington, in that she addresses similar themes of myth, dreams, Celticity, power and liminality. It is arguable that while Colquhoun identified as a Surrealist all of her life, and was one of the few women Surrealists who was completely comfortable with that label, she intersected many categories and the esoteric content of her art is as least as important, if not more so, than her Surrealism when evaluated in terms of a relationship to an overall movement. It may also be that the visual, cultural and theoretical matters which interest historians of Surrealism are uncomfortably realised in Colquhoun's work. So, while there are reasons to place her alongside other Surrealists the fit, as with many aspects of Colquhoun's life and work, will be somewhat awkward.

In a 1986 *New York Times* piece John Russell called 1936 the year that Surrealism truly dominated the international art scene.[7] Although

Surrealism had been challenging the art world on the Continent for twenty years, in 1936 three separate shows in New York, Paris and London took Surrealism to new audiences. The 1936 International Surrealist Exhibition in London must have been a breathtaking spectacle, and had a lasting impact on British art culture as well as providing some iconic visual moments. With 300 artists exhibiting at the Burlington Galleries in London, this was the first time that Surrealism had really hit Britain, and it intended to do so with a bang. The Tate notes that the Exhibition had over 23,000 visitors, and most of the superstar figures associated with Surrealism were present, delivering lectures and staging events: André Breton, Yves Tanguy, Dalí, Max Ernst and Man Ray were all there. This period also brought the emergence of the Surrealist object, combining sculpture and sometimes performance in a way that overturned ideas about art and also forced a new level of engagement from the viewer. There was, of course, the infamous occasion on which Dalí had to be rescued from his diving suit during his own lecture. Ithell Colquhoun was there, and it was here that Surrealism really sunk its claws into her, and a lifetime's relationship was born.

> Only in 1936 did the movement make its full impact on me; I had returned to London and was present on July 1st when Dali spoke at the first International Exhibition of Surrealism in Britain in the New Burlington Galleries. Dali, arrayed in a heavy diving-suit (skin diving gear was not yet invented) entered with two wolf-hounds on a leash. He mounted the dais and tried to remove his helmet but it had stuck fast. He was beginning to suffocate when his wife, Gala, (who had once been married to Paul Eluard – also present but soon to quarrel with Breton) sprang up to release him.[8]

Surrealism was not a comfortable fit in Britain. Some of it was seen as too theoretical and its eclecticism chafed at traditional British artistic sensibilities, which preferred landscapes and powerful scenes of natural beauty. This was not true of everyone, of course, and a number of artists had already been engaging with the ideas of Surrealism, Modernism and other challenges to the traditional British art world. The International Exhibition was the brainchild of writer David Gascoyne and Roland Penrose, who wanted to shake London up with a wild Surrealist happening. The *Guardian* reviewer who covered the Exhibition called many of the paintings on display 'silly' and seemed to care little for its theoretical orientation. However, many of the pieces were meant to challenge the viewer. The Exhibition was also an important chance for the emerging British Surrealist movement to flex its muscles on the international stage, with pieces from Eileen Agar, Penrose, and Gascoyne. The event helped create both the physical and conceptual space for the development of Surrealism in Britain, and it was here that Colquhoun found a spiritual and artistic base.

The 1936 International Surrealist Exhibition inspired greater cohesion among British Surrealists, spearheaded by the arrival of the showy and passionate Belgian art promoter Edouard Mesens. Mesens was a force to be reckoned with, a strong personality with a talent for organisation, and he intended to shape the British Surrealists into a unified force, even if it required heavy-handed tactics. His Surrealist network was almost unrivalled, and his dedication to the cause was tremendous. He was the agent and promoter for René Magritte, and he made his mark as a Surrealist leader in the 1930s, with his gallery in Brussels promoting Surrealism through exhibitions and events. Mesens settled in London in 1938 to help build a culture of Surrealism, and along with Roland Penrose, gallery owner Anton Zwemmer and wealthy patron Peter Watson, he became one of the directors of the London Gallery and proceeded to turn it into the hub of British Surrealism.

Much of the thrust for the development of British Surrealism came from the wealthy collector, artist and promoter Ronald Penrose. Penrose was steeped in *avant garde* and Modernist art circles and spent much of the 1920s and early 1930s in Paris where he befriended a number of prominent artists. Throughout the 1930s he continued to develop his Surrealist network, famously having a star-studded Surrealist jaunt to Cornwall in 1937 with such luminaries as Leonora Carrington, Lee Miller, Max Ernst, Man Ray and Paul Éluard, among others. He also had his share of Surrealist lovers, including Carrington, Peggy Guggenheim, and Miller, whom he eventually married. Penrose was not a prolific painter, although he did produce some iconic Surrealist images such as the 1937 *Winged Domino* and *Octavia* from 1939. Yet his talents in cultivating community served him well in constructing the foundations of British Surrealism, staging the International Surrealist Exhibition and founding the London Gallery with Mesens and others.

The 1936 Exhibition unlocked Colquhoun artistically, and her style shifted to a recognisably Surrealist visual language. Her earliest Surrealist-inspired works were a clear nod to the highly representational, dream-based imagery of Dalí, but she was building on her interest in the natural world and an increasing interest in delving into the mythic and the erotic. The work of Dalí provided a perfect framework for her slide into the Surreal:

> At the Slade School one was taught to draw in the style of Michelangelo but to paint in that of the French Impressionists. I could not see how to combine these disparate modes so I painted to match the drawing in monochrome with superimposed glazes of colour. The themes of my early works reflect those set for Slade compositions, which were usually taken from Classical or Biblical mythology. The portraits I painted also continued the Head-Life classes of my student days. The influence of Dali's technique took root naturally in this ground, and can also be seen (prophetically, almost) in my studies of exotic plants.[9]

From this point, Colquhoun's work progressed into more explicitly erotic themes and she continued to explore bolder depictions of both the male and female forms, which she saw mirrored in the sensual, curving forms of vegetation. *Double Coconut* (1936) and *Pitcher Plant* (c. 1936) are lightly veiled visual euphemisms for a close encounter with explicit sexuality.

Colquhoun started to engage with the Surrealist community more actively around 1938. Colquhoun was already involved with artistic circles in London, and she recounts in biographical notes that she was introduced to Mesens by Paul Nash in 1937 or 1938.[10] It is really in 1938 that we see her first deep dive into alchemical sexual imagery. She produces a positively tumescent *Aloe* (1938), and the now famous *Scylla* (1938) which features a view of the ocean framed with giant rocks, doubling as a woman's knees in the bath, with a small boat gliding not so innocently between them. This is also the year when she creates two rather delightful chalk figures, *Death's Head and Foot* (1938) and *Heart* (1938), which have the smooth dripping features one might see in Dalí's work. Unfortunately, these two sculptural pieces are anomalies in Colquhoun's work; we don't have any evidence that she ever produced anything else like them.

In 1939 Colquhoun's artistic style was to undergo two seismic shifts. The first was the beginning of her thematic exploration of mythic themes and male bodies, and the second was her introduction to automatism, which changed her art and spiritual practice for the rest of her life. In many ways this was the real breakout year for Colquhoun's new direction, and it was the point at which there was the potential for her to become a leading light of British Surrealism. She was showing quite a lot, mainly contributing single works or several at a time to larger exhibitions, but it was her joint exhibition with Roland Penrose in June of 1939 at the Mayor Gallery which was the stunner. She contributed 16 pieces, 14 paintings and her two charming 'objects'. A review called her work 'Post-Freudian' and 'Fastidious, infinitely smooth and caressing, and her colour sweet.'[11]

All of Colquhoun's paintings in the Mayor Gallery exhibition were relatively recent, with one from 1936, and the rest from 1937, 1938 and 1939, indicating shifts in her artistic direction, and her growing concentration on big universal themes of sex, magic, death and decay. It included several major new works and the *Mediteranée* series of seven pieces, including *Beau Gosse* (1939), *Rivières Tièdes* (1939), *Gouffres Amers* (1939)

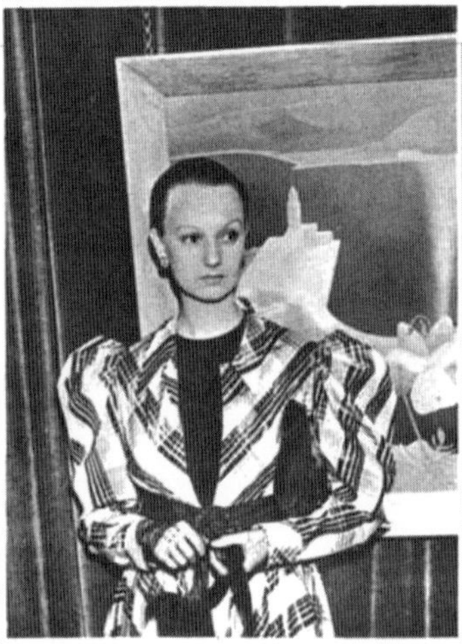

Paintings by MISS ITHELL COLQUHOUN *are on view at the Mayor Galleries. The painter is well suited by this picturesque checked silk house-coat.*

ABOVE Colquhoun and her Mayor Gallery show featured in the high society journal *The Sketch*, 14 June 1939.

and *Le Phare* (1939). *Beau Gosse*, which is French slang for a good-looking man, here probably used with irony, and *Gouffres Amers* in particular were extraordinary for their depictions of wounded, crumbling, naked men that spared no explicit detail. *Le Phare* and *Rivières Tièdes* both featured creative imaginings of Mediterranean architecture, sparse, clean, empty, except for the slightest hint of an elemental force breaking through, a flower pierced by a sword in the midst of a cold, white, angular landscape of buildings, or rivulets of coloured liquid running down the steps of what appears to be a church. These works built on and transformed her previous Mediterranean images, fixing them in the realm of the mythic.

The catalogue for the exhibition was featured in the June 1939 issue of *The London Bulletin*, the *de facto* publication for British Surrealism at the time and the showcase for Surrealist and *avant garde* art, writing and culture in Britain. In so many ways, Colquhoun owned this issue. Her name was featured at the top of the list of star contributors on the cover, a distinction she shared that month with Man Ray, Magritte, Penrose, Picasso and de Sade. In addition to the announcement of the exhibition and the catalogue listing, Colquhoun had three written pieces, with a short essay, 'What Do I Need to Paint a Picture?', along with 'Volcano' and 'The Echoing Bruise'. The second two were short, vaguely Surrealist fiction pieces, more snapshot than story, both of which eventually found their way into *Goose of Hermogenes*.

RIGHT *Scylla* (1938)

'The Echoing Bruise' starts as a tale about a triumphant victory in a contest and ends with a vision of death and decay. It incorporates some visions of the absurd, but primarily jolts the reader's experience from a feeling of celebration to something more unsettling. This becomes a feature in many of

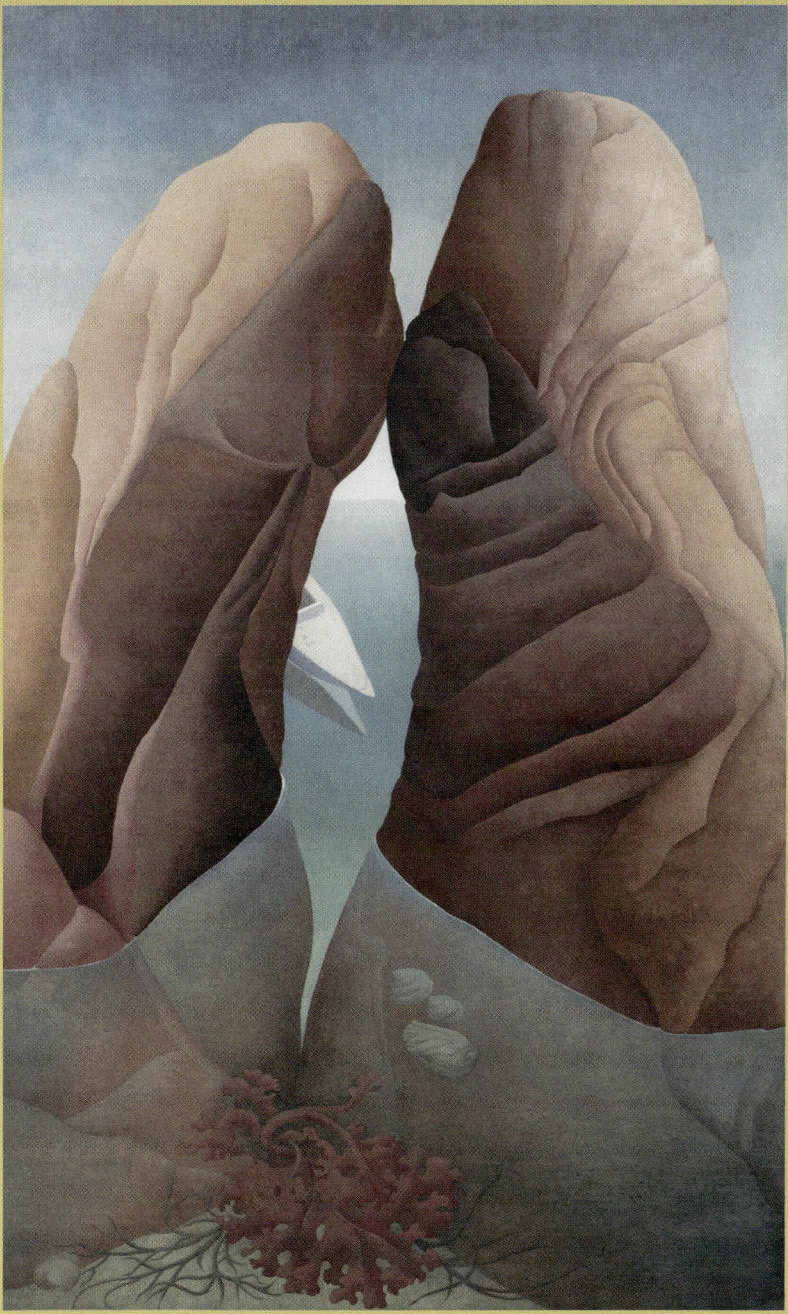

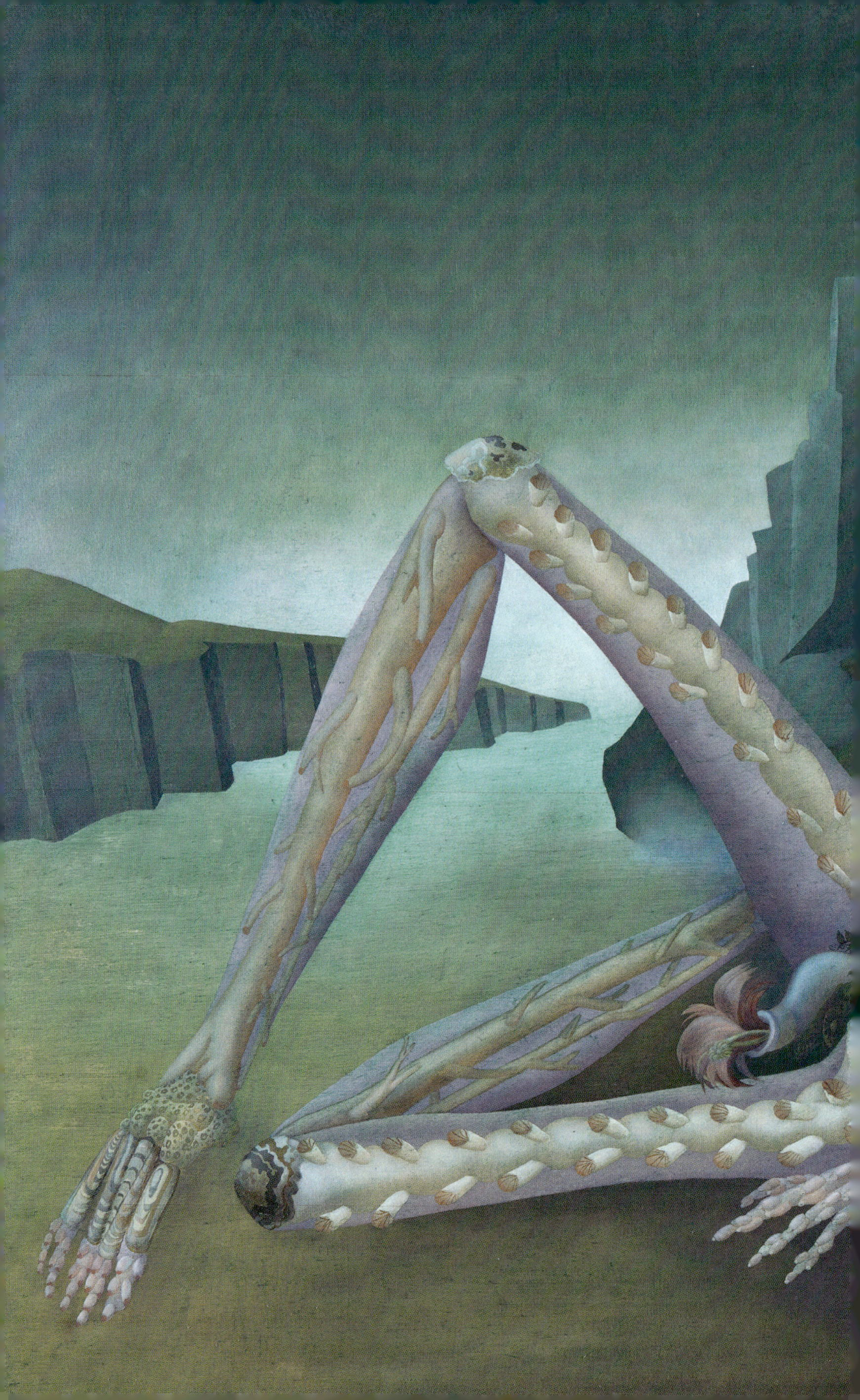

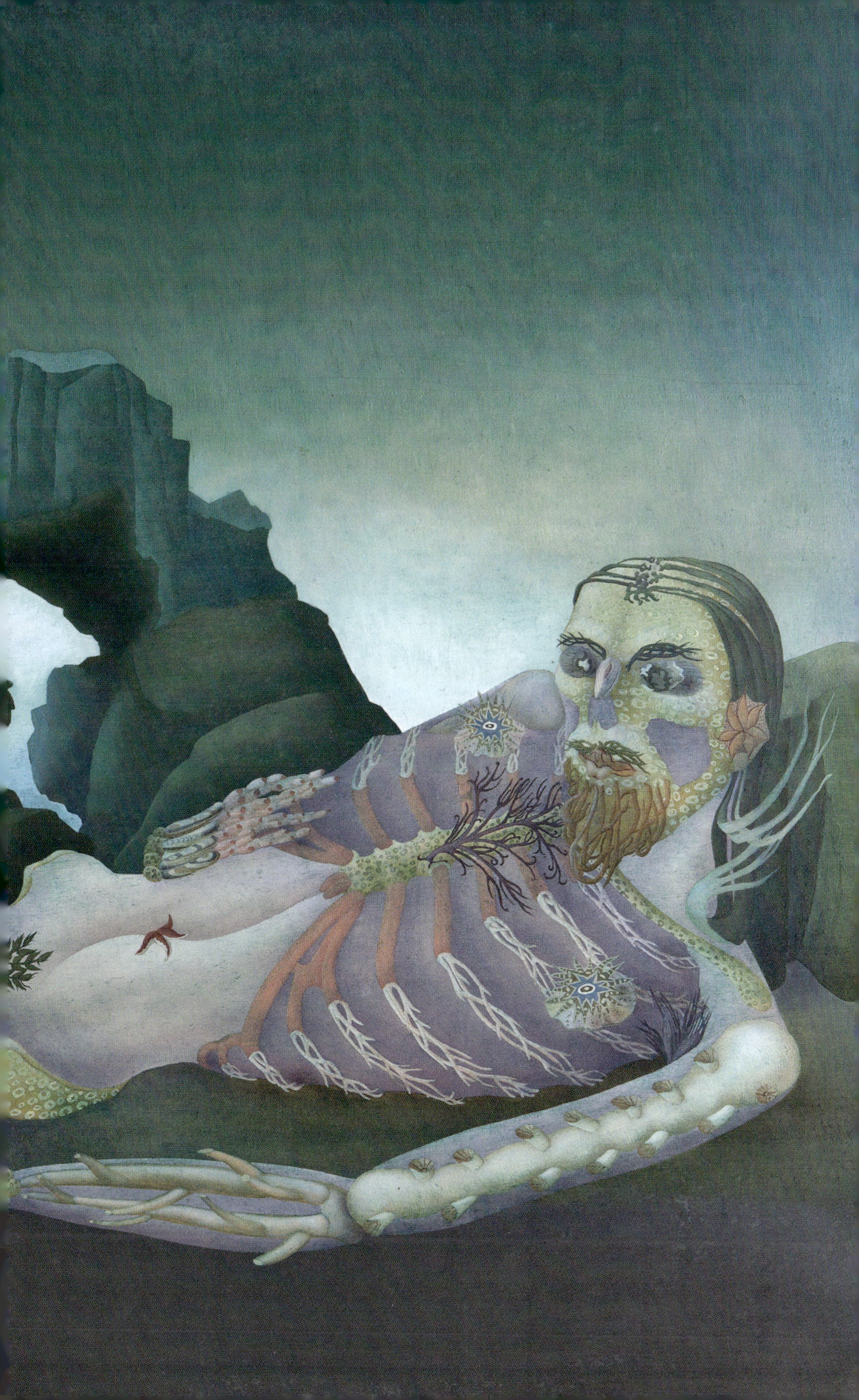

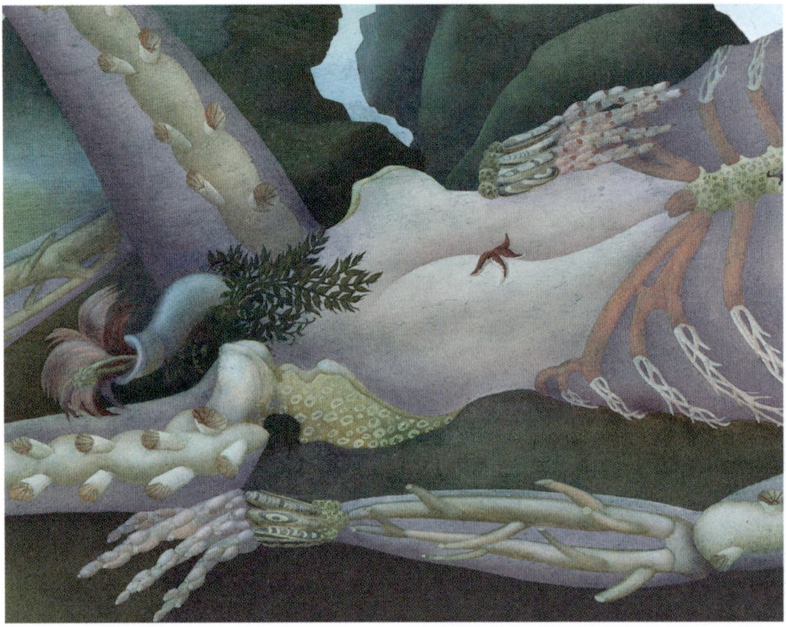

PREVIOUS PAGE & ABOVE (DETAIL)
Gouffres Amers (1939)

her writings, where Colquhoun interplays the quotidian with the grotesque. 'Volcano' is a snapshot of a glowing volcano in the middle of an island, ready to erupt, much like Colquhoun herself. Decades later, in the 1960s, Colquhoun explicitly adapted Breton's idea of 'convulsive beauty', or, the experience of that which is uncanny and jarring to reason in such a way as to cause a disruption of logic and order. Retrospectively, Colquhoun noted that her work with 'convulsive landscapes' started in 1939, but the highest concentration of them was in the 1960s, indicating her interest in the ability of landscape itself to prompt an experience of psychic shift. The volcano is perhaps the most convulsive of all landscapes, and she returns to it time and again throughout her life. This short piece, in some part signifying Colquhoun's own eruption into Surrealism, not only shows an early engagement with Breton's ideas about change and disruption, but it is an early point in the establishment of Colquhoun's personal symbolic language.

Colquhoun's third contribution was the short essay 'What do I need to Paint a Picture?' Compared to many of Colquhoun's other, later, theoretically based works about artistic production, 'What Do I Need to Paint a Picture?' feels positively tepid. It says very little about what moves her to paint or what lies behind her imagery, inspiration or techniques, and in that sense it hardly seems believable. 'What of inspiration? What can one say of it except that it comes and goes, is helped and hindered, is unbiddable and unpredictable?' Perhaps this restraint is because at this stage Colquhoun was still in a state of deep transformation regarding her direction, but this essay has so little of the force of will and spirit which seems to characterise her work throughout her life. By contrast, the illustrations surrounding the piece are anything but shy and retiring. It is surrounded by near pin-up photos of Colquhoun. One is her bathing topless on a beach, and another is her sunbathing in a bikini, in addition to a studio shot and another of her in a hat. She feels here like object rather than subject, and her essay reads as breathy and dull. Her voice is muted. In many ways this issue of *London Bulletin* was Colquhoun's Surrealist debut, and it gives mixed messages. Her exhibition work was bold, powerful and compelling, but the *London Bulletin* pieces don't reflect that strength. Yet she was about to find her way and her true compatriots in the Surrealist movement.

In the summer of 1939 Colquhoun again visited Paris and met André Breton and his wife for the first time, at his apartment. She recalled that Breton was interested in the development of psychomorphology, and this may have prompted her to attend the goings-on in Chemilieu.[12] In the summer of 1939, British artist Gordon Onslow Ford (1912–2003) rented a chateau called Chemilieu in Western France where a number of Surrealists met to work, play and let big ideas germinate. The summer at Chemilieu seemed like quite a party, and was an intensely creative environment. Breton, Yves Tanguy, Kay Sage, Roberto Matta, Colquhoun and Esteban Francés all flowed through the proceedings. It must have been a heady scene, yet one which was also overshadowed by the quickly escalating tensions in Europe and the impending war.

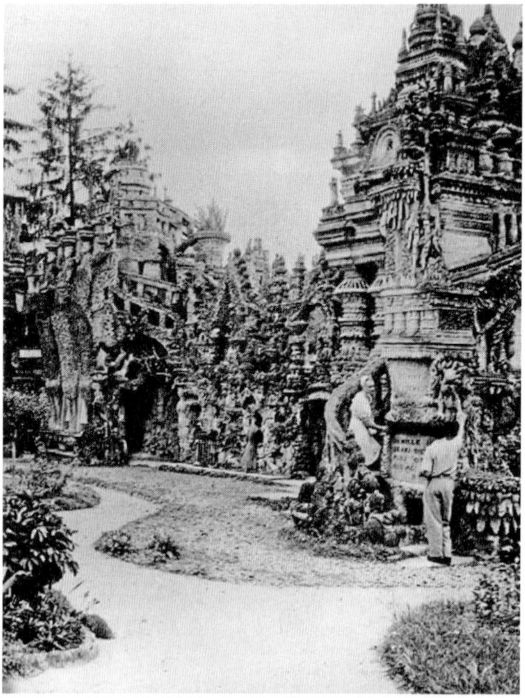

LEFT Colquhoun with Gordon Onslow Ford at the Ideal Palace of Facteur Cheval in Hauterives, France, 1939.

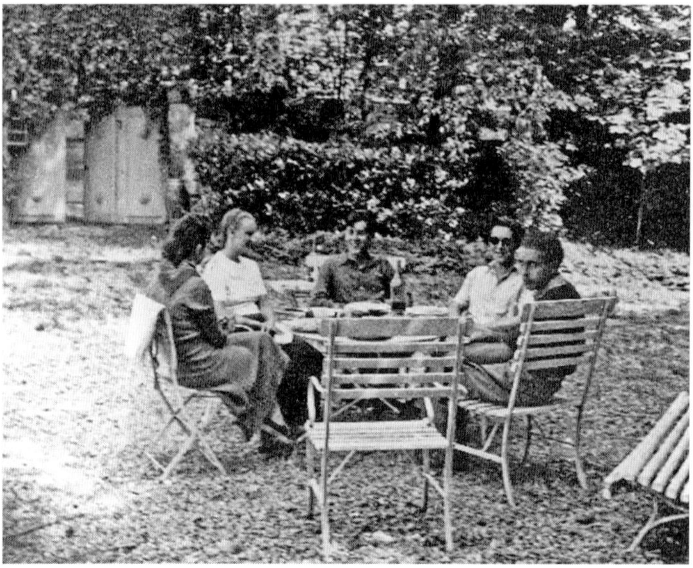

ABOVE The chateau at Chemilieu, France, 1939: L–R Ann Matta, Colquhoun, Roberto Matta, Gordon Onslow Ford, Esteban Francés. Photograph by Elisabeth Onslow Ford Rouslin.

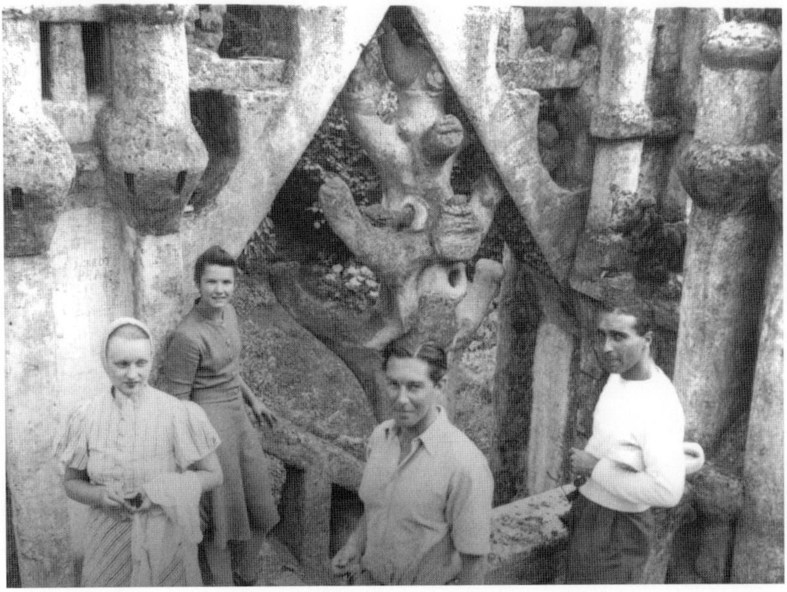

ABOVE At the Ideal Palace of Facteur Cheval in Hauterives, 1939: L–R: Colquhoun, Ann Matta, Gordon Onslow Ford, Esteban Francés.

It was through Onslow Ford and Chilean artist Roberto Matta (1911–2002) that Surrealism in general took a more metaphysical turn, one which informed Colquhoun's work for the rest of her life. Onslow Ford was a naval officer who came somewhat late to an artistic career, settling in Paris to pursue art in 1937. He met Roberto Matta there while Matta was working in the atelier of architect Le Corbusier. By 1938 the pair had started an artistic partnership partially fed by the works of P.D. Ouspensky, allowing for a deeper philosophy of automatism. Ouspensky characterised the artist as a magician, who helps the audience see what they cannot see themselves.

Matta and Colquhoun would have shared a number of foundational interests and perspectives, and she would have had a natural affinity for his particular take on Surrealism. Like Colquhoun, Matta had training and interest in design and architecture: 'Painting has one foot in architecture and one foot in the dream.'[13] Colquhoun had continued

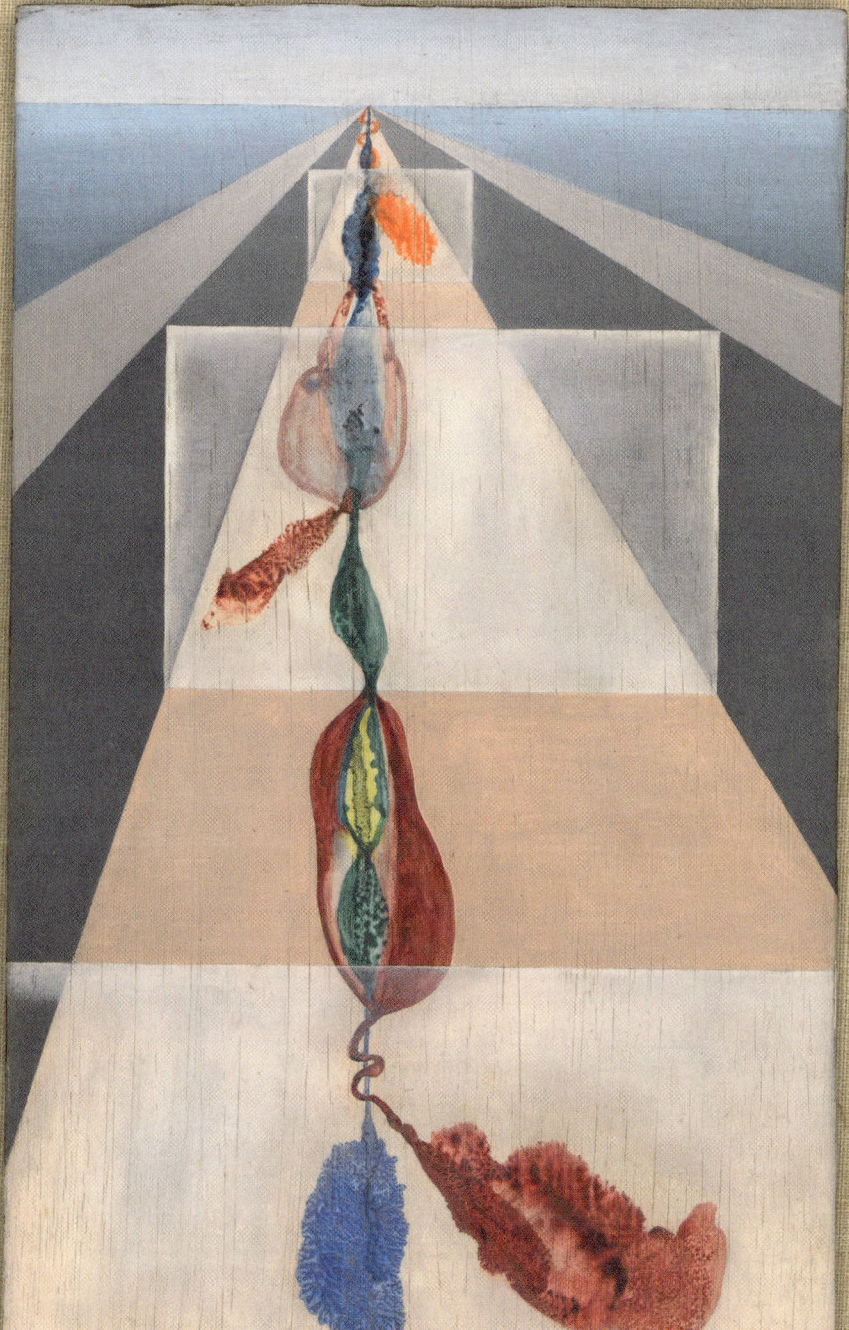
Colquhoun/44

to express this interest through her mural work, and had also extended her training in the field at the atelier of Amédée Ozenfant in the mid-1930s, although she mentions little about this time in her own notes about her life. Notably, Leonora Carrington also studied at Ozenfant's Academy. It is quite likely that Colquhoun and Carrington would have known each other, although their paths were not ultimately to be entwined, and both were interested not only in the structural impact of painting, but also in the theory of design in public spaces, outside a strictly fine art context.

Yet it was Matta's philosophical explorations that most influenced Colquhoun. Matta wanted to use automatism to probe beyond the unconscious or subconscious. He wanted to contact the ultimate. It was through Matta that the term 'psychological morphology' enters the vocabulary of Surrealism, a technique Colquhoun embraced until very late in her life, including in her all of her later enamel works and her Taro deck. Matta used psychological morphology in his creation of 'inscapes,' automatic works that probe the deep mind. Matta believed that psychological morphology, properly done, could bring about images that the thinking mind and the eyes did not have time to process or shape the meaning of during creation. He believed that this was the truest and most original form of automatism, and that the Surrealism under the influence of Dalí had become too Freudian.

LEFT

Ages of Man (1944)

This piece visually recalls Gordon Onslow Ford's 1939 enamel *Without Bounds*.

Matta also had an interest in sacred geometry, cubes and other dimensions, which makes sense for an artist who had a background in architecture. Matta believed that his painting was, in fact, an extension of his architecture, since he was using paintings to shape new 'walls' of perception. According to Miranda Lash, Matta believed that the structure of a cube could help promote a deeper vision for the viewer, as the cube symbolised the existence of multiple sides and perspectives. At the time Matta would have been in Chemilieu, his own work was not particularly linear, and in fact later in his career he started exploring the extradimensional possibilities of the cube visually. However, within several years his work became more focused on geometric forms, and he started to use dissected cubes as themes in his work.[14] Given the development of similar theories in Colquhoun's work, and their intersections with her occult work, it seems likely that she would have been compelled by Matta's thinking around this, and that she continued to be inspired by his direction after Chemilieu.

Although no written record of Colquhoun's thoughts during her time at Chemilieu has yet been found, the impact was clearly drastic. Although after her time there she continued to produce Dalí-inspired paintings that were representational, mythic and dreamlike, these ultimately fell away to be replaced by her embrace of automatic methods. Within a couple of years we start seeing early sketches of the esoteric Cube of Space and tesseracts, as she begins to consider the links between geometric forms, portals and other planes. It is at this point that her Surrealism and her occultism truly begin to support one another. If she had written 'What do I Need to Paint a Picture?' a year later, it might well have read completely differently. Colquhoun post-Chemilieu had a new direction, and before long she was redefining her relationship with her Surrealist tribe.

By September, the party at Chemilieu had scattered as France and Germany were going to war. British Surrealism was in danger of becoming unsettled in the middle of global conflict. Surrealism as a movement had always had a strange, club-like feel, with leaders like Breton demanding loyalty, and members falling out of favour and getting kicked out. Surrealism, with its manifestos and specialised techniques and vocabulary, had an oppositional stance from the start, poking a stick in the eye of the elite art establishment. It was meant to be revolutionary and political, and it was generally explicit about promoting the politics of the Left, but in the middle of intensive conflicts such as the Spanish Civil War and of course the Second World War, allegiances could easily shift. Dalí's ambiguous stance with regard to fascism alienated him from the Surrealists more than once.

There is no doubt that Mesens was a dedicated administrator of the British Surrealists, and he believed that the only way to ensure group survival was through complete cohesion. But despite the institutions that Mesens and others had worked to build, the group was never really cohesive. Mesens attempted to gain a very specific type of group coherence, one that would ensure the survival of Surrealism through the difficult times and tensions of war, and in 1940 he organised a meeting of affiliated Surrealist artists to discuss his aims. Colquhoun remembered that the meeting had less than auspicious beginnings: 'Cross-currents of hostility were perceptible from the beginning of the dinner; when it came to the speeches, John Buckland-Wright acted as Chairman and his impartiality provided a necessary calming influence.' Mesens required total ideological and practical commitment, and proposed a number of propositions which would form the basis of British Surrealism as a movement. One was that there would be no other group affiliation, and that all writing, art and publishing would be done in service to the aims of British Surrealism. Furthermore, Mesens wanted to assert that British Surrealism was politically in support of Communist and proletarian aims. His final edict was that art could not be produced for its own sake.

A number of the artists in attendance took issue with the propositions, including Colquhoun, Eileen Agar, Herbert Read, Grace Pailthorpe and Reuben Mednikoff. Colquhoun noted that she had problems with most of Mesens's directives. Although Shillitoe and Radcliffe both suggest Colquhoun's parting of the ways with the group was primarily about her commitment to the occult, and she herself noted that this was her primary area of dissent, in looking at Colquhoun's general orientation and temperament this may not have been the best club for her to have been a member of. Despite Colquhoun's membership in many groups over the course of her life, there is no doubt that Colquhoun was strong willed and uncompromising when it came to her deepest convictions, and she was not going to stay in any group that would attempt to clip her wings. Colquhoun rejected these propositions and thus her affiliation with the British Surrealists was short lived. It is worth noting, however, that British Surrealism was struggling even then, and Mesens's attempts were really a last-ditch effort to save the movement.

The London Gallery had closed the year before, and the *London Bulletin* stopped publication in 1940. So it's not as though Colquhoun was leaving a healthy movement; it was already somewhat in shambles.

Colquhoun's departure from the British Surrealists can be read in several ways. She was not the only one to have taken issue with the stipulations that Mesens was imposing; the strange psychological Surrealists Grace Pailthorpe and Reuben Mednikoff also left, being unwilling to abide by Mesens's directive of exclusivity. Eileen Agar ultimately relented and rejoined. Of course, Colquhoun intended to continue pursuing her spiritual activities, which would later involve more active group participation. Also, throughout her life, Colquhoun maintained that she held a nonpolitical stance, but this was not strictly true. She was not eager to support the business of electoral politics, but this does not imply that she did not hold strong positions which were highly political. And frankly, given her views and upbringing, it was highly unlikely that she would have been too sympathetic to a proletarian uprising. Colquhoun was generally not predisposed to a focus on the material and worldly, and even her own rather disguised 'political' manifestos, which would come a couple of years later, were focused on spiritual enlightenment as liberation. There are many ways in which this version of Surrealism was just not a good fit for Colquhoun, and while her initial rediscovery as the Lost Surrealist many years after her death focused on her work within the context of the Surrealist movement, perhaps this period is due for a reconsideration in terms of her life's work. There is no doubt that while from 1936 to 1940 many of Colquhoun's own artistic ideas took shape, that period would not define her. After she left that particular incarnation of British Surrealism, she sought to return to what she believed were the first principles of Surrealism, which for her were defined by mysticism and magic.

The Wasteland

From 1939 to 1941 Colquhoun genuinely refined certain aspects of her Surrealist vision, ranging from representational works dealing with sexual and mythic themes to experiments with automatism. She was amazingly prolific during this period, not only creating a number of important Surrealist works, but beginning a number of esoteric projects related to sex, sacred landscapes and otherworldly dimensions that, while drawing on many of the theories she would have discussed with her Surrealist compatriots, do not seem to fit with her other Surrealist pieces. Most of the work she completed during this period was heavily sexual and erotic in nature, even when the sexual nature of the piece is distressing, such as her portrayals of decaying male bodies and castration. Colquhoun's work regarding sex and gender always had a subversive and resistant quality; we can see it in her earliest large canvases and it became a key characteristic of all of her work throughout her life. The questioning of assumptions surrounding the nature of women and gender would also affect the way in which Colquhoun conceptualised the role of gender in magic, spiritual attainment and societal evolution.

Beginning in 1939, Colquhoun became very invested in what is probably a mythic exploration in representing male vitality and impotence, and she did not shy away from portraying the male body explicitly. In fact, in 1941 one of her nude males caused controversy at an exhibition in Harrogate.[15] She challenged women's roles and repression, and portraying the bodies of naked men in a variety of states and stages was an indicator of her own sexual agency. Castration, male sexual disfigurement, and male impotence was also an early theme in a number of works. While many of her more explicit pieces depicting women's sexuality are lush and inviting, such as *Scylla*, pieces such as *Beau Gosse*, and *Gouffres Amers* show men in a state of decay. *Cucumber* (1938), a depiction of a half of a sliced cucumber somewhat wilting in a jar, is even more graphic in its suggestion, as she appears to move towards a fixation with castration. By the time we get to *The Pine Family* (1940), Colquhoun is deep into the exploration of the disfigured and mutilated male. *The Pine Family* depicts a castrated male, a female and a hermaphrodite where all genitalia have been disfigured, yet the trio are lying together looking more like driftwood on a beach, rather than dismembered figures. They are trunks without feet, hands, or heads, but they are labelled: the male is the castrated Greek vegetation deity 'Atthis', the female is *'celle ce boite'* or 'the one who limps,' and the third figure is labelled 'the circumcised hermaphrodite'. These pieces were mythic and probably archetypal, rather than an overall comment on her view of men. In fact, often, Colquhoun's depiction of sex was positive and inviting. Visual metaphors of sexuality inundate her work, and even the simplest sketch of a spoon in a glass can easily take on a very explicit character, and one which is much more playful.

Dawn Ades has argued that Colquhoun's representation of men as vegetation is almost a parody of the ways in which Surrealist artists have represented women as landscape, which Colquhoun also did at many stages of her career.[16] In a response to Ades, Colquhoun strongly denied this, and said that she believed that parody was a very low form of art and that she would never engage with it.[17] She said she painted what she liked, and that her subjects should be taken at face value. However, this does not imply that Colquhoun was not engaging with the male-dominated Surrealist canon. She was. There are clear visual and textual references to Surrealist culture throughout. First, quite simply, the style of text in the painting *The Pine Family* is similar to that which one might find in a Magritte. Whitney Chadwick also comments that the label *'Celle ce boite'* is a reference to the Surrealist passion for Wilhelm Jensen's novel *Gradiva*, known as 'she who strides' who in this case is clearly broken.[18] The third stump, the 'circumsised hermaphrodite' most directly references the *Poésies* of the Surrealist favourite Isidore Ducasse writing as Comte de Lautréamont. In the first section of this sweeping takedown of many of the literary figures of the late nineteenth century, Ducasse refers to the 'mannish', cross dressing, female writer George Sand as a 'circumsised hermaphrodite'.[19] *Pine Family* also recalls Penrose's *Octavia* with the inverted woman, chopped in half, and images of male impotence run through the work of Dalí. Almost certainly these references to the wider Surrealist culture were intentional, yet within Colquhoun's own magical and mythic projects at the time, *The Pine Family* speaks to Colquhoun's preoccupations concerning a state of deep societal decay in need of redemption. This is an excellent example of the ways in which Colquhoun echoed the themes and preoccupations of Surrealism, in this case sexuality and the tensions it can produce, and the realms of the unconscious, but explored them within her own framework of esoteric practice and understanding.

So, if this was not parody, what was driving these themes? Perhaps considering the historical period in which these works was created might give us a key. This was during the intense years of the Second World War, when the earth was literally scorched. For someone like Colquhoun, so concerned with ideas of redemption and the hope that humanity could return to an ideal and uncorrupted state, there was hardly a more striking opposite to a Golden Age. The world was going to hell. The Wasteland was a reality.

It seems likely that these paintings were part of a wider exploration of the myth of the fallen and resurrected god as popularised by J.G. Frazer, and specifically to the notion of the Arthurian Fisher King with his wounded 'thigh'. Colquhoun returned to studies of deities associated with this pattern occasionally, but in 1940 and 41 we see a concentration of this imagery. It is likely that Colquhoun would have been familiar with Jessie Weston's influential 1920 book *From Ritual to Romance*, a popular treatise on Frazer's theories specifically in an Arthurian context. Similar to the work of Margaret Murray, Weston proposed the existence of a mystery tradition that celebrated the death and resurrection of a native British vegetation deity, whose health and vitality was linked to the prosperity and fertility of the land. Weston's theories would have held a special resonance for Colquhoun, given her interest in the idea of native British responses to universal themes. For Colquhoun, the wounded king must be redeemed by the restoration of sexual activity, which suggests not only a restoration of health to the land, but also that it is through sexual union, and the union of male and female polarities, that humanity itself will be uplifted. She explores these themes in other series of visual works, and there are consonant ideas in her writings of the time, based on her readings of alchemy, Tantra, and Yeats's *A Vision*; she also explores them in more detail in other artistic experiments, mostly in works not meant for public consumption.

In 1940 Colquhoun was 34. Certainly, she had had romantic relationships, but nothing seems to have stuck or really approached serious. Many women of this era would have been all but relegated to 'spinster' status being unmarried at 34, but marriage and children did not seem to be a real priority for her. It is difficult to know if she faced family pressures on these matters, but she had an unconventional life, and she seemed to be seeking something else. Nevertheless, during this period she began her deeply intensive and feverish studies of sacred copulation, and sex magic. Was she possibly looking to find the partner that would help her to complete the Great Work, or was she wanting to find ways to come to peace with the fact that the best integration will be the type that happens within the self, unpartnered? The theoretical underpinnings of her work during these years will be explored in another section, but it seems safe to say that in the time between Colquhoun's separation from the British Surrealist movement and her relationship with Toni del Renzio she embarks on some very deep magical art projects, piecing together a world view based on earthly decay and esoteric redemption. Foremost was the production of hundreds of sketches of nudes and explicit sexual pairings. This was clearly an intense fixation for Colquhoun over a two-year period, and it is hard to look at these works without imagining that they must mirror the desires of the artist. Or, perhaps, she was finding a way to sublimate them. Still, even the strong-willed and independent Colquhoun could be vulnerable to a dashing and charismatic artist with a mysterious history, especially one who held the promise of reintegrating with her beloved Surrealism.

RIGHT
Sardine & Eggs (1941)

Toni del Renzio, full name Antonino Romanov del Renzio dei Rossi di Castellone e Venosa, appears to have been quite a charming and seductive man. Early photos show him to be dark eyed and brooding.

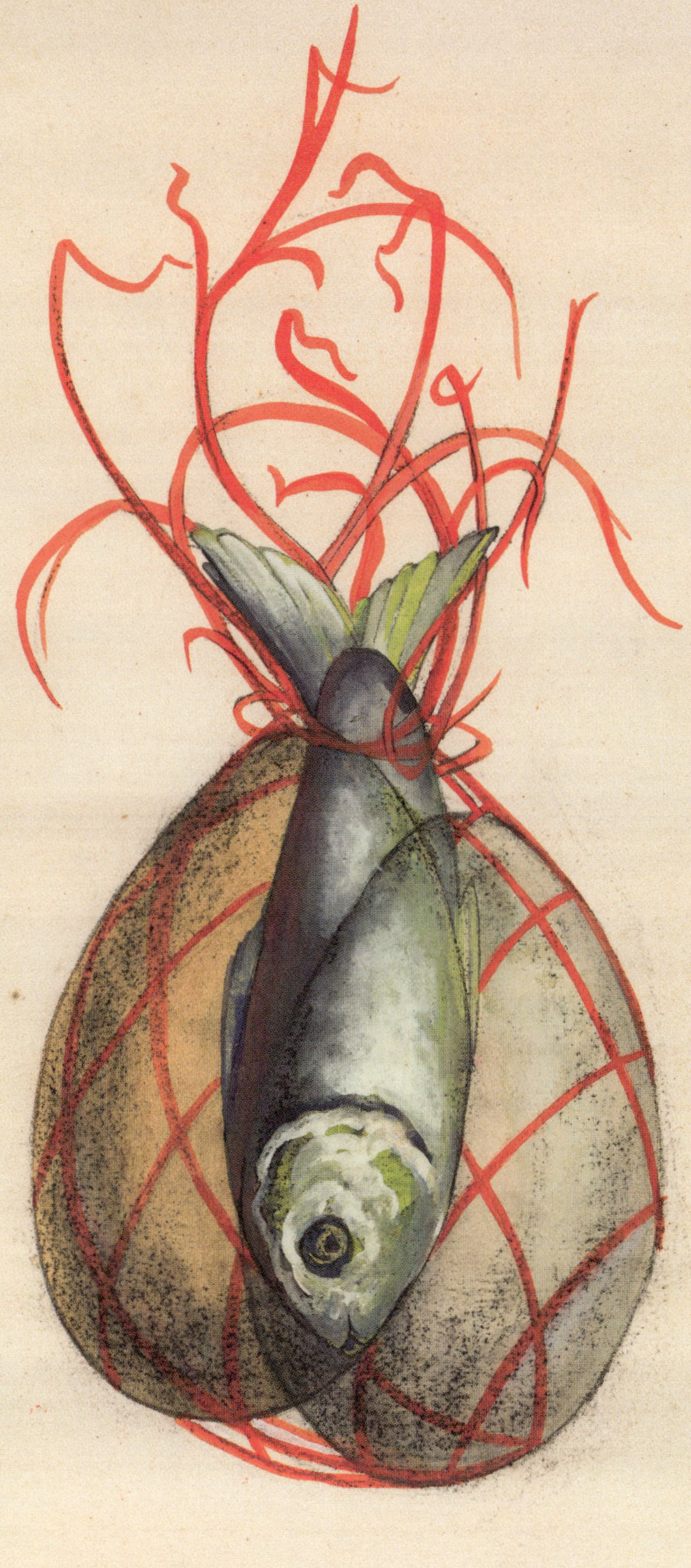

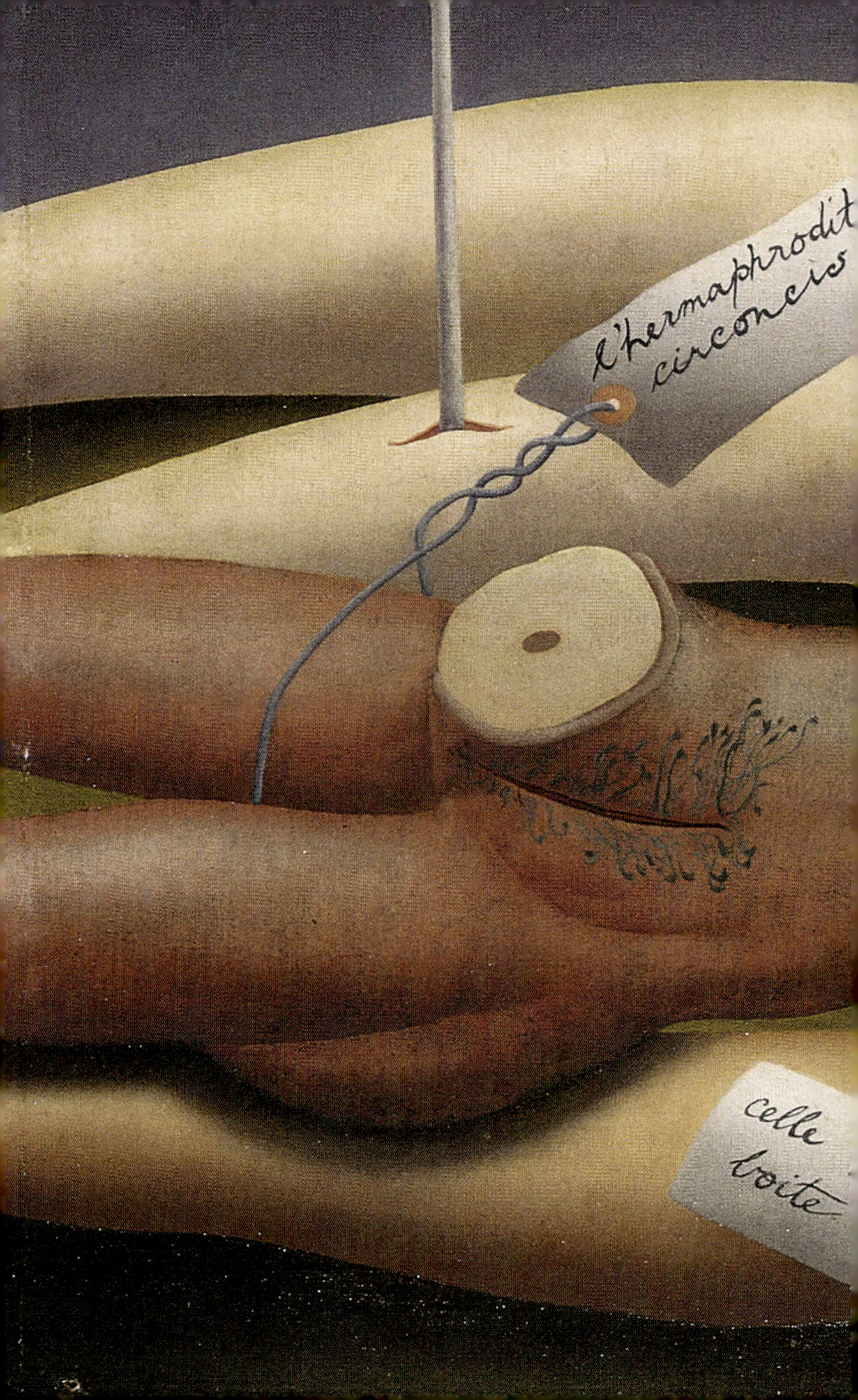
l'hermaphrodit
circoncis
celle
boite

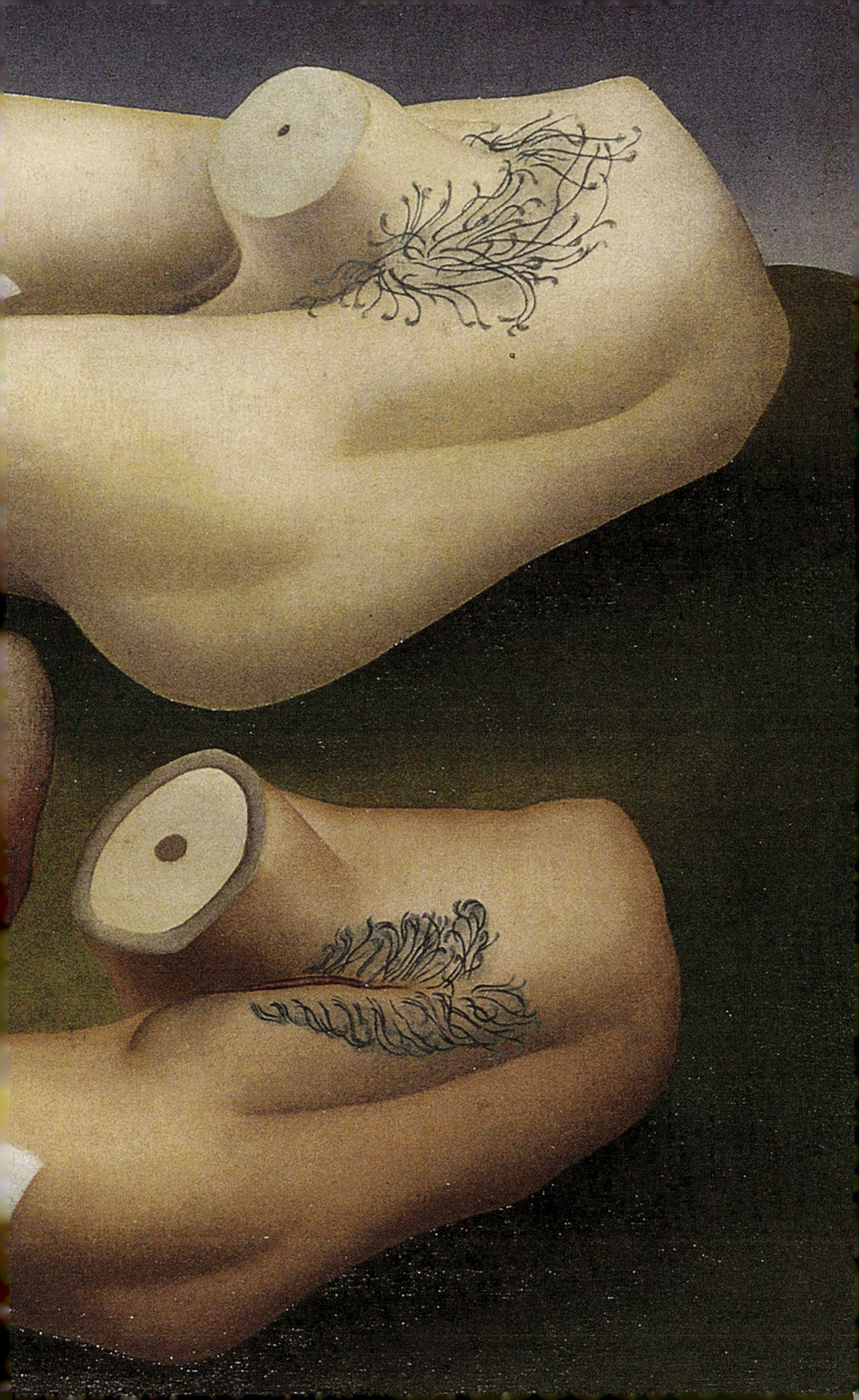

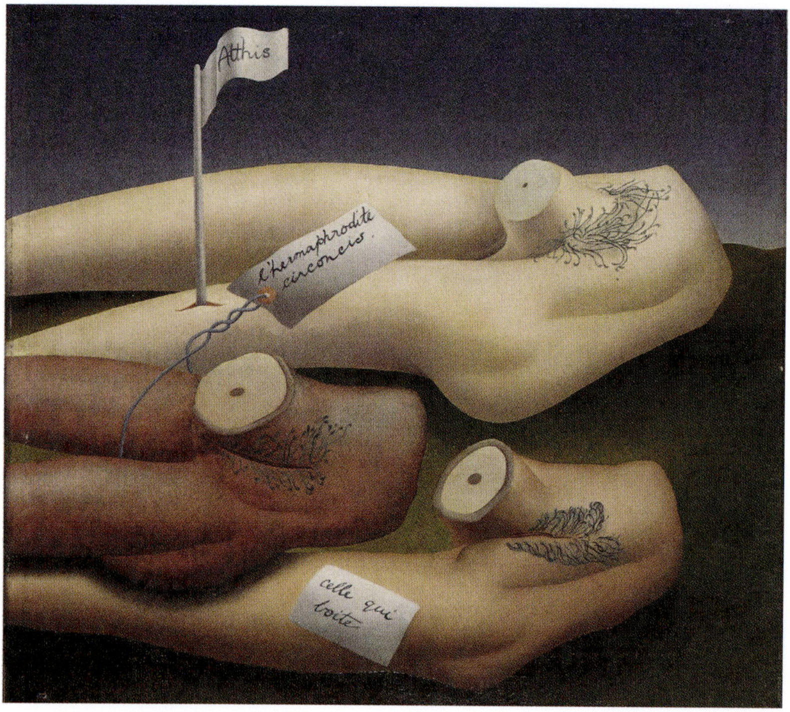

PREVIOUS PAGE & ABOVE
The Pine Family (1940)

His early life before Surrealism was, if true, straight out of an adventure film. He was born in 1915 to an aristocratic Russian family. His mother was a Romanov, and the revolution caused the family to flee to Italy where he had a comfortable youth. He was part of Mussolini's Second Abyssinian campaign in the late 1930s, but escaped on a camel train, disguised as a Bedouin. He crossed North Africa into Spain, where he fought against Franco in the Spanish Civil War, which he also fled in 1937. After a stay in Paris, with war once again encroaching on him, he ended up in England. In Paris he became involved in *avant garde* art communities and theatre design, and he had hoped to join up with the Surrealists in London, but by the time he arrived some of the key members had been drafted, and Mesens had effectively closed up shop.[20] Del Renzio saw this as a great opportunity to make a mark on the art world.

Socially, Colquhoun was rather at a loose end. She was considered unfit for National Service and the war took a toll on her fragile mental and physical health. Although Colquhoun had disaffiliated with the British Surrealists under Mesens, she was still very active in trying to carve out a place for herself in various art movements. After her split with the Surrealists, esoteric content starts to figure much more heavily in her visual work. We see her first forays into esoteric landscape studies, and a greater focus on alchemy, and the sexual conjuration of the Philosopher's Stone. In 1942 she paints the showstopping *Tree Anatomy*, a depiction of a tree knot which is explicitly vulvic in character, down to the clitoris and the pubic hair, which was exhibited at the Leicester Galleries in that same year. *Tree Anatomy* echoes the sexual character of *Pine Family*, but is not as barren or morbid. Colquhoun also turned her direction toward publishing and approached Henry Treece of the New Apocalypse movement to see how she could become involved. The New Apocalypse movement was rather short-lived and had little lasting impact, but Colquhoun may have been attracted by its non-political stance, a concern with mythology, mysticism and big, universal themes in addition to its general dislike of centralised control. As she had just been a victim of that with the Surrealists, it makes sense that she might gravitate toward a movement that championed autonomy. Additionally, according to Silvano Levy, Mesens was also trying to make more formal links with the New Apocalypse movement, which may have been ideologically appealing to Colquhoun.[21] But the movement wasn't exactly a great fit for her either, and the relationship never blossomed. She had hoped to take over an editorial position for the movement's publication *Kingdom Come* but her participation was vetoed by other members, and once again she was left wandering.[22]

Even after her split with the Surrealists, Colquhoun was still in contact with the Surrealist Conroy Maddox, and wrote to him of her interest in the New Apocalypse writers. Maddox was a member of the Birmingham Surrealists, a group that had initially taken issue with the London Surrealists, finding them too decadent to be committed to the original principles of the movement. They ultimately joined forces with the London group, but Maddox still had an earthy fundamentalist streak to him. Maddox knew the movers and shakers within the New Apocalypse movement, and while he was not all that keen on their theoretical thrust, he still contributed illustrations to some of their work from time to time, and was seen by some of their members as sharing their 'apocalyptic vision'.[23]

Writing to Colquhoun on 14 November 1941, Maddox mentioned a new Surrealist who had visited him in Birmingham, who had some 'interesting proposals' and paintings that were reminiscent of Dalí' but without the heavy sexual content.[24] By early 1942, Colquhoun herself was hoping to launch a Surrealist exhibition, but Maddox discouraged her, saying it would have been at odds with his own plans.[25] He followed up by telling her that he and this new Surrealist, Toni del Renzio, were launching a new Surrealist magazine together called *Arson*, which was due to appear that March.

Silvano Levy has noted that when del Renzio showed up in Britain eagerly wanting to participate in the Surrealist movement, the start of the war had created a lull, and the movement didn't have the activity and vibrance of several years earlier. When del Renzio arrived, his goal was to inject new life into the flagging British Surrealist movement, as well as trying to take it back to the philosophical roots laid down by Breton. It was his belief that many British Surrealists had lost their way, and that Mesens had let the movement lose its direction. According to Levy, del Renzio's first Surrealist encounter was Onslow Ford, whom he believed to be the most authentic and traditional of the British Surrealists. Del Renzio then made it his mission to spearhead an active international Surrealist community of artists who would want to return to the principles of Breton. Clearly in Maddox he found a sympathetic soul interested in first principles, and also a partner who was willing to invest the time to try to revive a Surrealism that had been badly hit by the war. It is noteworthy that del Renzio and Colquhoun had both been strongly influenced by the work and theories of Onslow Ford and Matta in what they considered should be the true direction of British

Surrealism, based on Breton's principles of automatism, and this may have provided another dynamic in the connection between them. Certainly the notion of trying to direct British Surrealism back to the philosophy of Breton would have been very attractive to Colquhoun as well, and the prospect of becoming involved in an artistic community again would also have been very compelling.

In March 1942 the one and only edition of *Arson* appeared, dedicated to 'four dear departed: Sade, Rimbaud, Lautréamont and Lenin in the concentration camps of heaven.'[26] *Arson* was meant to be a beacon of Surrealist activity among the ruins, and contributors included Maddox, Robert Melville, Eileen Agar, Edith Rimmington, Emmy Bridgwater, Breton, Nicolas Calas, Giorgio de Chirico, Esteban Francés, Pierre Mabille, Onslow Ford, and Marguerite Salle.[27] The issue was a manifesto of sorts, stating del Renzio's personal view of the Surrealist mission. Del Renzio actually takes a pot shot at Colquhoun's work, calling her paintings 'Sterile abstractions'. 'Miss Ithell Colquhoun has finally damned herself publicly with her admission of endeavouring to do in painting what the 'New Apoplexy' is doing in literature.'[28] Apparently, she didn't take this too seriously, and he may have used it as the basis for a flirtation. During this time del Renzio was romantically, or at least physically, involved with two other Surrealist artists, Emmy Bridgewater and Marguerite Salle, but before long he became involved with Colquhoun. She ultimately took on the debt of the publication and he, nine years her junior, moved into her flat.

Some of the financial arrangements between del Renzio and Colquhoun may have been eased by the death of her father in September 1942. She didn't fare particularly well. Her father left her the outcome of an insurance policy, but her brother was willed the family home and most of the estate. This may have provided her with enough of a cushion to feel she could take some risks. In November and December of 1942 del Renzio organised an exhibition at the International Arts Centre in London to which Colquhoun contributed, as well as several British and French Surrealists. This put del Renzio on the map.

With the war raging, it was a hard time for the arts in Britain. People and supplies were being diverted to the war effort, and paper for publishing was hard to come by. Poetry, short story collections and small limited run journals were keeping things alive. Retrospectives on the early 1940s in Britain often argue that not much of artistic merit was produced, with the constraints on materials and everyone existing at a high level of panic. Yet art did continue, and by 1943 Colquhoun and del Renzio were becoming involved in wider artistic circles, with the young and flashy del Renzio having been invited to start a Surrealist section of John Bayliss and Alex Comfort's *New Road* publication. Colquhoun and del Renzio married in July of 1943, witnessed by Conroy Maddox. In commemoration of their wedding, Colquhoun, del Renzio, Maddox, Lillian Melville, Robert Melville and Olive Bellamy constructed a Surrealist chain poem, here with the contributions of each labelled with their notes:

Do take cherries at the wedding
Did you take the salt of

Lillian Melville

A wax model with stale bread under her eyelids
And the crevice of her armpits sodden with leaves
Chased a tonsured priest in his underwear
Through the corridor of my mind

Conroy Maddox

The thoughts of the crowd disturbs my dream

Olive Bellamy

Ithell, the Bride, snow white and black as soot
And gold with isolated clamours
And revealing veil reminds me
That beauty is convulsive but not contorted

Robert Melville, with sincerity

'OBJECTIVE HAZARD': Surrealism

Laugh, O sword, and pay with rice.

ITHELL COLQUHOUN

All this I tell you leads us to express only our sex.

TONI DEL RENZIO for his bride, 10 July '43

It was during this period that Colquhoun was introduced to writer Derek Stanford, who ultimately became a lifelong friend and her literary executor. Stanford was a poet and literary critic most remembered for his writing about British literary culture in the 1940s, and a biography of the poet John Betjeman. He clearly had a great deal of affection for Colquhoun. His quirky memoirs of the New Apocalypse and Neo-Romantic literary movement of the 1930s and 40s, *Inside the Forties: Literary Memoirs, 1937–1957* provides a sympathetic portrait of Colquhoun that shows insight into this transitional period in her life and into her short-lived partnership with del Renzio. Stanford recalled that Colquhoun and del Renzio were united in 'revolutionary monogamy', deciding that their conventional relationship, perhaps in contrast to the partner swapping that regularly occurred among other Surrealists, would in fact be interpreted as somehow being *avant garde*. They worked to have a dynamic life together, enlivened by the comings and goings of artists and writers. In Stanford's memoirs he recalls attending parties of the literati with Colquhoun and del Renzio. The couple shared a studio flat in Chiswick which Stanford recalls as being bright with mobiles hanging from the ceiling and Colquhoun's esoteric art on the walls:

> From every high point and opening of the body radiated out in circling curves a line of astral force completely surrounding the man. The colouring was rainbow bright and the effect of the picture was both extremely sensuous and ethereal.[29]

Colquhoun herself cut an exotic figure, dressing in Indian saris, reflecting her family history and her own identity. 'She had large bright eyes' Stanford recalled, 'which led to my forming an image of her as some twilight hovering, pollen sipping moth.'

During this time Colquhoun was forging her own identity among artistic circles, and was becoming recognised for her occult knowledge. It was certainly playing more of a role in her art and creative writing in the early 1940s than it had previously. Del Renzio would occasionally use Hermetic allusions in his own works, but it is likely that where magic was concerned he was trying to come into her world.

Colquhoun was also engaging in differently flavoured political circles than before, and a number of the writers in her circle identified as anarchists, pacifists, nascent Libertarians and conscientious objectors. Given del Renzio's persistent attempts to evade military conflict, this might have had an appeal to him as well. Stanford, Bayliss and Comfort (who would eventually become better known as the author of *The Joy of Sex*) were generally of an anarchist tendency, and shaped a number of the publishing and cultural efforts that Colquhoun would contribute to during this period, including *The Fortune Anthology* and the 1943 and 1944 editions of *New Road: New Direction in Art and Letters*. While it is hard to say definitively how this circle affected Colquhoun's own perspectives, it may be that it was a more comfortable fit for her than the proletarian politics of Mesens's Surrealists. Colquhoun had always had an interest in promoting independence and individual liberty, and this group may have reinforced these sensibilities. Derek Stanford characterised the editions of *New Road* as capturing writers of an explicitly free-thinking nature: 'Apocalyptics, Surrealists, Neo-Romantics and Anarchists against that old popular front of the baddies, consisting of Marxists and Social Realists.'[30] We see a focus on the notion of liberty in Colquhoun's own contribution, 'Water Stone of the Wise', which she published in *New Road* 1943 as a response to Breton's concerns about the flagging Surrealist movement during wartime. A focus on individual liberty also featured in del Renzio's writing, and that of many of the writers associated with *New Road*. 'Water Stone of the Wise', a revolutionary essay replete with alchemical polemic, indicates that she was bringing her engagement with Surrealism into a different political and philosophical conversation, one which championed individual thought and the power of the mythic to reshape reality.

Del Renzio clearly inspired Colquhoun's revolutionary zeal and her engagement with international and particularly Francophone Surrealism, but these efforts would ultimately lead to even more heartbreak for Colquhoun. Silvano Levy describes in some detail the attempts that del Renzio made to take control of the British Surrealists, and Mesens's increasing anger at this.[31] Colquhoun and del Renzio were investing a lot of energy trying to counter what they felt was Mesens's failure in letting British Surrealism become so degraded. From 1942 to 1944 the pair organised poetry readings designed to showcase their own vision of Surrealism. The intention was to rekindle public interest through readings designed to promote the original vision of the Surrealists. The selection of readings was quite varied, including works from Surrealist canon authors such as Tzara and Breton, occult works, and their own material. On one occasion in 1943 she read pieces from the Welsh alchemist Thomas Vaughan (aka Eugenius Philalethes), who was a significant influence on her during this period, a selection from her Surrealist alchemical novel *Goose of Hermogenes*, Rimbaud, Jarry and Lautréamont. Del Renzio read Lewis Carroll's 'Jabberwocky', and selections from Blake and Apollinaire among others. Here Colquhoun saw her opportunity to help shape and influence the direction of the movement, selecting foundational texts which to her captured the spirit and essence of Surrealism.

The couple's efforts inspired Mesens to regroup, and to try to counter their threat. It all came to a terrible conclusion in 1944 when, during a reading at the International Arts Centre in Bayswater, Mesens and a number of the British Surrealists including old friends such as Conroy Maddox, Emmy Bridgewater, and Edith Rimmington stormed the venue with the express intent of humiliating Colquhoun and del Renzio. The participation of Maddox must have been particularly painful. Colquhoun reported that the mob all took on fake names and did their best to disrupt the performance, finally pelting them with projectiles and causing them to shelter behind a piano. It is clear that this event affected Colquhoun deeply, and certainly she felt the betrayal of her former Surrealist colleagues. Del Renzio continued to wage attacks on Mesens throughout 1944, publishing yet another manifesto, *Incendiary Innocence*, where he restates the centrality of automatism to the Surrealist project. Much of his characterisation of automatism seems, if not influenced directly by Colquhoun's own perceptions, certainly derived from a common source, in the focus on using the subconscious to contact other objective realities. For del Renzio, this indicated his own implicit loyalty to Breton above all else, but the impact of Colquhoun's synthesis of automatism with Hermetic principles should not be underestimated or erased. Accounts of del Renzio's machinations rarely take Colquhoun's artistic influence into account, especially the ways in which her own understanding of automatism as an occult process was developing at the time.

Mesens continued to antagonise del Renzio, organizing exhibitions and publications that excluded both him and Colquhoun, and would even directly attack him. Many of Colquhoun's relationships with her former friends, including Maddox, never fully recovered. Colquhoun and del Renzio had a couple of limited Surrealist gestures in their remaining years as a couple. He tried unsuccessfully to gather pieces around the theme of the suicide of Sonia Araquistain, believing that her death was a perfect example of Bretonian Surrealist disruptive violence. Colquhoun produced a painting, *Dreaming Leaps: in Homage to Sonia Araquistain*, but the collection never happened. Del Renzio had certainly been effective in reuniting the British Surrealists, but not in the ways he had hoped, and Colquhoun's continuing participation with them was one of the greatest casualties of his attempts at revolution.

In later years, del Renzio claimed that the cause of Mesens's hatred for him was sexual jealousy. del Renzio believed that Mesens was sexually interested in Colquhoun, which could be substantiated by the odd pictorial of her in the 1939 *London Bulletin*. Del Renzio also claimed that Mesens was also attracted to him, but that he had no intention of becoming his lover.

The marriage between Colquhoun and del Renzio ended in 1947. Although the circumstances surrounding the ending of the marriage are not clear, there is some suspicion that it may have been due to infidelity on his part, possibly with other men. Derek Stanford wrote that she never recovered from the breakup of the marriage, and although she had other lovers in her life, and other romantic interests, she never partnered again. One thing that is certain is that her relationship with del Renzio completely and utterly severed her relationship with the British Surrealist movement, probably to an even greater degree than her official split with Mesens in 1940. Yet in the relationship with del Renzio we see the recurring theme of championing orthodoxy and embracing the notion of an original 'current', which becomes prevalent later in her occult work.

Colquhoun would have loved the idea that she had a partner who would help reformulate Surrealism in its first, best and least corrupted image, for that is what drove most of Colquhoun's most radical acts. After the dissolution of her marriage, she continued this quest for the pure Surrealist current alone. It is likely that she spent some time recovering from the breakup in a rest home. As for del Renzio, his marriage to Colquhoun seems to have been a blip in his personal history. Although his early life could hardly have been more colourful, he settled down into a somewhat staid career in design and eventually taught art history. But as a final dramatic act, when he was 70, he fathered quadruplets.

By end of the 1940s, although Colquhoun was still committed to the techniques and revelations of Surrealism, she began to change direction: we see a new emphasis in her life as her relationship with her London artistic community shifts and she begins to seek out occult community. However, her relationship with Surrealism was far from finished, and, unfettered from a movement that demanded strict compliance, Colquhoun was free to develop her use of Surrealist techniques in a way that was well integrated theoretically into a variety of esoteric interests. Almost predicting Colquhoun's development, reporting on the 1936 International Surrealist Exhibition, *The Guardian* rather presciently asked: 'To what extent can a man turn his subconscious imagery into consciously created form and colour? Does not the very act of laying hands on the subconscious bring it into the field of consciousness and thereby destroy its very nature? Would not true Surrealist art consist rather in those queer little drawings that one involuntarily makes on blotting-paper during the course of a telephone conversation?' Ultimately, of course, this is the direction in which Colquhoun would go.

By the late 1940s, Colquhoun had fully embraced automatism. Surrealist automatism was somewhat inspired by, yet different from, mediumistic automatism, the primary aim of which was to be a vehicle for spirit communication. The source of automatic images in Surrealism was initially not believed to be spirits, but the psyche itself releasing repressed desires and impulses. Within Surrealism, automatic writing and drawing preceded any attempts to apply automatic methods to painting. In fact, it was initially believed that painting was not a suitable medium for automatic processes to be well realised. As the Surrealist experiment expanded, automatic techniques were based on seemingly random applications of paint to canvas or paper to see what emerged, after which the artist would be able to shape the final image using her conscious mind. Other automatistic forms included collage, found objects (as she explains in 'The Mantic Stain', Colquhoun considered collage and found works to be automatistic because of their element of chance), found poems, frottage or rubbings, and a number of other techniques designed to incorporate elements of chance and play into the creative process. Yet Colquhoun, inspired by Matta, would move her automatism in a direction that brought it more in line with mediumistic automatism.

Some of Colquhoun's more significant early decalcomania oils were produced during the years of her marriage, and she would continue to refine her automatism throughout her life. *A Visitation 1* and *A Visitation 2*, both from 1945, and refined from the same initial print, indicate her development of technique and the ways in which she was starting to use decalcomania to express ineffable themes about energy and movement. The effect is to create an atmosphere with paint that is billowy and otherworldly. *Gorgon* from 1946 is a lush but threatening decalcomania that has been worked and detailed with a small brush to provide an atmosphere of realism and recognisability to a shape that is completely unreal. *Gorgon* captures the essence of a terrifying angel with wings and a face you cannot and should not look at. By contrast, *Alcove* from 1946 is a luminous celebration of blues, yellows and greens encased in what seem to be fleshy vaginal folds in various shades of pink. Colquhoun frequently used geological metaphors such as caves or volcanoes to refer to the vulva, and this representation is warm and inviting. The counterpart to this, using the same base sheet, was reworked into *Alcove 2* and is dated 1948.[32]

Automatism became increasingly integral to Colquhoun's spiritual practice as she moved further away from her affiliation with the Surrealist movement and began the next phase of her life. 1947 was bookended by two shows at the Mayor Gallery in London, one focused on drawing and a second, a retrospective of paintings from 1942–1947, showing some of her more dramatic oils. Those shows must have been somewhat of a boost in what would otherwise have been a horrible and traumatic year. Perhaps one of the more striking pieces exhibited at the Mayor Gallery would have been her 1947 *Attributes of the Moon*. This astonishing piece uses some of the same vulvic framing and colouring as *Alcove*, with lush folds of pink surrounding and encasing a female figure that is part mermaid, part moon goddess and part Mary. This picture may be an attempt to place Mary within a wider framework of lunar and oceanic goddesses, a theme she expanded in *Goose of Hermogenes*. The clear referent is to the longstanding visual tradition of the Immaculate Conception, picturing Mary on a crescent moon crowned with a halo of stars, which comes out of Revelation 12:1, 'And there appeared a great wonder in heaven; a woman clothed with the sun, and the moon under her feet, and upon her head a crown of twelve stars.' Colquhoun here takes the *vesica piscis* which frequently surrounds Mary and makes the womb aspect explicit, as she emerges from the state of primordial Goddess. Her crown is of ten orbs, not twelve as usually depicted, which may refer to the ten sephiroth of the tree of life. It is one of the more explicit works Colquhoun creates with a vaguely anthropomorphic representation of the Divine Feminine.

Colquhoun noted much later in life that she had bounced back quickly from the pain of her divorce. While that may or may not have been the case, she continued forward. In 1948 she had a wonderful opportunity to present her automatic techniques on a BBC television programme called *Eye of the Artist* in an episode titled 'Fantastic Art' which also included Eileen Agar. Colquhoun demonstrated and described automatic techniques including *fumage*, decalcomania, and *parsemage* (her own invention). Colquhoun made other attempts to contribute to BBC programs later in the 1950s and 1960s, but never seemed to have another shot quite like this one. This occasion allowed her a fine platform to articulate her artistic methodologies and process, one that she would soon flesh out more fully.

RIGHT
Attributes of the Moon (1947)

In 1949 Colquhoun was two years on from her divorce and, while not healed from it, she was getting back on her feet, having found her first studio in Lamorna, Cornwall, where she settled part time. In that year she wrote her initial treatise on automatism, 'The Mantic Stain', for *Enquiry*[33] and she expanded and followed it up with 'Children of the Mantic Stain' published in *Athene*[34] in 1951. Both essays set out to explain various forms of automatism and how, when properly used, they can tap into the unconscious mind of the artist or practitioner. In these essays she sets out her own personal vision of automatism as a process which she conceived as essentially divinatory in nature. Here, Colquhoun explicitly fashions herself as the seer, the clairvoyant. Through her magic and refinement of the self she could potentially

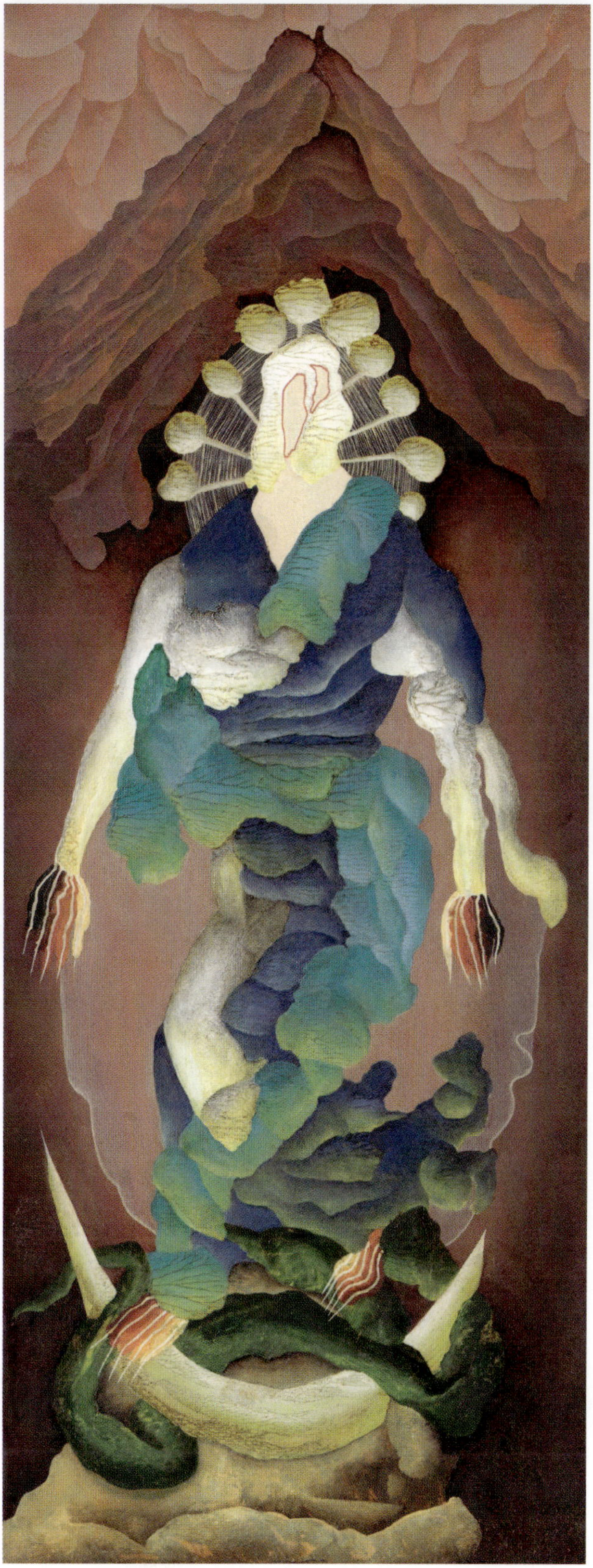

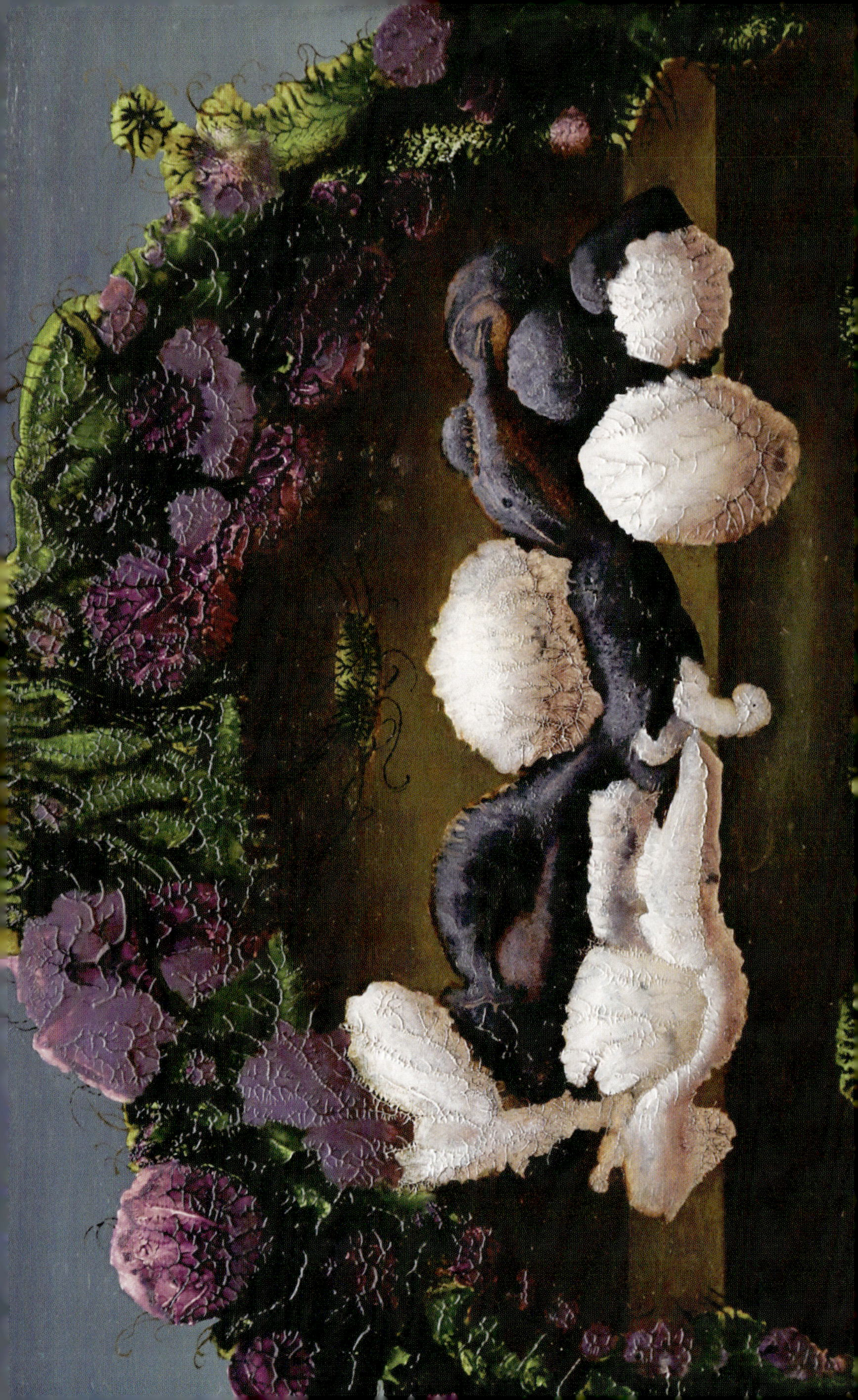

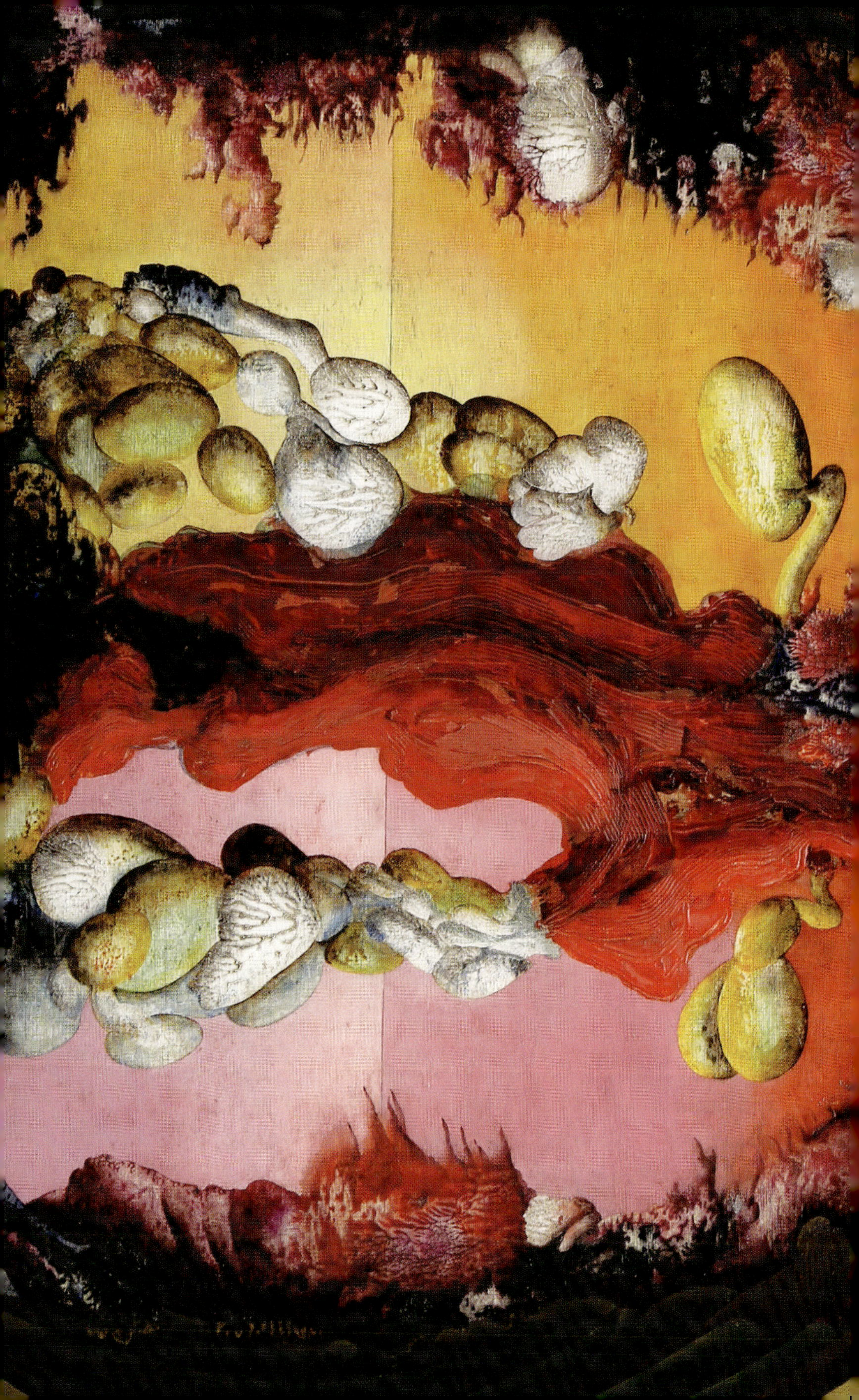

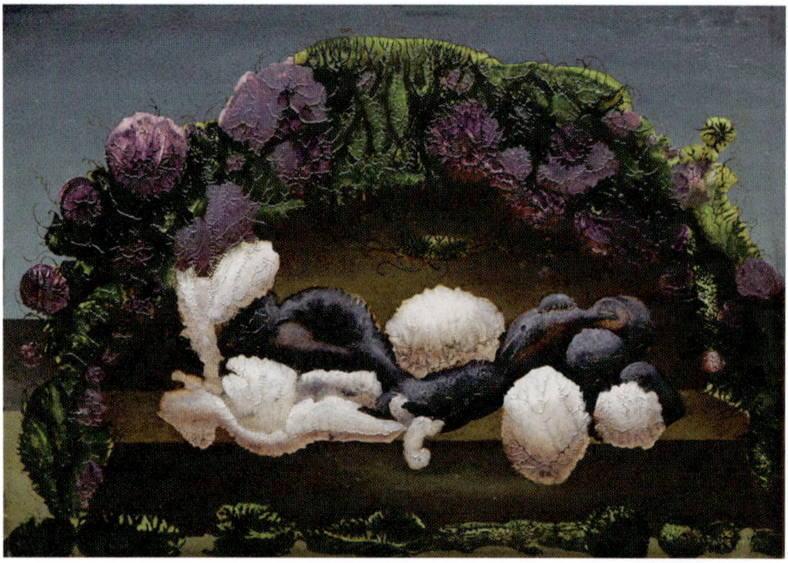

ABOVE & PREVIOUS SPREAD
Arbour (1946)

paint the unseen, and automatism would provide the vehicle. Her essay also recalls a section from the work of her cousin Edward Garstin's alchemical work, *The Secret Fire*:

> Here the allusion is to the Sacred Trance, the Mantic state, when, after the Alchemical Solution, the Soul or Spirit, withdrawing from the lower vehicles, penetrates into the hidden worlds. Therefore, the warning not to attempt to draw the Veil of Isis until the necessary purgations have been successfully performed, for She is not lightly to be profaned. Nor must the soul be led away by the delusive and phantasmal appearances which beset it on its passage through the Astral World wherein continually lieth a faithless Depth, delighting in unintelligible Images.[35]

What seems to be a primary difference in Colquhoun's development of Surrealist techniques is that her conception of the spaces one could reach using automatic processes would be inhabited by real entities and specific beings, contacted using a variety of esoteric languages.

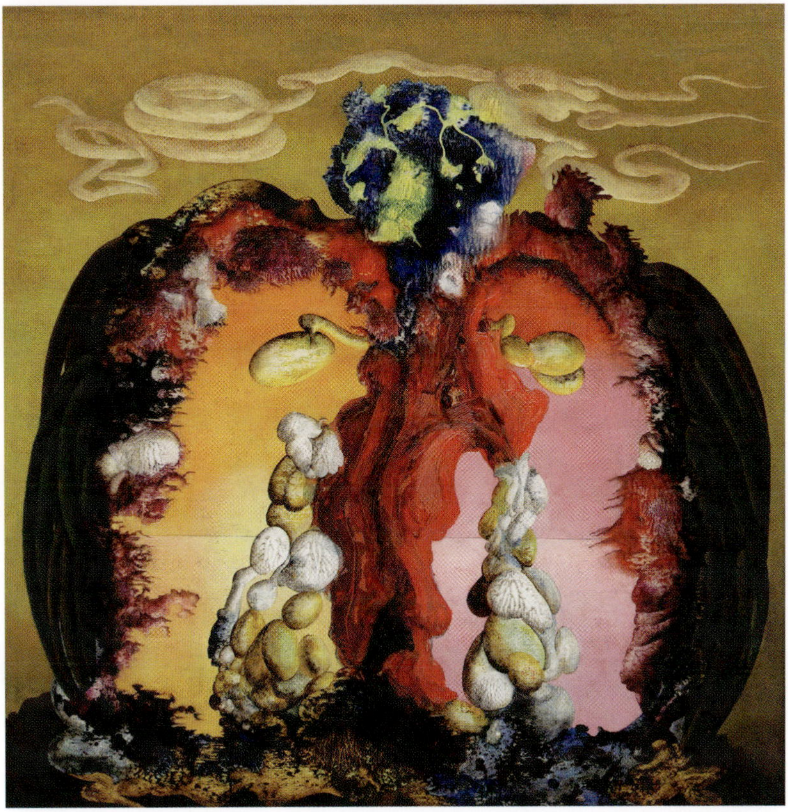

ABOVE & PREVIOUS SPREAD
Gorgon (1946)

She did not just use these techniques to see what came out of them with her mind in a state unfettered by logic and rationality, or to explore subconscious desires. It was about moving entirely beyond the self and establishing links with different planes. These other planes and entities had things to communicate to her, and as such her art was part of her road to enlightenment and served as invocation and ritual. This point is not explicitly articulated in the essays, where she mainly refers to the unconscious mind, but what was unwritten is Colquhoun's very real conception of the relationship between the unconscious mind and other realms.

Colquhoun's automatism was Hermetic in nature. For instance, she interpreted the four major automatic processes as corresponding to the four elements: *fumage* (which is developing figures from a canvas or paper which has been previously smoked) to Fire; *écrimage* or *parsemage* (which is when in the first instance oil and in the second charcoal or pastel are floated on water and then gently applied to paper) to Water; techniques where things are blown on paper, such as charcoal, paint or pastel, to Air; and *decalcomania*, where prints are either transferred or superimposed from one surface to another, to Earth. Therefore, when she chose which process she would use, she was in some way prescribing intent or focus into the artistic outcome.[36] Additionally, throughout the course of her own development of automatism, Colquhoun would also use specific colours that had magical correspondences, frequently based on Kabbalistic sources. This is most beautifully realised toward the end of her life in her Taro series (1977) and the *Decad of Intelligence* (1978–79). Further, she not only believed that this way of working would connect her with other planes of reality, but that this experience would be transferred to the viewer.

Many of Colquhoun's automatic works were decalcomanias, where she would place paint on a canvas and then place cardboard or another sturdy surface on top to create shapes, which she would then work up with a smaller brush to clarify forms. In the late 1940s and early 1950s we see Colquhoun expanding more skilfully into other forms of automatism, including superautomatism, *fumage* and *parsemage*. She was particularly skilled at reworking initial automatic designs with delicate pen or brush work to emphasise and bring out forms, as in *Depression* (1947). Her skill with *fumage* in particular became quite accomplished, although she never exhibited her best. *Fumage* is created from flames burning the paper ever so slightly to create an image, and as one might imagine the room for error is small. Although her archives show a number of attempts at making lines and shapes, at one stage she was able to execute a

RIGHT

Autumnal Equinox (1949)

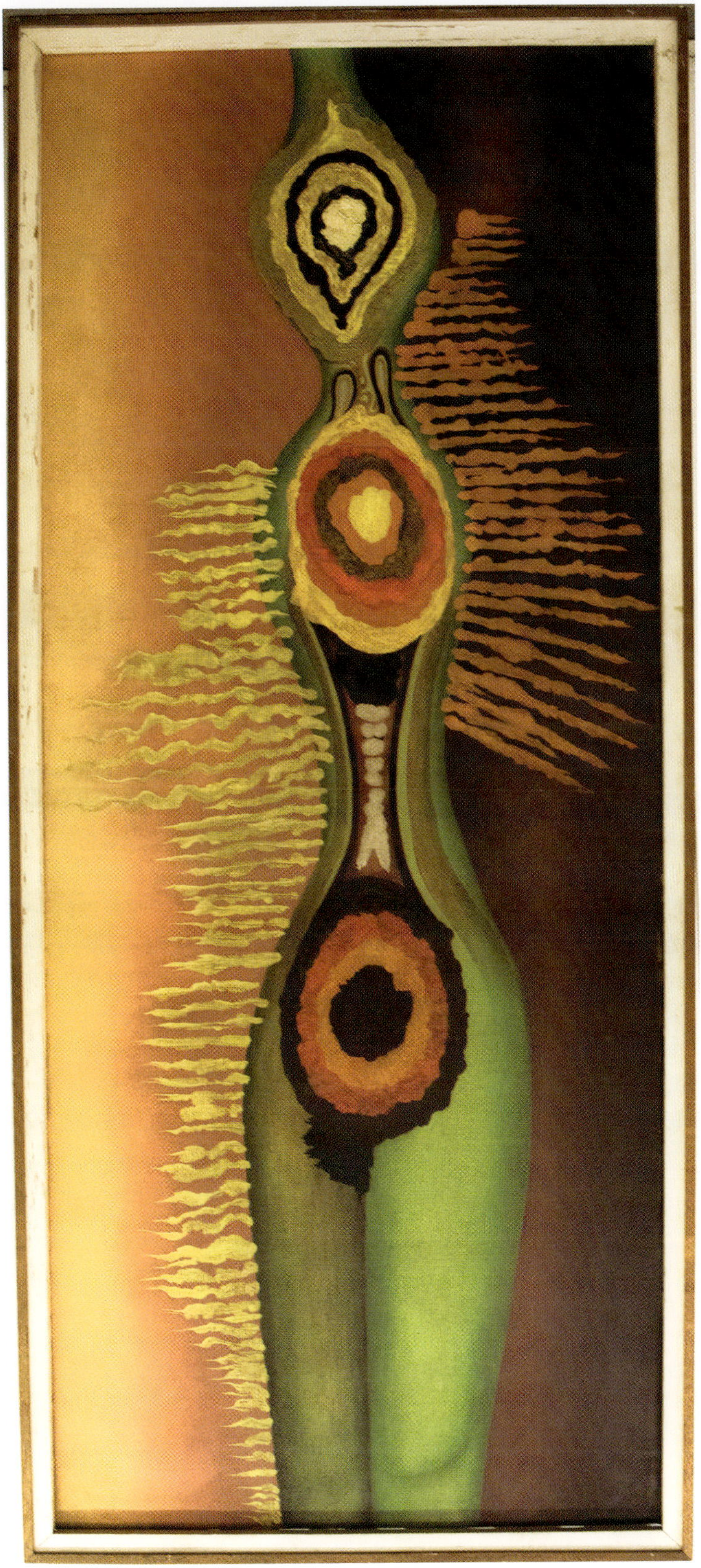

recognisable self-portrait in this manner, probably dating from the late 1940s or early 1950s.

Colquhoun experimented with and mastered a variety of automatic techniques. *Autumnal Equinox* (1949) is perhaps her most striking example of frottage, which is executed by rubbing some sort of pigment over a rough surface. In this case, Colquhoun applied paint to an old door to create an image that almost looks as though a spirit is trying to emerge from the richly textured spirals. In the 1960s she experimented with a variety of other types of automatism around the time when she was working heavily in *Merz* collage. In 1970 and 1971 she completed a series of graphomanias, which involved connecting dots with a pen using curved lines. She also completed several very accomplished stillomancies, although these were somewhat rare in her collection. Stillomancies are created by applying ink or paint to paper and then folding the surface in half to obtain roughly symmetrical images on both sides of the centre line. She would then work the images with fine detail to create images of deities and spirits that are unusual in her later corpus as they are clearly animate and representational. Her stillomancies frequently dealt with mythic figures, including *Horus* (c. 1957) and several other pieces from two decades later, including what have been labelled by auctioneers as *Nude with Orange Sky* and *Green Figure with Wings*. Not only are most of her stillomancies charming and alluring, but they have a psychological resonance similar to a Rorschach pattern: an aspect she might have enjoyed.

Colquhoun also used automatic techniques in her writing, mainly in constructing her poetry. When she was working in the Surrealist cultural milieu, she would create chain poems along with other Surrealists, where one person would generate a line or two and then pass it on to another for inspiration.[37] She appeared to have enjoyed the 'Question and Answer' variety where one person would pose a question, the following person would respond and then pose a question to the next person in line. In 1973 she wrote a short essay on the chain poem, explaining that it is yet another way of exploring the subconscious, and also connecting with others. She also wrote that if the party consisted of an equal number of men and women then the sexual tension would further arouse and heighten any E.S.P. faculties.[38]

Sometimes Colquhoun would create 'found poems' by rearranging or framing words and phrases she would find in other texts such as grammar books. In a 1980 essay on automatism for *Melmoth*, Colquhoun wrote that she would find poems in lists, grammars, and tables of contents, essentially removing phrases from books, and reframing them as poems, causing the reader to draw new connections and focus on the beauty of what might otherwise be a pedestrian list.[39] She used Gaelic grammars for these on a number of occasions, and one resulting poem was titled 'Exercise for Translation from a Gaelic Lesson Book by John Mac Kechnie', which, unsurprisingly for Colquhoun, ends up reading as a sensual encounter.[40] One example of an automatic poem crossing several forms was 'Hypnagogic Interior' which was generated from a list of names of moths, another creature with which Colquhoun was fascinated. She noted that this poem was created through 'automatism, decoupage, collage, objective hazard.' She had taken words from newspapers and glued them together to form the lines of the poem, which was eventually published in 1983 in her small collection *Osmazone*:

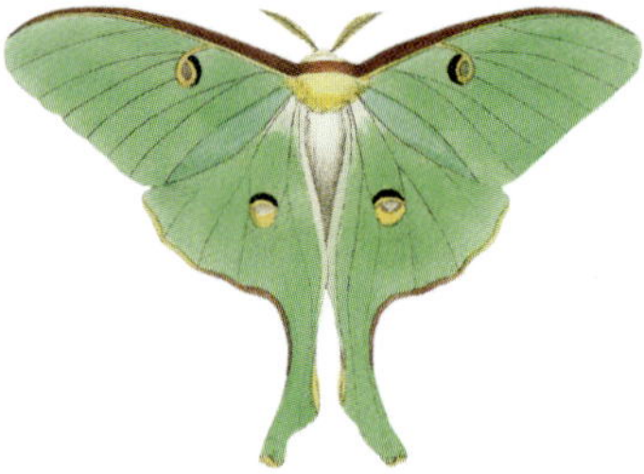

Silvery arches
Small angle shades
Scarce burnished brass
Small argent and sable

Water ermine
Narrow five-spot burnet
Brown argus
Barred chestnut

Great brocade
(Hidden wolf-light?)
Pale shining brown

ABOVE
Luna Moth

She would also pull out advertisement texts and short sections of magazines that she found poetic to highlight their beauty, turn of phrase, or strangeness. As she refined her position and her craft throughout her life, automatism became the means by which Colquhoun could realise her wider world view; she became the mediator and the medium, sometimes connecting the viewer to other worlds and sometimes simply turning a spotlight on that which might otherwise go unnoticed.

Dreams

Colquhoun's dreamtime was as significant as her waking life to her. She was deeply interested in the language, nature and reality of dreams as doorways to inner workings of the mind, and to other worlds beyond. Jungian dream interpretation was a significant feature in both her spiritual and artistic practice and the results can be seen strongly in her work in the 1950s and 1960s. She kept an active dream journal, and throughout her life many of her paintings and writings used her dreams as a basis. This was another area where the culture and practice of Surrealism supported her esoteric practice, and they worked in tandem. Surrealist practice around dreams focused on the facility of the artist to access the subconscious, which it was believed naturally extended into capturing one's dreams. Surrealists would also foster the capacity for dreaming since dreams may hold the keys not only to the unconscious but also to a superconscious world of shared images and archetypes. In many ways 'dream-like imagery' has become synonymous with Surrealist art, especially as imagined by Dalí, whose repeating visual motifs suggest a wider reality of images which force the unseen and unacknowledged into being. Breton's treatise on dreams, *Communicating Vessels* (1932), which lent its title to one of Colquhoun's paintings in 1941, suggested that the dream formed the link between the inner worlds and reality, the rational and the non-rational, and that the Surrealist should develop the facility to move from one state to the other.[41]

Given that scientific experts still don't know how dreams function, it is little wonder that these vivid experiences and visions have generated

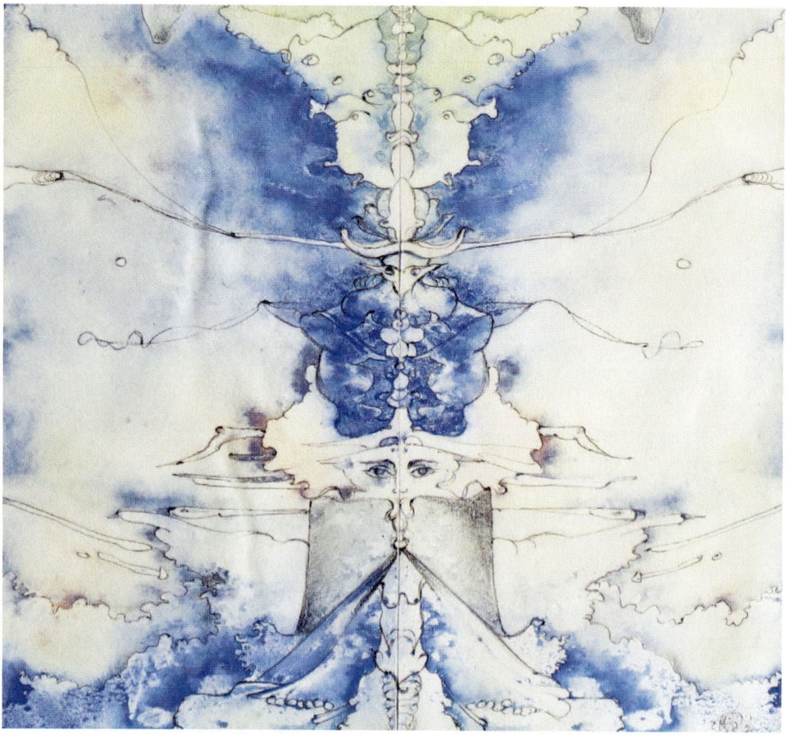

ABOVE
Oread (1970)

various esoteric explanations over the centuries. Some historical explanations suggest that the dream world constitutes a distinct and separate reality where the dreamer can cultivate a state through which she or he can receive divinely inspired messages or revelations. A number of esoteric systems still teach that, with training and practice, dreams can be a gateway to the astral plane, which contains its own reality, and where one can receive messages or have contacts from other entities. Additionally, occult practitioners might attempt to coordinate their activities to meet in a common dream space. Colquhoun experimented with this as well, contributing to her own identity as both artist and mystic. And as with her work with automatism, Colquhoun sought to take her dream work to different planes and levels than other Surrealists, using dreams to explore outer as well as inner worlds.

Colquhoun's focus expanded not only to facilitating communication between different parts of the mind or consciousness, which was a common Surrealist understanding of dream space, but she explored the belief that in the dream state the dreamer has the ability to move to different planes of reality. Dreams become the portals through which one passes from one reality into another. Not only can dreams help one to explore the inner landscape of emotions and desires through the interpretation of symbols, but one might also be able to move through time, with dreams as portents of future events.

Colquhoun believed that dreams could be used ritually, to help seed magical activity and to sharpen the magician's aim and understanding. She cited her richly textured 1952 painting *Grotto of the Sun and the Moon, Nicaragua* as an example of a revelation of the inner planes through dreams. The initial dream on which the painting was based was from 1941, where Colquhoun believed she had been shown the physical details of a magical alchemical order based in Nicaragua. On her therapist's advice, she painted it. She ultimately concluded that this was a direct message from the Order, which may or may not have ever existed in Nicaragua, trying to communicate its continuing existence to her, and its values of the eternal balance of male and female.

An important fellow traveller on Colquhoun's dream journeys was a London-based Jungian psychotherapist named Alice Buck, who conducted some rather unconventional research on dreams. Buck served as Colquhoun's dream therapist and interpreter, and the pair were already collaborating on dream interpretation as early as 1950. The notes between them indicate that this work created quite an intimate friendship. Buck was interested in dreams as an output or indicator of psychic activity, and from 1952 to 1955 Buck was working in America with the Parapsychology Laboratory at Duke University, researching distance precognition.[42] In addition to dream research, Buck also seems to have been conducting research with Zener cards (which resemble playing cards with simple graphics on them, designed to test for the capacity to either send or receive images).

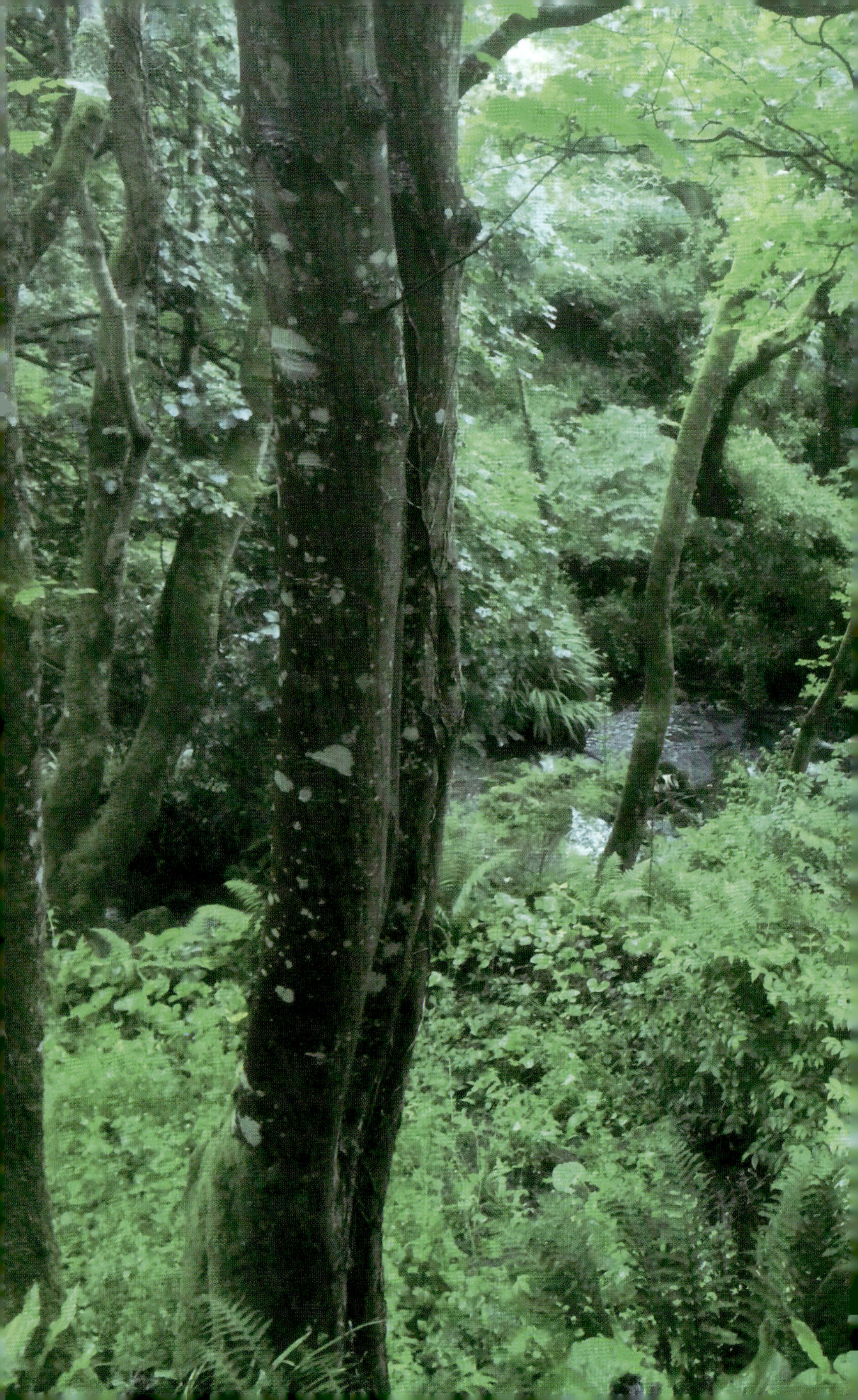

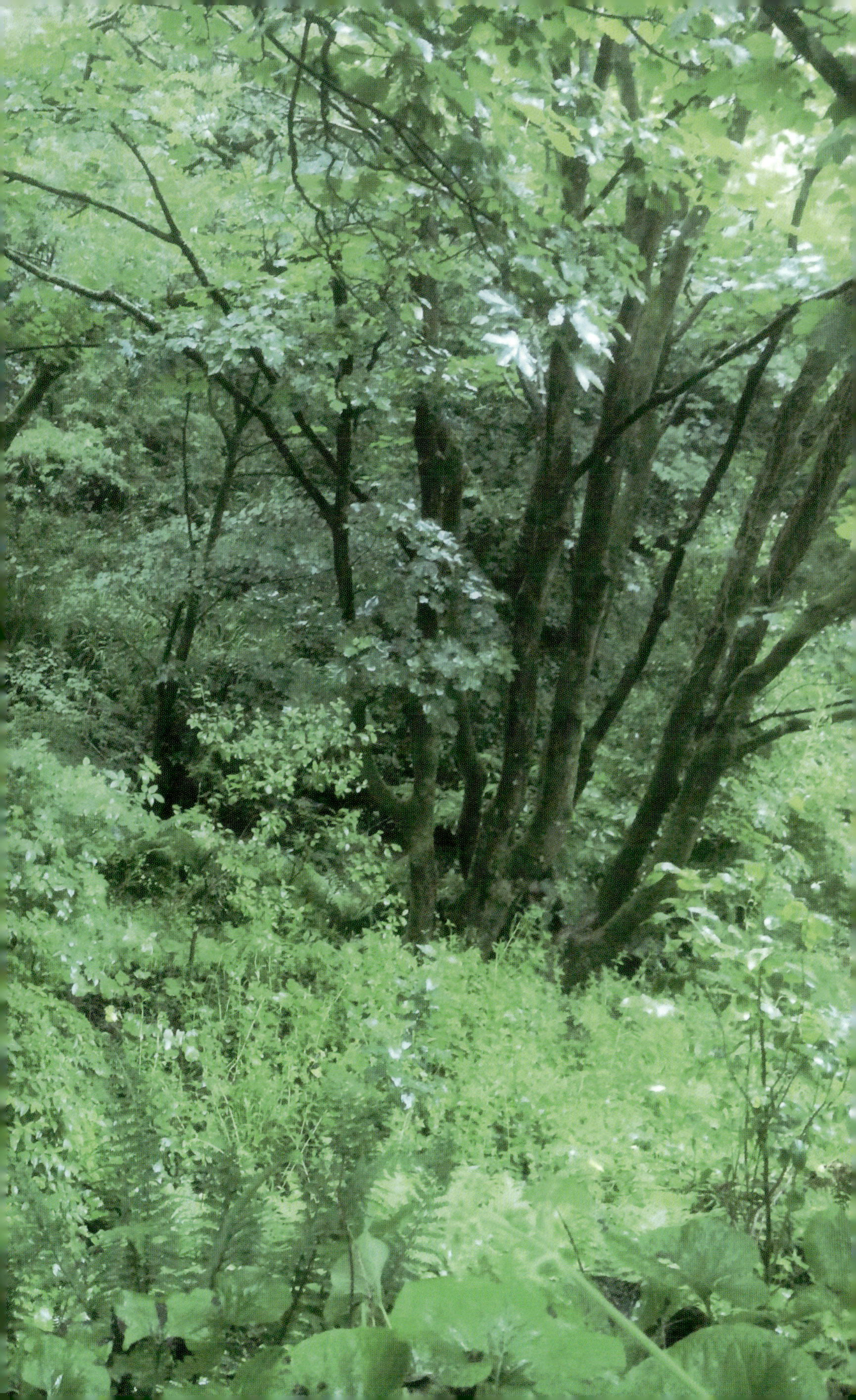

Perhaps Colquhoun was also part of this research. For over a decade Colquhoun was sending Buck dreams and sharing with her details of relationships and magical experiments, and Buck would provide coaching to help her understand her own psyche and where her dreams may have originated. Apparently, Buck's research also took an interest in the occult and, thinking of Colquhoun's own magical endeavours in the early 1950s, Buck indicated that while she was in the U.S. she would like to try to contact members of the O.T.O., or Ordo Templi Orientis, the magical order most commonly associated with Aleister Crowley.[43] The friendship continued through the 1950s, with Colquhoun designing the cover for a 1956 book that Buck and F. Claude Palmer published with Peter Owen. By 1961, Buck had placed herself into a convent for a retreat, and started calling herself Sister Alice Emily, commenting that Colquhoun's sensibility was closer to Catholic than Anglican.[44] Sadly, much of Buck's research has been lost, although some, regarding the religious implications of dreams, has been cited in Christian dream research. According to several medical registers she was still in practice in London in the late 1990s, and she may live on as a partial inspiration for Colquhoun's dream-based novel *I Saw Water*.

Colquhoun also had correspondence with an American philosophy professor named Raymond Frank Piper. Piper taught philosophy at Syracuse University from 1917 to 1954, and later in his career took an early interest in artists working with otherworldly realms, and in what might be now termed 'visionary art'. Visionary art today intersects with esoteric art to a degree, but is generally thought of as being created by untrained artists whose work is purely based on visionary experience or contact with otherworldly entities. In 1956 Piper wrote a book called *The Hungry Eye: An Introduction to Cosmic Art*, and Colquhoun's correspondence with him lasted from 1952 to 1961. Colquhoun's work with both Buck and Piper shows the degree to which she would have characterised herself as a seer, with regard to her work, and why 'The Mantic Stain' reveals more about her process than just being a primer

PREVIOUS SPREAD
The lushness of the fern loved gully, Lamorna.

about automatic techniques and divination. Through dreams and other means, she was working to cultivate these talents in herself, and wanted feedback from professionals who were possibly working to use and study these phenomena in distinctly modern contexts using modern means. As evident from her interests in the science behind extra dimensions, it's clear that Colquhoun, despite her disdain for progress that disrupted nature in any way, wanted to engage with scientific inquiry. To that end, in 1955, she wrote a piece for the *London Broadsheet*, 'Divination up to Date', chronicling the progression of paranormal work.

Although Colquhoun drew from her dreams occasionally as inspirations for her paintings, her dreams were more important for her fiction, short stories and poems. In fact, dreams form the basis for most of the episodes which are found in her Surrealist fiction. Colquhoun kept detailed dream notes, sometimes scribbled on tiny lined notebook sheets that she would pull out and rearrange for various projects. Often, she would weave together dream sequences from quite disparate time frames to help her clarify various themes. This gives her writing an overall otherworldly effect. The reader is meant to experience these tales as being dramas enacted on an archetypal level. This technique may also contribute to a certain stylistic coldness that pervades her writing. She writes of strange things happening to strange people, often motivated by cosmic themes. As a result, her writing is often rich in description and symbolism, but the style is sterile and the characters' motives are hard to relate to. However, it is supposed to operate on the level of revelation rather than entertainment.

Vow Cave and Lamorna

Although Colquhoun was visiting Cornwall during the war, partly to escape the Blitz, she began the process of settling there, part-time, in the late 1940s. She kept a residence in North London until the late 1950s, and commuted back and forth, which must have been no small expense. In 1947 she started renting Vow Cave, the small, rough studio that was to be her Cornish base until she moved to the village of Paul near Newlyn and Penzance in the 1950s. There were a variety of reasons why she ultimately chose Cornwall as a home: her love of the Celts and her attraction to sacred landscapes and rural tranquillity was perhaps a primary one, but there is no doubt that the artistic heritage of Cornwall, and especially the eccentric Lamorna valley, would have made it a suitable home, even though her relationship with the arts communities which were already established in Cornwall was a somewhat awkward one. Her artistic style and sensibilities did not exactly fit but she somehow managed to carve out a place for herself.

Cornwall is often touted as a home for artists and the creatively offbeat, and studies of artists and writers who settled in Cornwall are legion. But it's good to keep in mind that this view of Cornwall as a quirky, arty isthmus is not shared by everyone, and for many it is not the most significant story to tell of Cornwall and its people. West Cornwall is a stunningly beautiful place, but in the wake of the decline of the traditional industries of mining and fishing, it suffers from a most picturesque form of rural poverty. In particular, the art colonies which settled in West Cornwall from the nineteenth century onward have been a rather uncomfortable topic for scholars of Cornwall. While the growth of the creative economy has certainly been a boon in many ways, there is no doubt that the influx of artists in the late nineteenth century was occurring in the shadow of the death throes of Cornish native industries, and that pain was still very much present among the local population, evidenced by mass migration and a swiftly declining economy. In many ways the phenomenon of the arrival of English artists reinforced much of the Otherness of Cornwall that made it attractive to artists, especially when they were coming in to immortalize the dying industries of a population that seemed removed from them by culture and by class. But what is indisputable is that the art movements of West Cornwall economically and culturally transformed the landscape in ways that are still shaping the character of that area, even if this development is contested.[45]

There were two primary art movements in Cornwall that formed the background of the artistic milieu in West Cornwall in which Colquhoun lived and worked for the second half of her life. The first was the Newlyn School, which operated from around the 1880s until the 1920s. Newlyn is a fishing village adjacent to Penzance, dramatically overlooking the Atlantic. In the late nineteenth century artists such as Stanhope Forbes, who had previously been working in Brittany, began to settle in Cornwall to capture the lives and activities of the fishing community there, believing that they were witnessing the end of an era. Forbes, his wife Elizabeth, and Walter Langley are the most recognised names from the Newlyn School, and Forbes started an art school in 1899 focused on the study of the figure. Newlyn artists worked *en plein air* and focused on dramatic moments of industry, trying to preserve the moment that a shoal of fish was netted, a conversation between fish sellers on the docks, or the aftermath of a fishing tragedy. The subject was gritty, yet the Newlyn painters managed to be romantic in their approach, creating scenes bathed in pastel pinks and soothing light aqua tones. Although the artists generally believed that they were advancing social realism in portraying the labours of the working class, there is still a sense that they were comfortably removed from the reality of the lives they were painting. Although the Newlyn School had seen its day by the time Colquhoun was its neighbour, the artists had made a lasting impact. In a slightly earthier vein, the Newlyn Industrial Class was a development out of the Newlyn School that lasted from the 1890s to the outbreak of the Second World War and was designed to retrain members of the fishing community in Newlyn in craft production that would help to supplement their incomes. Newlyn Copper was the primary recognisable outcome of this programme, with artisans creating Arts-and-Crafts-inspired designs that reflected the themes of the landscape and community, often beautifully spiralling fish. It was a member of this programme, Francis Cargeeg, who later crafted Colquhoun's magic mirror as well as the regalia of the Cornish *Gorseth*.

The second arts colony in proximity to Colquhoun, and the one which would have defined much of the character of West Cornwall during Colquhoun's life, was at St. Ives. There had been arts activity at St. Ives from the late nineteenth century, and the St. Ives School of Painting was established in 1938, but it was really the development through the war and after that had the most lasting cultural impact. It is hard to know which would have grated against Colquhoun's artistic sensibilities more, the sentimentality of the Newlyn School or the abstraction of the St. Ives Modernists. Unlike the school at Newlyn, the St. Ives group had much less coherence as an artistic movement. What they did share, however, was their love of a small and immensely picturesque fishing village in the West of Cornwall that had been hit hard by the decline of the fishing industry, and which was known for its spectacular light. St. Ives is a truly stunning village, with tightly packed houses and winding complex alley ways crisscrossing from one harbour to another. It is easy to see why these artists believed they had discovered a slice of paradise.

Although the styles of St. Ives and Newlyn painters couldn't be more different, the artists settling in Cornwall all shared a fascination with what they perceived as the native, naïve, primitive and 'authentic', a dynamic which has shaped the relationship of arts production to Cornwall up to the present day, and which was certainly an attraction for Colquhoun. In 1928 artist Ben Nicholson came upon self-taught Cornish artist Alfred Wallis, a fisherman who created scenes of St. Ives and fishing boats on wooden planks. Nicholson loved the 'primitive' quality of his work. Partially inspired by the seeming abstraction of Wallis's paintings, Nicholson and his wife, sculptor Barbara Hepworth, settled in Cornwall in 1939 and helped to foster a developing community of artists inspired by cubism, using bold lines and bright colours in their own abstractions of the Cornish landscape. Significant artists in the community included potter Bernard Leach, Terry Frost, Wilhelmina Barns-Graham and Peter Lanyon, one of the few native Cornish artists affiliated with the group. As Cornwall was a popular relocation spot for Londoners during the war, these artists chose to ride out WWII in the relative isolation of this small village, and of course their presence impacted the character of the area. Yet the St. Ives school flourished most after the war, in the 1950s, when even more artists flocked there. Welsh writer Denys Val Baker's 1959 book

Britain's Art Colony by the Sea was one of the first to capture the spirit of the community, but by that time the movement was on the wane, and ceased to be a real force by the mid-1960s.

Regardless of Colquhoun's own artistic path, which was unique by comparison to these others, each of these historical communities that had so shaped West Cornwall also shaped her. But Colquhoun's initial landing spot in Cornwall, the lush and stunning valley and cove of Lamorna, had its own artistic history that Colquhoun became a part of. Lamorna, like many coves in Cornwall, was initially known as a shipping port for quarried stone. It was owned and developed by a single owner, Colonel Paynter, who supported the development of an artists' colony in the earliest years of the 20th century. Paynter was reportedly opposed to any sales of his land, so he rented out his properties to artists. He allowed Colquhoun to make alterations and improvements to Vow Cave. In *The Living Stones* Colquhoun writes that Paynter was actually one of the first people she met in Cornwall, and was amused that she ended up renting out Vow Cave Studio from him a couple of years later.

What is known as the Lamorna Colony had historical links to the Newlyn School, but it had its own development that encouraged a variety of artists who were not as stylistically aligned with one school or another, such as one might find at Newlyn or St. Ives. Samuel 'Lamorna' Birch was a prominent Newlyn School artist who settled in Lamorna, followed by other Newlyn-aligned artists who themselves started a small colony. Eventually a variety of other artists and writers moved to Lamorna Cove, making it a dynamic yet small scene. Although it may seem isolated, from the perspective of an outsider, Colquhoun's artistic milieu in Cornwall would have been a rather heady mix and she would have had varied neighbours. So, although she may have been escaping the big city when she was away from London in Cornwall, it's useful to keep in mind that she still had the ability to be right in the middle of things. Lamorna may feel remote, but it was still exceptionally connected. It is easy to imagine peace-loving Colquhoun

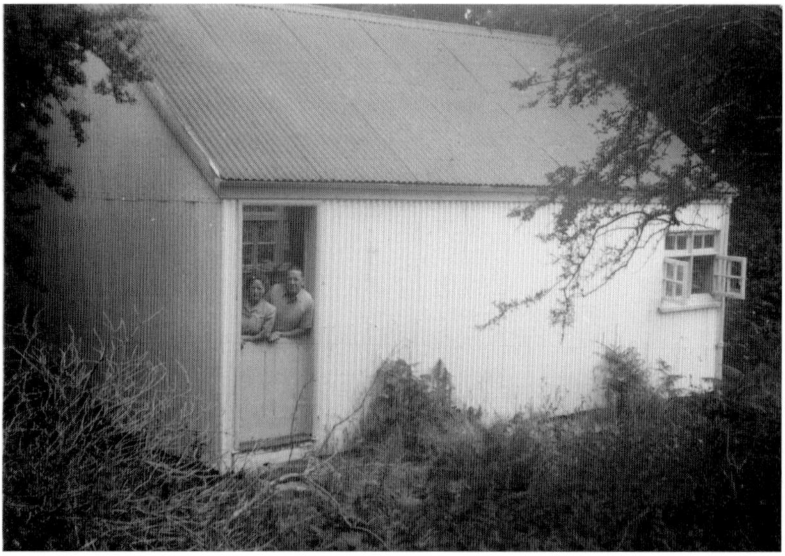

ABOVE Colquhoun's studio in Lamorna, Vow Cave.

in isolation, in her primitive shack, but her reality may have been more socially connected, and her shack more comfortable than primitive.

In *The Living Stones*, Colquhoun portrays a rather alternative and unconventional side of Lamorna when she tells the story of The Woodcutters, whom we might conceptualise as early hippies living a somewhat communal life-style, making crafts and living off the land as conscientious objectors during the war. Interestingly, The Woodcutters' values may mirror those of the artistic community of anarchists and conscientious objectors who Colquhoun was working with in the early 1940s, so there may have been a resonance there. We see here the portrayal of Cornwall as a haven for the offbeat, weird and unusual at quite an early stage, and West Cornwall was in the thick of it, providing spaces for those on the margins. In an unpublished short story Colquhoun wrote about Lamorna called 'The Streams of St. Bride' she captures what seems to have been a hotbed of social activity, affairs and machinations typical of any small community, but perhaps particularly amplified by the big personalities of artists, writers and

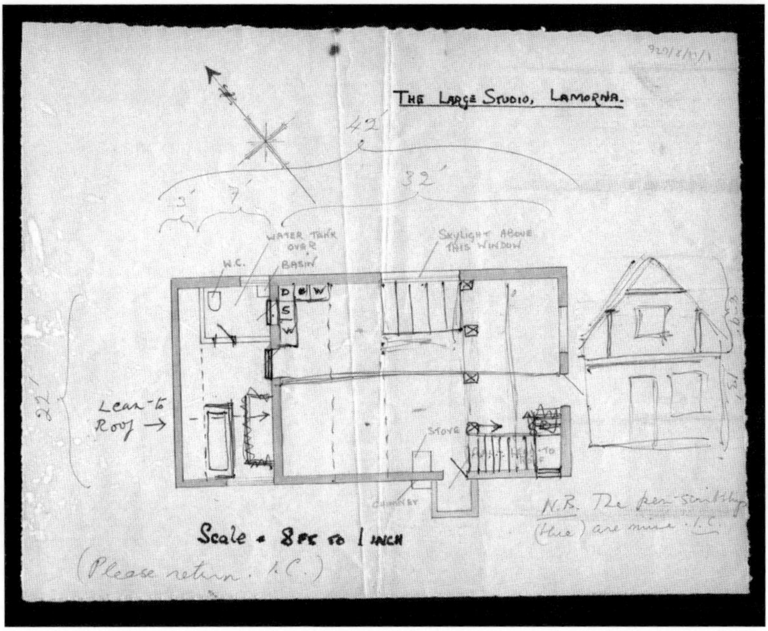

ABOVE Architectural drawings for the improvement of Vow Cave.

other dropouts. Yet in Colquhoun's retelling of how she took possession of Vow Cave in *The Living Stones* we hear little about Lamorna's status as an artists' colony, just the occasional mention of all the homes with studios.

A variety of artists lived in Lamorna during the time Colquhoun was there, and she would have had many things in common with her Lamorna compatriots. She very likely knew John Tunnard from his loose affiliation with British Surrealism, and although he was living in the nearby village of Zennor when Colquhoun arrived in Lamorna, he moved there in 1953. One unconventional and richly uncompromising neighbour was Hannah Gluckstein, better known simply as Gluck: 'No prefix, suffix, or quotes'. Gluck was an open lesbian from a very wealthy background, known for dressing in a 'mannish' fashion, and an artist who refused to be confined to any artistic labels. Her subjects ranged from beautifully realistic still life compositions of flowers to portraits of wealthy women. She had a number of properties that she spent time in, but she appeared to live freely and openly in Lamorna with her partners. One long term partner, Edith Shackleton Heald, was one of Yeats's lovers. Gluck and Colquhoun had a friendship that lasted until the end of Gluck's life in 1978, and Colquhoun purchased Gluck's Bolton House studio at Windmill Hill in Hampstead from her in 1949 for £2,500. Marlow Moss was another lesbian artist of a 'mannish' disposition working in Lamorna, a Constructivist with a background in architecture. It is possible that Colquhoun knew of her from earlier trips to Paris and of her work with Amédée Ozenfant. She was also clearly a friend, and Colquhoun kept the catalogues of her shows in Mousehole and London.

Colquhoun's retelling of her arrival into Lamorna in *The Living Stones*, with its focus on characters, antiquities and Celts, paints a picture of a woman embracing the 'primitive' and the wild in an ancient and haunted land. But we should keep in mind that Colquhoun still had her home in London and was able to go back and forth between Cornwall and London as she chose. Peter Owen characterised her studio in London as well appointed, spacious and certainly comfortable. Colquhoun had the means to choose to live somewhat raw in Cornwall, and either home could serve as an escape. While her love of Cornwall was certain, she was still, for quite some time, between spaces. Cornwall may have been her love, but she had not yet fully submitted.

After she started living in Cornwall part-time, Colquhoun focused more of her energies on trying to get published. While she had always been a writer, the circumstances during wartime were not as conducive to major publishing efforts such as novels, and many of her efforts were seen as too risky or not marketable. In addition to novels she worked on a number of short stories and dream-inspired Surrealist vignettes, with varying levels of success. Colquhoun was still running with her old literary crowd, and started publishing various items with Antony Borrow, who knew of her friend Derek Stanford at least through his poetry readings. Joshua Blu Buhs, chronicler of Bigfoot and eccentrics, characterises Borrow as a 'Fortean', having joined the Fortean Society in 1948, which would have given him common ground with Colquhoun.[46] He was a chemist by trade who had an interest in the occult and later in science fiction. Borrow started *The Glass*, a small literary magazine, in 1948, and Colquhoun published her 'The Myth of Santa Warna' in the first issue. Borrow may also have intersected with Colquhoun's occult circles. He knew of and published Ross Nichols, who was on the poetry reading circuit at the time, and this may well have been one of the channels through which Nichols and Colquhoun initially interacted. Borrow later went on to publish the *London Broadsheet*, in 1954, to which Colquhoun also contributed.

Many of Colquhoun's most important publishing efforts came about as a result of her personal relationship with the publisher Peter Owen. His firm, which started in 1951, has always prided itself on having an independent, uncompromising and high-quality catalogue, taking chances on worthy authors and books which may have had trouble finding a home. One example of Owen's keen eye was the publication of Herman Hesse's *Siddhartha*. In 2003, Owen recalled that he had met Colquhoun at a pub in 1950 and their friendship was bolstered by their mutual social circle of artists and writers. The writer Muriel Spark, at that time the partner of Colquhoun's longtime friend Derek Stanford, was the first editor for Peter Owen when the company started in 1951. Colquhoun was focusing more on her efforts at publication during this time, and Owen recalled that Colquhoun had initially approached him about publishing *Goose of Hermogenes*, but he was unsure of the market for it, and gently put her off for over a decade. However, Colquhoun worked for him as an illustrator, and created a number of book covers, including one for her friend Alice Buck. When she had mentioned her interest in writing a travelogue about Ireland, Owen commissioned it, and followed up with *The Living Stones*. Based on the success of these, he felt more comfortable taking a chance on *Goose of Hermogenes*, which was finally published in 1961 after rather continual prompting from Colquhoun.

Later work

Colquhoun's visual work decreases dramatically in the 1960s, as much of her artistic production moves into writing and also into magical imagery associated with various magical projects. Colquhoun was never going to be bound by fashion or trend, and she created the art that she wanted to create. Although she engaged in artistic communities, she was independent and had no allegiance to a movement. In 1964, inspired by the *Merz* collages of Kurt Schwitters, she began primary focus on collage and found art which continued for the better part of the decade. This, too, she related to her occult practice since she believed that Moina Mathers was one of the first collage artists, and that collage also unlocked the potential of the subconscious. In an unpublished 1969 essay about Schwitters, Colquhoun recalled that they had met twice in London during the war, and she found him 'without pretention'. Although it took some time for her to adopt *Merz* collage as part of her artistic repertoire, and many of her attempts were less than polished, she still claimed Schwitters as a primary influence on her later work. 'If "Che lives", then so does Kurt, even in the poets who now pack the Albert Hall with imitations of his style, but often lack his wit.'[47]

In the mid-1960s, perhaps buoyed by her successes with Peter Owen, Colquhoun was working to spread her wings as a Surrealist writer. However, success eluded her. She worked with literary agents on publishing her novels and short stories, and sent out manuscripts, yet her work was simply too occult, and too hard to relate to, for commercial success. Her letters from the later period of her life show that she was frequently lonely and depressed, and as an artist she may have been more isolated from a social network. She suffered greatly from asthma, and went through periods where asthma relief was a focus of her attention. Cornwall is not the most hospitable climate for asthma sufferers, being cold and windy, and Colquhoun was isolated in Paul, with medical attention not being quickly obtainable. But her health and isolation did not diminish her focus and dedication. She continued to exhibit and create until her final years. In the 1970s she exhibited works both old and new, held solo shows of new work and Surrealist retrospectives, and participated in a number of group exhibitions. From 1977 to 1981 she was the focus of several exhibitions featuring much earlier work. Her artistic focus returned to automatism, and many of her experiments became more visually refined. She made a thematic return to images and ideas that she had worked with through her life with flowers and the natural world. In 1971 she completed several remarkable stillomancies, and in her later years she also returned to volcano imagery. In her younger years this may have been a metaphor for the changing world, but it is hard to know how she saw herself in relationship to the bursting creative earth in her final decade. Some of her later Surrealist works may represent the most complete synthesis of her esoteric work and her Surrealist processes.

Toward the end of her life she once again engaged with the Surrealist community and even came back into the orbit of her old friend Conroy Maddox. In 1979 the short-lived Melmoth project emerged, which included Maddox, outsider art proponent Roger Cardinal, Tony Pusey and Iraqi writer and activist Haifa Zangana. According to Silvano Levy, the aim of the group was to promote Surrealist action in everyday life.[48] In 1980, under the editorship of Zangana, Colquhoun contributed three poems and 'Notes on Automatism' to *Melmoth* 2. Later, in 1983, Tony Pusey helped Colquhoun to publish a poetry anthology, *Osmazone*, which featured a small collection of her prose poems from a much earlier period. It was perhaps not the anthology she had always hoped for, but this small contribution ensured that the power of her voice was heard. The title was a reference to J.K. Huysman's 1884 novel *A Rebours* (Against the Grain) where he refers to the prose poem as the distillate of the novel, 'the osmazone of literature'. Colquhoun wrote a lot of prose poems, and clearly her aim was to convey the essence of a moment. The print run was small, only 200, and it was very slim, nearly a pamphlet. Many of the poems came from earlier in her career, some composed as early as World War Two. Shillitoe notes that many of the selections have a transgressive theme, dealing with bodily fluids and even condoms.[49] One piece, 'Divination', was originally written as a section of her autobiography, *Until Twelve*, and shows her radical view of the power of menstruation:

> This is what must be done, even though it will make civilisation turn over. It is harmful to attempt a normal appearance – business, housework, the catching of trains – when normality is absent and its place taken by intensified sensibility to hidden springs. It is the mood to divine buried treasure, to speak the oracular words, to consummate the ritual marriage. It is a natural break in outward routine and to neglect this rhythm brings age, harshness, irritation, the loss of beauty and peace. Through retirement I have become reconciled to the moon.[50]

This collection would have been published when Colquhoun was 77 years old. And while we know many of these pieces to have been written by a much younger Colquhoun, it may, in fact, be even more radical that this emerged as the poetic voice of an older woman, one who was not going to succumb to easy themes. She was always going to be a force to be reckoned with.

Atlantean currents:

IV – Celticism

NEXT PAGE Mên-an-Tol
from J.T. Blight's 1893
A Week at the Land's End.

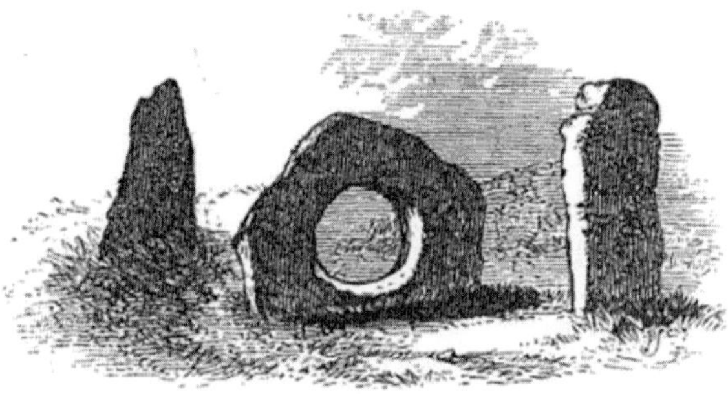

THE MÊN-AN-TOL.

IV

Ithell Colquhoun was what Marion Bowman would call a 'Cardiac Celt': she was not raised within a Celtic culture, but her Celtic soul was a matter of deepest conviction. For Colquhoun her sense of what was Celtic was deeply entwined with her spirituality and artistic expression that ran alongside her Hermetic pursuits. Her love of the Celts started early with her own ancestral researches, and eventually caused her to settle in Cornwall in the late 1940s, after her divorce. She believed that her Celtic ancestry predisposed her to second sight and the visionary states that would make her Surrealism more successful, and that Cornwall would allow her to be surrounded by sacred landscape and Celtic culture. Like the other Surrealists fascinated with the Celts, Colquhoun's attraction stemmed from her attraction to Celtic otherworldliness and, rightly or wrongly, she believed that as someone of both Scottish and Irish ancestry, she was heir to that otherworldliness. By extension this formed the basis of her connection to and love of Cornwall.

Colquhoun's personal interest in Celtic cultures mirrors the general development of Celtic spiritual and political movements in the second half of the twentieth century. Her deep attachment to the Cornish landscape and her ideas about Celtic mysticism inspired her involvement with a variety of emerging Celtic groups and movements. She participated in a variety of Celtic themed spiritual organisations at key moments in their development, encompassing Druidry, varieties of Celtic orthodox Catholicism and, later in life, groups dedicated to Celtic mysticism. Colquhoun's Celtic interests and identity form an important strand of her overall work and spiritual practice, yet because they did not result in a significant body of paintings, this part of her magical biography has not received as much attention as her Hermetic work. Yet her Celticity was important in her understanding of herself as a Surrealist, and she was a writer as much as she was a painter. Her Celtic interests inspired poetry, essays, and two books which are now considered groundbreaking in the earth mysteries genre.

However, Colquhoun's love of the Celts is not unproblematic. It was of the highly romantic type frequently found in English Celtophiles, and it didn't always sit comfortably with ethnically Celtic communities. Colquhoun's beliefs about Celts' essential nature, as earth-loving, artistic, psychic, and spiritual, are, as Malcolm Chapman showed in his still controversial 1992 book *The Celts, Construction of a Myth*, at their core a construction of cultural 'Otherness', that have contributed to social, cultural and economic marginalisation in addition to internal colonisation. The Celts have been historically portrayed as 'noble savages' in opposition to the practical, logical, Anglo-Saxons with whom they are frequently contrasted. Celts are historically painted as naturally poetic people who are inherently soulful, and therefore incapable of self-governance. The idea of 'The Celt', and particularly 'The Ancient Briton' has, since the eighteenth century, become emblematic for a nation trying to unite under a cultural substrate by promoting a sense of Celtic British indigeneity. In the twentieth century we see the growth of this position within the development of various forms of Celtic spirituality, where English people who were not raised in culturally Celtic areas could still, as British, claim a Celtic cultural inheritance. The results of that exercise have been uneven at best, but Colquhoun believed in the spiritual ideal while simultaneously, and importantly, recognising the impact of English colonisation on Celtic peoples and places. Colquhoun was explicitly against the English colonisation of Celtic areas. She despised the colonisers and what they stole and she particularly resented any English historical suppression of Celtic languages and Celtic customs. Yet her own beliefs about Celts and the magical nature of Celtic landscapes were clearly generated by a highly romanticised view.

A Preservationist Outlook

Much of the motivation for Colquhoun's engagement with what is now more broadly known as 'Celtic spirituality' was her belief in the existence of a Celtic wisdom tradition that flowed in the veins and the land of Celtic peoples. Archaeologist Michael Dietler has defined Celticity as a 'phenomenon centered around a global spiritual connection to the idea of Celtic identity'. He distinguishes this from Celticism, which he defines as 'self-conscious attempts to construct ethnicised forms of collective memory and communal identity that are territorially bounded and embedded in overt political projects and ideologies.' Colquhoun's Celtic identity was more firmly situated in the first category, although with one caveat: Dietler suggests that Celticity is not built on rhetorical strategies of race and ethnicity, yet many 'Cardiac Celts' believe that their relationship to the Celts is one of 'race', and can be activated by 'race memory', especially if they believe that the Celts formed the deepest ancestral substrata of Britain. Colquhoun was certainly in this category.

As a Perennialist who moved between spiritual systems and practices, Colquhoun would have interpreted her Celtic pursuits as one way to 'The Truth' out of many. 'Celtic spirituality' is a modern umbrella term with both Pagan and Christian articulations, and both are relevant to understanding Colquhoun's Celtic spiritual pursuits, which seem oddly contradictory at times . Although 'Celtic spirituality' tends not to be a label of self-ascription, Druidry, earth mysteries, Contemporary Celtic Christianity, and even in some cases Wicca have all been incorporated under it. Celtic spirituality can be characterised as broadly nativist in British, Irish and Scottish contexts, with a focus on institutions and practices that are believed to be indigenous, and in a Christian context frequently set apart from incursions of Roman Catholicism. Spiritual activities may include pilgrimage and the veneration of sacred landscapes, ritual activity around saints (even in a non-Catholic context) or local pre-Christian deities, celebration of saints' days or the revival of agricultural festivals, and the incorporation of Celtic myth, folklore or folk practices into ritual or liturgy. In both a Christian and non-Christian context, environmentalism and the veneration of the Divine Feminine have been adopted as values which are imagined to reflect the values of indigenous, pre-Christian British peoples, and thus have shaped the ethics and practices of Celtic spirituality. Many of these features drove Colquhoun's expressions of a Celtic spiritual identity, particularly her interest in Celtic myth and above all in building a connection with sacred sites and landscapes.

When looking at the context for Colquhoun's spiritual and even political convictions related to Celtic cultures, we must understand that her sentiments were fiercely antimodern. She believed Celtic peoples were closest to their own nature when not subjected to modernising influences or outside philosophies that would dilute their unique cultural properties, such as her belief that they had more natural psychic ability.

> There was no need for written history because past and present were not sharply distinguished, and man could enter the ever-present record if need be, since all veils were thin. One with his race, whether living or dead, he still retained kinship with supernatural races.[51]

Since Modernism and civilisation interfere with the otherworldly access of the Celt, Colquhoun believed Celtic primitivism needed to be preserved at all costs. She particularly resented the intrusions of civilisation on Celtic sacred sites and landscapes, with which she felt a psychic and ancestral connection. In her life in Cornwall, especially at first, she cultivated the veneer of extreme simplicity, despite being able to retreat to her well-appointed London studio. For many years in her studio in Lamorna she had no plumbing or electricity, and no doubt this was to help her achieve a sense of authentic experience in a Celtic setting: she felt modern life was simply too encroaching and too loud. Yet as she admitted in *The Living Stones*, she never spent a full year in Lamorna, only visiting when time afforded.

Colquhoun maintained that she did not engage in politics, but while she may not have been actively involved in electoral politics, she most certainly had political views, and her forays into Celtic activism were preservationist in character. Colquhoun was a self-described Traditionalist, and understanding this sheds some light on the decisions that she made regarding her spiritual and artistic practices. Colquhoun was well aware of the philosophical school of the same name, and was deeply inspired by some of its key thinkers, particularly the esotericist René Guénon, who certainly influenced her relationship with Celtic peoples and Celtic spirituality. Traditionalism is a philosophical movement which emerged in the early 20th century and is associated with a group of European esoteric philosophers including René Guénon and Julius Evola. It is driven by a critique of modernity, and a belief in a return to a 'Traditional' society, based on spiritual principles which once guided the development and governing of ancient civilisations, and were handed down to elites through initiatory traditions. According to Traditionalists, the roots of this 'Tradition' can still be seen in some latter-day faith systems, notably those of the East, in Hinduism, Islam or Orthodox Christianity. Traditionalists critique modern society as deeply degraded, chaotic, and corrupt, and argue that only through a return to traditional social structures, values, and belief systems can the world be redeemed and returned to the state of divine order. This view characterises Colquhoun's view of the world, and her view of Celtic cultures and her vision of them. Certainly, by the 1950s she had read Guénon. She was also influenced by his predecessor, Oswald Spengler, whose 1918 publication *Decline of the West* was an early, and extremely popular, work describing the rise and fall of civilisations within a comparative framework. Spengler's view was aristocratic and driven by an early anti-capitalist critique of democracy, the Enlightenment and the notion of individual freedom. Spengler must have reinforced Colquhoun's strong feelings about the moral bankruptcy of a modern society in the throes of decay.

Much of Colquhoun's Traditionalist and antimodern view of the world can be traced to her interest in W.B. Yeats, one of the deepest theoretical influences on her. Yeats was also a Traditionalist. Toward the end of his life he was influenced by the writings of the Indian art historian and Perennialist Ananda Coomaraswamy, who was chiefly responsible for introducing Indian art to Europeans. Yeats's writings, notably the channelled text *A Vision* that he completed with his wife Georgie, frequently feature concepts of the eternal cycles of time and the breakdown of society, both of which characterise a Traditionalist perspective. Yeats's commitment to the rebuilding of a truly Celtic Ireland drove much of his artistic, spiritual and political activity, and Colquhoun emulated this model, having been inspired by Yeats from a very young age.

Understanding Colquhoun's interest in Yeats's work and his views about Ireland and the Celts in general is crucial to interpreting her Celtic body of work. She may have believed that she was carrying on his work, and throughout her life her poetry was criticised as too derivative of his. Much has been written on Yeats's political views, particularly his attraction to fascism, but it is important not to conflate all Traditionalism with overt fascist sympathies. Yeats did not live to witness the horrors perpetrated by fascist regimes during the Second World War. His views about the potential of fascism understandably seem horrific to modern audiences, who do not want to associate such an odious political stance with the much-admired poet who so powerfully articulated the dread of watching things fall apart. Yet there is certainly an uncomfortable connection between expressions of nativist spirituality and the sorts of exclusionary ethnic politics that emerge in right-wing nationalism, and this is, indeed, one strand of Traditionalist inspired spirituality. There is no doubt that the politics of 'ethnic purity' were an undercurrent of several of the Celtic flavoured groups with which Colquhoun was affiliated.

The White Goddess

Many of Colquhoun's influences centred around themes of the playing out of eternal sacred stories, and systems of thought that reveal the deep structure and pattern of the cosmos as retold in a variety of contexts. To Colquhoun correspondences were everything, and the more she could find, the more the truths about the deep structure of existence were affirmed. Another lasting influence in Colquhoun's interpretation of Celticity was Robert Graves' *The White Goddess. The White Goddess* was published in 1948, just prior to the wider promotion of Druidry and Wicca as 'Celtic'-based native British spiritualities. Despite the many flaws in Graves' theories, this work, which expanded on James Frazer's ideas about an overarching mythological cycle expressing the relationship between a Mother Goddess and her son/lover, revitalised the British popular imagination about the power and influence of the Divine Feminine. The fact that Graves centred so much of his theorising around Welsh and Irish medieval narrative also helped invigourate post-war cultural and spiritual movements seeking to claim an ancient Celtic spiritual heritage for all of Britain. However, Graves' 'inspirations' about pre-Christian Celtic cultures and religions were often taken as historical fact despite Graves' own characterisation of his work as primarily based in 'revelation' and not history. Graves' 'Celtic Tree Alphabet' and his musings about the nature of the Goddess certainly took hold of many imaginations and had a powerful impact on the growth of British Paganism. We see references to the themes and ideas of *The White Goddess* in Colquhoun's wider work and her esoteric interests, not only in her interest in the Divine Feminine, but in showing the foundational potential of Celtic mythology to reveal yet another instance of the sacred structure of the cosmos.

So, to sum up: Colquhoun had philosophical and cultural influences which shaped the way she saw many of her Celtic activities. Celtic peoples were the inheritors of an ancient wisdom tradition, which over time became lost to humanity. Much of this tradition had to do with the relationship of people to landscape. She believed that the esoteric current between people and their lands can and should be contacted and restored, to regenerate the people and the land.

Celtic Cornwall

Cornwall has an attraction for the seeker, bearing as it does traces of those sunken countries, Lyonesse and Atlantis, which are lost in the depths of every mind. This 'end of the land' exerts a magical pull on those who are dissatisfied with themselves or their environment: It proposes something other than a mere humdrum existence. This explains why so many people from 'up country' come to settle here after retirement; others cannot wait for that, but, irresistibly drawn, will jettison their prospects and come down here to find not only a living, but a life worth living.[52]

Cornwall sits right in the middle of the romanticised construction of Celtic peoples and places. The peninsula at the Western tip of Britain was colonised by the ninth century, and although it retained independent political structures as late as the nineteenth century, the revived nature of Cornish language communities and Cornwall's governance as an English county has created a tension: while many ethnically Cornish people feel wholly un-English, many English people experience simultaneously a sense of belonging and an otherness in Cornwall that creates the perfect conditions for an accessible Celtic Otherworld. This has been the foundation for the portrayal of Cornwall since the late nineteenth century, when the collapse of the Cornish tin- and copper-mining industry created a gaping hole in the formerly robust Cornish economy. The newly developing tourism industry swooped in, and promotional efforts by the Great Western Railway enticed tourists, writers, artists and spiritual pilgrims to flood into Cornwall to escape the urban and embrace somewhere mythic.

Contrary to popular belief about Cornwall's supposed isolation, there have always been people coming and going. From London, Cornwall may be perceived as marginal and difficult to reach, but by sea Cornwall is in the centre of the Atlantic Arc, linking routes ranging from Ireland, to Spain and North Africa. Its significance as a crossroads for international trade is well established, and centuries of metal mining fed a worldwide market. Even after the retreat of the mining industry, the Cornish diaspora settled in Cornish communities as far flung as South Australia, North America, Mexico and South Africa. Yet Cornwall still has an undeserved reputation for being culturally isolated, a place of pre-literate and pre-rational magical survivals, housing a population still gripped by superstition and backwardness. Some Cornish bristle at these characterisations, yet this particular imagining of Cornwall continues to fuel tourism and the settlement of people looking for a 'simpler life'.

As one might expect, the relationships between settlers into Cornwall and the ethnic Cornish have not always been congenial. Toward the end of the twentieth century and into the twenty first, second home ownership and a focus on tourism has created an entrenched economic disparity and a lack of sustainable development. The Cornish economy has lagged behind the rest of the UK for decades, and it has been argued that this is a result of a desire to fashion Cornwall as a tourist destination and playground for the wealthy, at the expense of its native Celtic population.

Cornish history is not well represented in most of the British curricula, but Cornwall has resisted cultural and economic assimilation into a wider English state for centuries, and this resistance is key to understanding the cultural difference which is often understood as 'Celtic'. It is often forgotten that Cornwall was its own sovereign territory until the 9th century. The mining economy in Cornwall also supported a separate native legal system known as the Stannary Parliament until the nineteenth century. Many know that Cornwall has its own language, Cornish, related to Welsh and Breton. Fewer know that Cornwall has a long history of religious and electoral deviations from the English norm. These distinctions tended to be shaped by Methodism from the eighteenth century onward, which influenced the development of Cornish culture in ways ranging from greater Liberal voting patterns to brass bands and tea treats. At the end of the nineteenth century, Cornish cultural activists started to form allegiances with the emerging Pan-Celtic movement, and by the middle of the twentieth century, Cornish nationalist politics had extended further into electoral politics. In 1951 the nationalist party *Mebyon Kernow* was formed and the party has remained an important pro-Cornish voice in the British political landscape, despite a general lack of electoral success at a national level. So, while many treat Cornwall as a beautiful 'English' peninsula jutting outward into the Atlantic, centuries of cultural difference from England have created a frequently unrecognised nation within a nation.

Although many Cornish people had always felt culturally different from the English, it was only after the second world war that a cultural and political movement arose to help consolidate that experience. As this process continued into the twentieth century it created tensions with in-migrants who felt a sense of ownership of Cornwall and in many cases did not recognise a distinctive Cornish identity. The result is that even in the twenty-first century there are a variety of peoples in Cornwall who claim affinity with a Celtic heritage, sometimes adopting icons such as an affiliation with King Arthur or megalithic monuments but frequently for different reasons. 'Celticity' can either reflect an expression of ethnicity, or a deep spiritual conviction.

It is into this milieu that Ithell Colquhoun started settling into Cornwall in the late 1940s. Since her first incursions into the Duchy, she not only sought mystical Cornwall, but had a clear desire to participate in promoting its Celtic difference. At the time of her arrival, the Cornish were beginning the process of ethnically redefining themselves as Celts on a wider scale and finding common cause in the Pan-Celtic movement with other peoples and nations who were seeking their own sovereignty and asserting their distinctive identities. This project did not have widespread success in Cornwall until the 1980s and 1990s, but from the 1950s onward, after the disruption of the war on Celtic-based organisations, we start seeing the impact of the slow consolidation of Celtic political identities through the reinvigouration of the Celtic Congress and in 1961 the establishment of the Celtic League. Although Colquhoun certainly had some allegiances with Cornish nationalist politics, primarily through social networks, her main interests were spiritual. The people with whom she shared her Celtic-based spiritual and artistic interests over the decades frequently had uneasy relationships with Celtic nationalist activists, ranging from the failed attempts of Colin Murray to recruit Celtic political activists to the cause of Celtic mysticism, in the 1970s, to Colquhoun's own rejection from the Cornish *Gorseth*.

Yet Colquhoun's relationship with Cornwall was uncompromisingly enduring and passionate. She was connected with the place for over half her life. She was primarily a spiritually motivated incomer, and her love of Cornwall intersects with several of the reasons people commonly move there: the long history of artists and creatives, a Celtic cultural heritage, and importantly for Colquhoun, a history of alternative spiritual settlements and esotericists. Cornwall to this day has a reputation as a land of ghosts, witches and paranormal activity, and throughout the twentieth century Cornwall's 'Otherworldliness' made it a magnet for settlements of occultists, Pagans and earth mysteries enthusiasts who still continue to affect the character of Cornwall. But it is equally important to acknowledge Colquhoun's own sense of displacement from the place of her birth in India, and how she longed to find a spiritual home that would support her own animist identity. She believed that Cornwall was this place, and the betweenness of Cornwall's own identity helped support her own sense of liminality.

According to one of Colquhoun's early biographers, Eric Ratcliffe, she started visiting West Cornwall as a child on holiday, and like so many became enchanted with it. It is hard to know exactly when Colquhoun started visiting Cornwall as an adult, but in *The Living Stones* she noted that she, like many London residents, moved to Cornwall during the Blitz. She gave her Lamorna Studio, Vow Cave, an interesting and somewhat redundant choice of name, since 'vow' means 'cave' in Cornish, but the studio also had the feel of a monastic sanctuary which may have also been appealing to her, perhaps replicating an idealised cave of a Celtic saint. Vow Cave was a one-room studio with a tin roof and few amenities, that she adopted as a place to paint, write and escape from the city. She loved the sparseness of her studio tucked away in the woods, and the ways in which it forced her to do without modern convenience, although she did make just enough architectural changes to it to make it comfortable and aesthetically pleasing. However, it is important to remember that this was a cultivated asceticism. She still maintained a residence in London for many years, until fully moving in 1959 to Stone Cross Cottage in Paul, where she remained until her death. This allowed her to enjoy the established artists' colony at Lamorna, while still maintaining her social networks in London, which would have been central to the magical connections she was developing in the late 1940s and early 1950s. Colquhoun claimed a deep Celtic affinity, yet she was often able to enjoy it from a safe distance without the experience of disadvantage and poverty that was so common in communities in which she lived.

Sacred sites and landscapes

Colquhoun had a passion for landscape antiquities, and this passion was part of her bond to Cornwall and other Celtic areas. Ancient monuments were, for her, evidence of the genius of early humans, and a visual reminder of all that humans have forgotten about living in harmony with the land and harnessing its powers. The ways in which the land could serve as a conduit for sacred experiences was a recurring theme in both her visual work and her writing, and she felt that the Celtic people had a closer, less alienated relationship to the natural environment.

The ancient stone sites of Britain and Ireland have historically played a significant role in imaginings of a Celtic past, and of a Celtic priesthood believed to have possessed advanced magical skills and technology. While this is not true, it has fuelled romantic beliefs about the Celts for centuries. While we know today that megalithic monuments were not artifacts of a specifically Celtic civilisation, the idea that the Celts were the inheritors of an ancient mystery tradition of the West, probably transmitted to them by the mythical super-human inhabitants of the sunken land of Atlantis, has never stopped being part of the lore of Western Esotericism, particularly in Britain. Although these monuments were built by pre-Celtic peoples, and their function has never been truly determined, they have had an enduring role in creating the image of an advanced civilisation of the past that merged spirituality with technologies now lost. It is likely that the megalithic monuments, holy wells and remnants of medieval sacred sites that Colquhoun would have encountered in her early visits to Cornwall inspired her interests in sacred landscapes and even what would later be known as earth mysteries. Colquhoun's early writings on sacred sites in Ireland, Cornwall and later Egypt, brought together a number of cultural influences of the early to mid-20th century, including an interest in pilgrimages to sacred sites in Britain, ley lines, and ideas about electromagnetic currents under the earth's surface. These theories merged in British subculture with the earth mysteries movement in the 1960s, but as early as the 1940s Colquhoun was exploring ideas about the ways ancient monuments might serve as portals to other dimensions.

Colquhoun's interest in sacred sites and their power was ahead of her time. She synthesised a number of beliefs and fringe intellectual currents in Britain and Europe regarding the origins and functions of sacred sites, including megalithic monuments, ancient churches and stone crosses. It was in this milieu of ideas in the early 1940s, combined with her interest in other dimensions, that Colquhoun developed her theories about stone circles. In 1925 Alfred Watkins published what is considered to be the first book on ley lines, *The Old Straight Track*. The idea of an ancient aligned network of tracks connecting key sacred sites, used by traders and travellers, caught the imagination of the British public and antiquarians. However, ley lines did not take on supernatural associations until the publication of John Michell's *The New View Over Atlantis* in 1969. Yet Colquhoun's paintings and writings, with their references to wells of subterranean energy, are consistent with the early twentieth century stirrings of what today is referred to as 'alternative archaeology', where the past function of sites is speculated on using unconventional or intuitive means. Frederick Bligh Bond's use of gematria and psychic readings at Glastonbury

Abbey published in 1919 is an early example, with which Colquhoun would have been familiar. While this was not considered acceptable practice in the archaeological community, the idea that sacred sites reflect ancient wisdom traditions of the ancient inhabitants of Britain, or even Atlantis, was not uncommon in esoteric circles. In her 1934 *Glastonbury: Avalon of the Heart*, Dion Fortune suggested that megalithic monuments and ancient Christian sites were built on power spots which would act as channels to higher consciousness for the visitor, and which demonstrated the application of ancient spiritual technologies. Likely, Fortune's theories inspired Colquhoun's.

Much later, in 1979, Colquhoun published an essay in *Sangreal* magazine which outlines her theories about the energies which flow under sacred sites, and how one might tap into them:

> Over the earth's surface are to be found localities which the ancients called 'Fountains out of Hecate.' To tap these chthonic power-centres it is essential to be near them at the times when they erupt as geysers of energy. Certain places have an affinity with certain times – of the day, of the week, of the year, of the cycle. Many of these are still to be discovered, or rediscovered; mythology and folklore provide clues, calendrical observances being especially useful. One's own hunches about the atmosphere of certain places are often worth following up. Short of becoming a wandering 'venerable,' it is important to live (or at least occasionally to stay) near one of these 'Fountains.' In this way one can gradually come to know the seasons when its stream of power wells up most strongly. One can immerse oneself in it, even if one lacks the knowledge to direct it to other purposes.[53]

There is no shortage of 'Fountains of Hecate' in West Cornwall.

The Neolithic/Bronze Age stone monuments dotting the landscape of Cornwall have inspired the antiquarian and esoteric imagination in

Britain since at least the 17th century, when early researchers linked them to the Druids and hypothesised that these were the ritual or astronomical sites of the ancient Britons. Researchers and spiritual pilgrims have tried to penetrate the mysteries of these sites, recover their original function, and tap into whatever energies they may be harnessing. Cornwall has one of the densest concentrations of megalithic monuments in Western Europe, which has only added to the mystical lure of the area and reinforced the belief that there is something ancient and powerful lurking just below the earth. Colquhoun was evidently taken with the mystical fascination around these monuments, and produced many studies of Cornish stones over the central decades of her life. Around 1940 she completed some rough watercolour sketches of a couple of monuments located in West Cornwall known as the Mên-an-Tol and Lanyon Quoit. Within a couple of years she developed some unique full studies of the Nine Maidens/Merry Maidens and the Mên-an-Tol that suggest the merging of a number of complex esoteric theories about the nature and role of the monuments, ranging from wells of energy coming from the earth to, perhaps, her researches into other dimensions.

In 1941/42 Colquhoun completed two outstanding paintings of Neolithic or Bronze Age monuments, *The Dance of the Nine Opals* and *The Sunset Birth*, which display the most sophisticated articulation of Colquhoun's theories around sacred sites. In these luminous, visually complicated paintings she explored a wealth of ideas around megalithic monuments – primarily how they function as energy conduits at points in the earth that can act upon the energy centres present in the human body – and we can chart how they intersect with her wider esoteric thinking at the time. In the early 1940s Colquhoun was concentrating theoretically and artistically on energy flows and portals, and these take shape in a number of her artistic projects at the time, including these particular works on Cornish stone monuments. These complex paintings include a number of ideas and theories that Colquhoun was working on quite feverishly, yet they never seemed to blossom into a major body of work regarding her theories about sacred landscapes. Her lifelong obsession with the fourth dimension and tesseracts also gets reflected in the sketches of *Dance of the Nine Opals*. These paintings are early visual articulations of what Colquhoun would later poetically refer to as 'The living stones', a phrase which may have its source in Ouspensky's *Tertium Organum*, with a nod to Peter 2:5: 'Ye also, as lively stones, are built up a spiritual house, an holy priesthood, to offer up spiritual sacrifices, acceptable to God by Jesus Christ.'

In these paintings we see a synthesis of her theories about extra dimensions and energy flows, regarding both human bodies and landscapes, and we can see a confluence of her work on tesseracts, sex magic and sacred sites. In some watercolour sketches from around 1941 Colquhoun encapsulates these stone monuments within a tesseract using the same colour schemes that she used for her other tesseract and cube of space sketches. Was she suggesting that these megalithic monuments were also extradimensional portals?

Dance of the Nine Opals is multi-sourced in its inspiration, and like a number of her magical landscapes comprises a collage of features which she imaginatively recombined to generate the visual result she was looking for. The physical structure on which it is modelled is probably the beautiful Merry Maidens stone circle in West Cornwall. The Merry Maidens circle contains nineteen stones, not nine as in Colquhoun's painting, with a well-trodden pathway running through the centre. This pathway is probably the result of modern travellers as it was not part of the original structure. Outside the circle are two larger stones known as 'The Pipers', and in Colquhoun's rendering two stones stand as guardians to the main circle on either side of the pathway bisecting the monument. It is notable that there are a number of stone monuments in Britain called 'The Nine Maidens', including two in Cornwall, which probably appealed to Colquhoun's mythic sensibilities around the number nine. The lore of these sites, as with many stone circles, was that the stones were women turned to stone for dancing on the Sabbath. Colquhoun calls this a '*hexentanz*' or Witches' Dance, another theme which recurs in later essays. In 1942 she also completed some delicate watercolour-enhanced sketches on onion skin paper showing beautiful naked women frozen in the stones, mid-dance. It is likely that the fables of the dancing women and the number nine were both magically compelling to Colquhoun, but the remaining circles did not have the visual and energetic elements she wanted to explore so she painted her own ideal circle.

Colquhoun wrote a short essay to describe the complexity and variety of visual themes in *Dance of the Nine Opals*. There is no one unifying idea behind it, and it reads more like an ephemeral collection of short theories, but it is clear that she is perfectly comfortable reading her own painting in a complex, multi-causal way, as if her work here is not entirely born from her own conscious mind. The painting features a circle of nine crystalline stones, with whirls of primary colours mingling at the centre. The earth beneath them is red, the sky is a dark indigo and they are surrounded by white mountains, which are fictional to this landscape in Cornwall, giving the work an even more liminal quality. The stones are linked by a green ring, with a green central causeway bisecting the circle, originating in the distance and extending out into the mountainous landscape, passing through the centre of the two pillar stones, perhaps suggesting that this monument is only one on a well-worn path. From under the centre of the stone circle emerges a golden fountain which cascades back down underground, creating a sphere of thin yellow lines connecting each of the stones. The stones are also connected to each other through an intricate web of red threads.

Although Colquhoun's essay is vague in terms of a single motivating theory, the image itself reveals a clear set of underlying principles, namely that the stones are in some way animated intelligences, that they conduct energy, and that these sites themselves are conduits for some sort of subterranean electromagnetic currents. Given that these ideas only enter the wider earth mysteries movement in the 1960s, Colquhoun's exploration of them here is an early articulation of ideas about energy sources under the earth connected with some sort of energy current. In her essay about the painting she refers to the golden fountain of energy as a 'Fountain of Hecate'. This phrase was later adopted by Kenneth Grant, but here Colquhoun refers to the idea which entered Western Esotericism through the popularisation of the Chaldean Oracles that there are power centres of the earth associated with the Goddess Hecate, presented in the Oracles as a life-giving force.

Other suggestions for the form of the painting that Colquhoun addresses in her essay are, as was her nature, recursive and reiterative, and reinforce the idea that these sites were built on top of power sites already existing in the landscape that early peoples were in some way attuned to; for instance, the idea that witches would meet at these sites for their rites, or that they were locations for fertility rituals such as a Maypole dance. For Colquhoun the more correspondences that any given circumstance or image can be tied to is more evidence of its significance. She also notes that the number nine is that of the astrological planets plus Vulcan and Pluto, and that it is the number of the earthbound sephiroth under the more ethereal Kether, and the nine months of human gestation, which again reinforces the idea of fertility.

The second subject of Colquhoun's landscape energy studies is the Mên-an-Tol, a highly unusual monument consisting of a granite ring flanked by two short pillars. The Mên-an-Tol, which in Cornish means 'holed stone', sits alone on a gentle, barren hill in West Cornwall. It is quite small, and emerges as a breathtaking surprise when one comes upon it. When Cornish antiquarian William Borlase sketched the monument in the late 18th century, the alignment was different, with the holed stone to the side of the two pillars. It has been suggested that initially these were part of a larger stone monument with as many as 22 standing stones, but that the primary stones were dispersed by local farmers. These unusual stones have had a long local association with healing. They are said to be able to heal every condition from rickets to infertility as long as the afflicted passes through the centre stone in the right way at the correct hour. Borlase related some of these folk traditions in his 18th century text, although he himself believed that megalithic monuments had their true origins in Druidic rites. By the middle of the nineteenth century the stones had been rearranged and brought into an alignment with the two small pillars flanking the central holed stone, which is the arrangement they are in today.

The Sunset Birth has similar features to *Dance of the Nine Opals*, yet Colquhoun was clearly looking at different energetic aspects of the monuments. The primary distinction is that *The Sunset Birth* references the impact of the monument on the energy centres of the body. Here we can see the result of intense theorising on sex magic, and Colquhoun's other visual attempts to represent the magical sexual act by an abstracted conjunction of energy channels in conjoined human bodies.

The stones in *The Sunset Birth* are not the crystalline crucibles we see in *Dance of the Nine Opals*. The landscape and sky are very sparse, but the stones themselves are bright. The stone on the left is a deep blue, the stone on the right is a yellow orange, and the centre ring is red, echoing the trinity of primary colours which represent synthesis of polarities and fulfilment of unity. As with *Dance of the Nine Opals*, the stones are linked by pulsing subterranean energy lines. There is a faintly visible figure of a woman passing through the centre stone, almost levitating, clutching the pillar stones on either end with her hands and feet. We don't see her flesh, only her energy, which remains in streams of red, yellow and blue activated by her connections with the stones. The Mên-an-Tol here functions as a sort of extradimensional battery acting upon the energy channels of the human body.

Although Colquhoun visually revisits the stone monuments of Cornwall in her work throughout her life, these two representations reveal a much deeper sense of esoteric theory about sacred landscapes than we see in her other work, but we can still see how her ideas echo in other areas of her work around sex and the human body. She saw these stones, and the very landscape itself, as alive and surging with energy. If people can cultivate the right attunement with nature and themselves, they can access a beneficial spiritual relationship with these sacred monuments, which Colquhoun believed to be evidence of an enlightened Celtic spiritual system which was not entirely lost to the world.

Writing the Celts

Although Colquhoun was becoming known within her own literary circles as an expert on Celtic matters during her marriage to del Renzio, it was after the marriage ended in 1947 that she started to explore Celtic topics more vigourously. Interestingly, Colquhoun did not frequently focus on Celtic mythology in her artwork. In 1949 she completed a delightful decalcomania, *The Battle Fury of Cuchullin*, depicting the Irish hero in full 'warp spasm' with one of his eyes bugged out of his head, and a stream of red energy emerging from his crown like a fountain. In 1950 she produced a frottage called *Woman of Beare*, a legendary old woman in Ireland who was associated with various Irish stone monuments. But the bulk of Colquhoun's works which might be considered 'Celtic' were landscapes and antiquities. From very early on she had created sketches of her experiences in the Irish landscape, some of which became wonderfully abstracted as illustrations for *Crying of the Wind*. She completed many studies of Cornish landscapes, megaliths and stone crosses as illustrations for *The Living Stones*. These were less abstracted than the illustrations she used for *Crying of the Wind*, several being quite delicate and detailed. Others were highly sexualised. Among the studies for *The Living Stones* were several successive studies for a cave which eventually became a watercolour sketch of a massive labia.

Peter Owen published *The Crying of the Wind* and *The Living Stones* within two years of each other, in 1955 and 1957, and they represent an extension of Colquhoun's growing fascination with Celtic traditions, peoples, and their relationship with the lands in which they lived. They are basically quirky travel journals, records of her observations of place, people and landscape. They hold interest for the reader with an interest in the development of earth

RIGHT
Dance of the Nine Opals (1942)

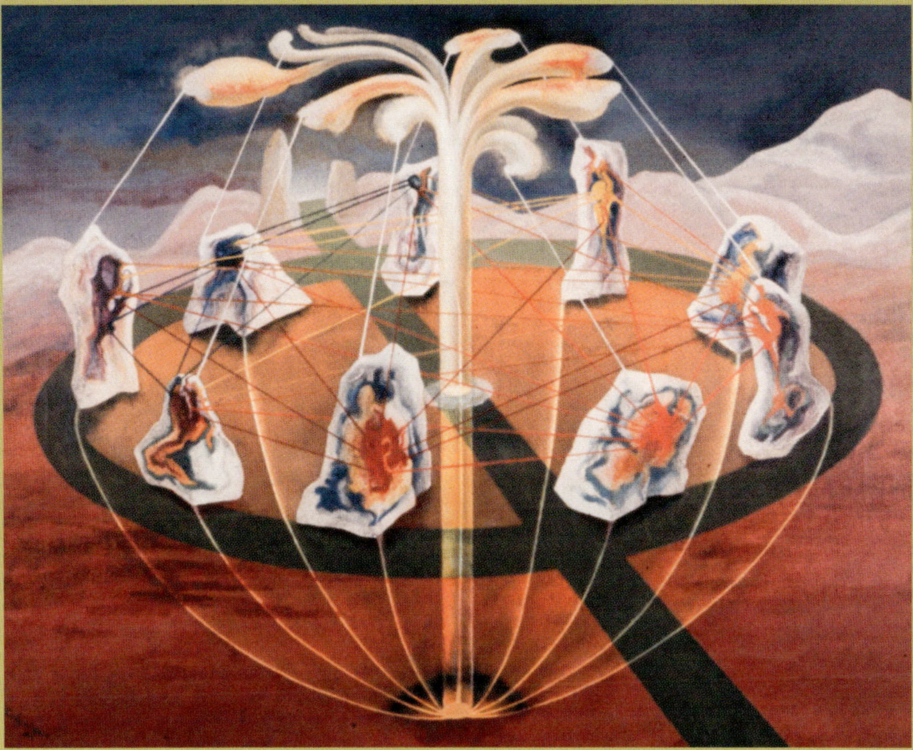

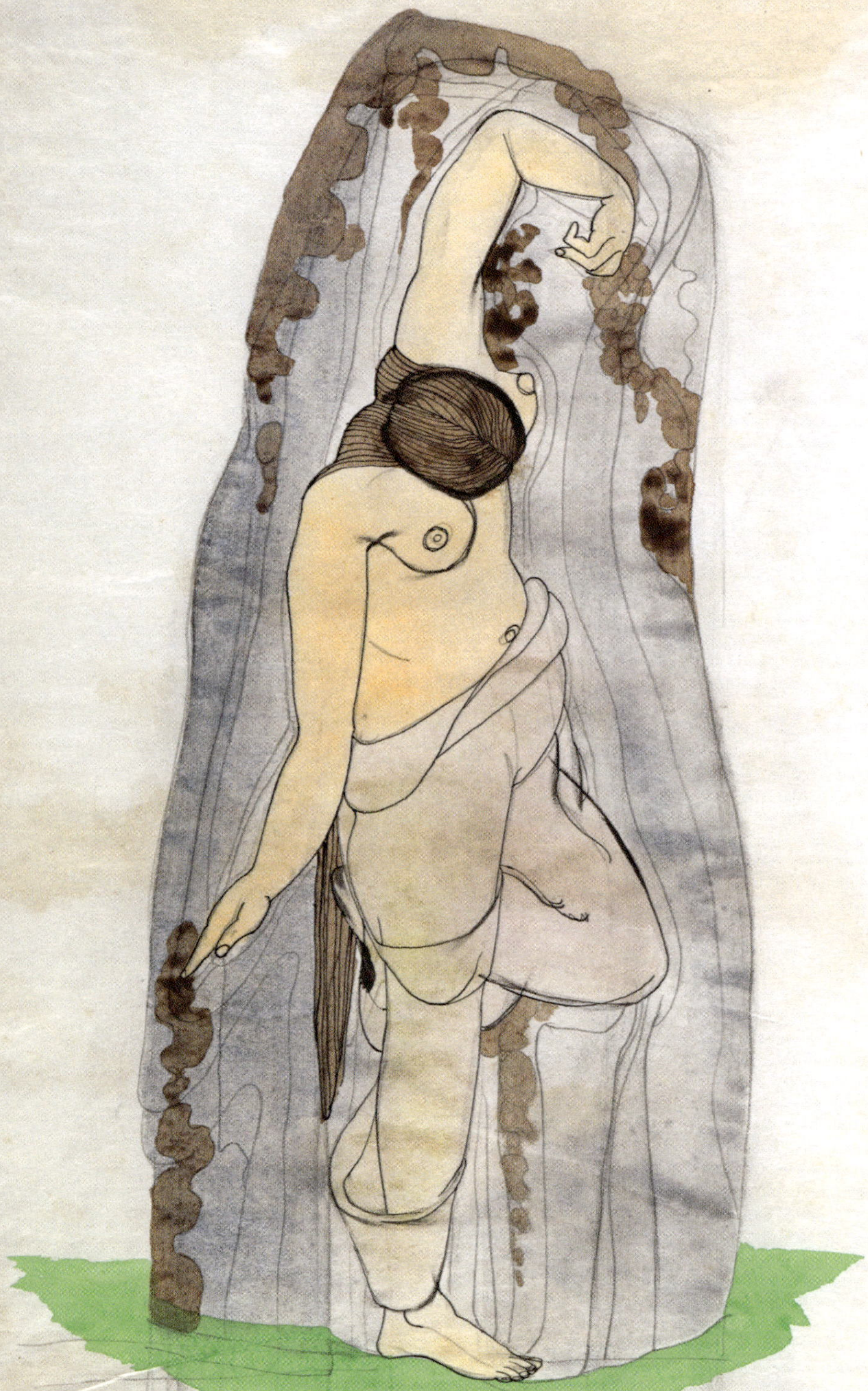

mysteries and the development of 20th century Celtic spirituality as personal revelatory texts, providing a snapshot of the ways in which the landscapes and sacred sites of Cornwall and Ireland were conceived to possess a mystical characteristic for spiritually inclined travellers at the time. When they were written, Colquhoun was part of an early wave of post-war writers who were actively seeking the experience of spiritualised landscapes, and collectively working to reclaim an ancient British sacrality that had been muted by the devastation of war. She was certainly not alone in this project. For example, Wellesley Tudor Pole, who established the Chalice Well Trust in Glastonbury in 1959, was actively promoting a re-enchantment of the British landscape by encouraging pilgrimages to Britain's sacred sites, particularly those associated with St. Michael. Likely inspired by Dion Fortune's enthusiasms for pilgrimage, Tudor Pole believed that this would help usher in a New Age of spiritual redemption for Europe, with Britain leading the way. Colquhoun mentions these pilgrimages in *The Living Stones*, as well as her own inspirational journeys to the Michael sites of Cornwall, and it's clear that these two books are artifacts of this sort of response to the landscape, particularly that which is rural, unspoiled and innocent.

LEFT From the series *Dance of the Nine Maidens* (1940) showing women dancing on the Sabbath frozen in the stones.

The Crying of the Wind: Ireland

Colquhoun had a life-long relationship with Ireland, and *The Crying of the Wind* reveals both her love of the country and a deep ambivalence about the direction of its development. The text is alternately effusive and grumpy. Her maternal relatives hailed from Ireland, and she had visited from a relatively young age and evidently experienced a bond. She visited Ireland in the 1940s and again in 1954, collecting material and completing landscape illustrations of the Irish countryside. It is likely she was also working with Yeats's archives during at least one these visits, following up his work synthesising Hermetic and Celtic magical systems. As is characteristic of her writing, the book is a very personal and opinionated account of the Irish cultural condition at the middle of the twentieth century. It isn't simply a journey of Colquhoun's earth mysticism, but a challenging and sometimes angry depiction of an Ireland in decay, victim of the forces of the modern world and centuries of conflict and colonisation. The book itself is rather unpolished and reads like an unedited, and certainly uncensored, travel diary. It gives little context for Colquhoun's travel or observations. She jumps right in, with a description of her stay in the Liffey Valley. We don't know why she is there, what year it is, how long her stay is, or who her companions are. It is only at the end of the first chapter that we learn the year is 1954, and she is renting studio spaces for drawing.

Although much of the delight in the text comes from her unusual turn of phrase and thick description of places and flora, she includes a great deal of commentary and observation, some of which reads uncomfortably in a modern context. She notes how run down many of the buildings seemed to be, and comments on the low living standards of the people. It is clear that she followed Yeats's opinion of the direction of the still relatively new Irish Republic. She was derisory of the role of Catholicism in the culture, and believed that it suppressed the Celtic spirit of the people. She was consistently critical of the poverty in mid-century Ireland, and the revelation of her classism throughout the text is somewhat surprising. Her disparaging characterisation of gay men also may leave the modern reader with a less than pleasant taste. By the end of the book it is clear that she felt the Anglo-Irish got short shrift in the political fallout which established the Republic, and she laments their lack of cultural and political influence in its development. The text is brimming with antimodernist sentiment, and her opinions on the impact of modernisation on Ireland's landscape and population consistently seep through.

RIGHT & NEXT PAGE (DETAIL)
Stalactite (1962)

Colquhoun writes longingly of a pre-Christian time in Ireland, one soaked in mythology, where the people were more in tune with 'their race' and with the beings of the otherworld, reflecting the belief that

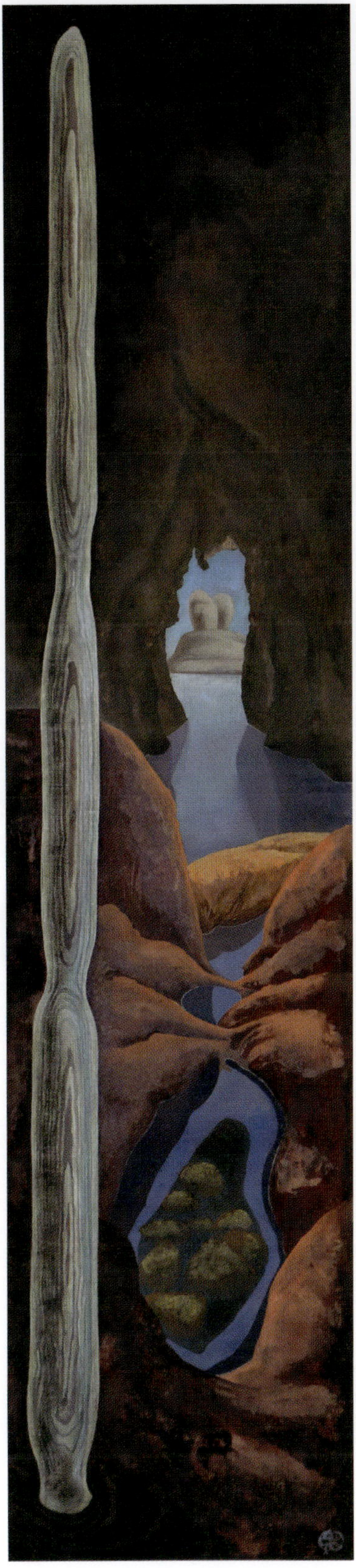

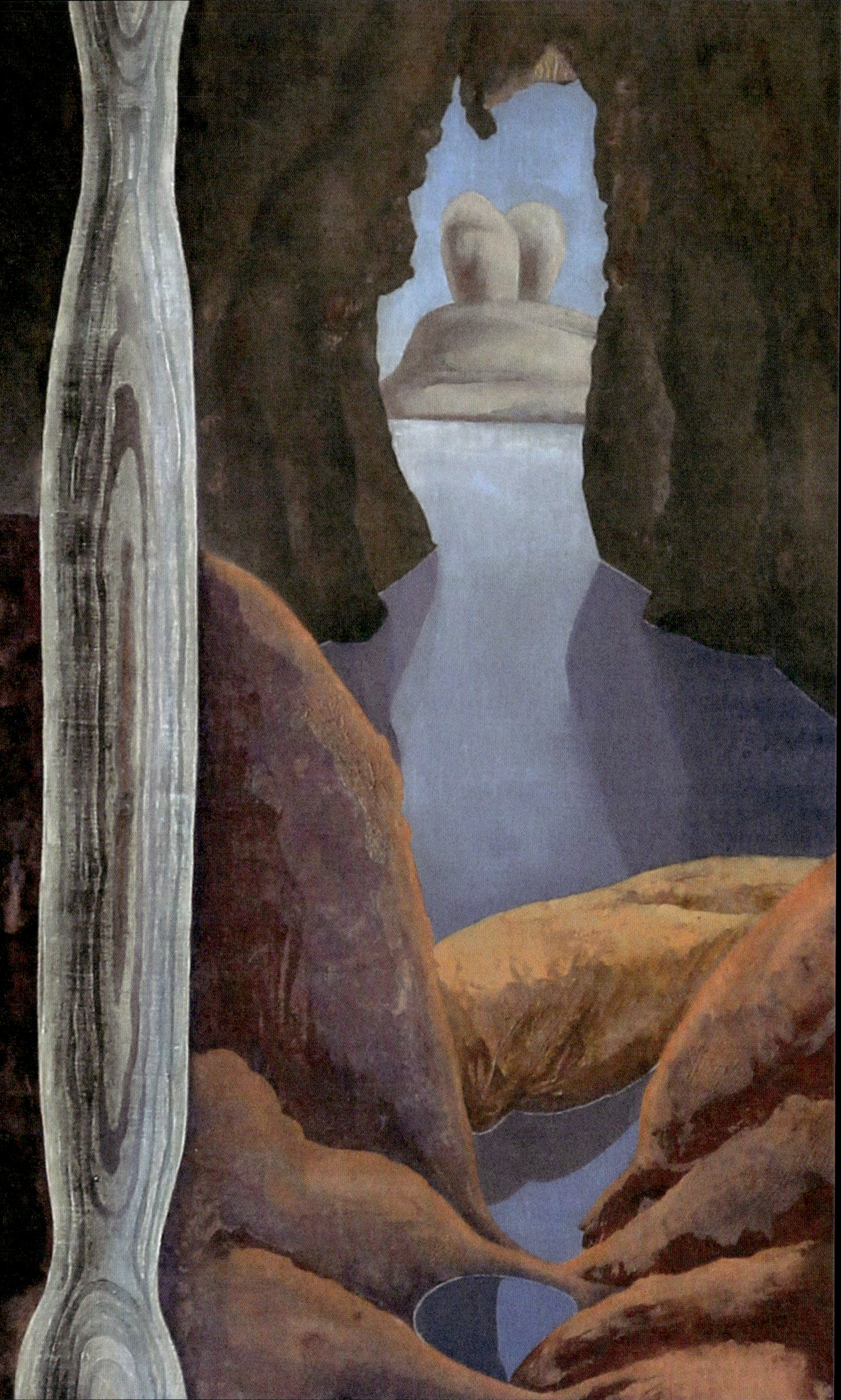

Celtic peoples flow easily between different realities and exist most naturally in a 'time out of time':

> The same is true of all Celtic countries in so far as the same causes operate. The past is present in the holy unconscious, and in regions not yet entirely divorced from it, essential care is not for ambition and the rationalized outlook. The sense of individualized indemnity is softened, the 'ego' tending to sink and be engulfed in the 'id'. Achievement scarcely counts: existence in relation to the moment is all. No wonder that time loses its anxiety or rather has reached in the anxious pitch; the angles of space also bathed in an age-old ambience, leave aside their sharpness.[54]

Colquhoun found solace from her discomforts and frustrations when she could retreat into the embrace of the Irish landscape and antiquities, and she would make spiritual connection with sacred monuments when she could find them. She wrote of finding a basin stone on top of a carn and leaving a sprig of heather in offering, and she commented that the only way to truly understand the meaning of such monuments is to silently commune with them.

The Living Stones: Cornwall

The Living Stones, by contrast, is Colquhoun's love letter to Cornwall. It has a different tone and colour to *Crying of the Wind*, in that it is more positive and upbeat. The writing is full of life and colour, whereas in *Crying of the Wind* one frequently senses her endurance. In *Crying of the Wind* she often compared Ireland to Cornwall, the latter being her spiritual centre, and Cornwall generally comes out the better of the two. *The Living Stones* was published in 1957 and chronicles events and experiences from the previous decade, along with odd historical and cultural facts. This text was also illustrated with Colquhoun's vision of the sacred landscape, but here many of the illustrations take on an explicitly erotic feel. The cover of the book is a rather suggestive reading of the famed Mên Scryfa, an 8th century inscribed stone commemorating a Cornish petty king known as Rialobran, or 'Royal Raven'. Colquhoun depicts the stone as being in congress with the earth, turgid and ringed with pubic hair, possibly an artifact of what Colquhoun believed was the existence of an ancient, universal, phallic cult.

Colquhoun dedicates *The Living Stones* to another traveller on the early earth mysteries path, Margaret Keturah Fulleylove Thornley, who was also known by the name she took when she was made a Cornish Bard in 1953, 'Maghteth Myghal', 'Daughter of Michael.' Thornley, based near St. Ives, was the wife of the naturalist and Anglican vicar Rev. Alfred Thornley and she was committed to the idea of eradicating spiritual darkness from the British landscape. In 2012 dowser Sally Kunis recalled that in the 1950s Thornley would ride out to the 'dark places' in Dartmoor with her father, a Dartmoor guide, to heal the areas of bad energies. Thornley was deeply dedicated to the idea of the St. Michael pilgrimage and visited 151 Michael sites throughout Britain, Ireland and elsewhere in Europe. She worked on this mission with Wellesley Tudor Pole and in 1952 collaborated with Tudor Pole, Cornish cultural activist Robert Morton Nance, and several others on a pamphlet published by J.W. Watkins titled *Michael: Prince of Heaven, Captain of the Angelic Hosts*, extolling the modern relevance of the Michael pilgrimage. At one point there was a plaque at Chapel Carn Brea near Redruth noting the importance of Thornley's Michael pilgrimages to the preservation of the hill. While Colquhoun was ahead of her time in exploring the ideas of wells of energy under the landscape, she was not alone.

The Living Stones covers a wide variety of topics in addition to sacred monuments, providing the reader with a unique snapshot of West Cornwall in the 1940s and 50s: Druidry and the Cornish *Gorseth*, the persistence of witchcraft and legends of Aleister Crowley, and early settlements of alternative cultures and communes. It reflects Colquhoun's vision of a Bohemian 'Celtic' Cornwall, one that attracts mystics, artists and people with deep sympathetic character. She doesn't linger on the industry that shaped so much of Cornwall's modern history; she is following a different thread.

Colquhoun also wrote of her own moving experiences and intimate connections with sacred places in Cornwall. She comments on the recent trend of pilgrimages to St. Michael sites and goes on to describe her own experiences while visiting them. She believed these hilltop sites reflected very old spiritual settlements and places of ritual activity, probably associated with solar worship, and powered by reservoirs of magnetism located within the earth. If this was true of all the ancient sites in Cornwall, then the ancient peoples who built them, and those who later rebuilt them (in her view only lightly Christianised), were in touch with a deep spiritual and physical energy. That she characterises witchcraft in Cornwall as not being far under the cultural surface suggests that the potential to access this energy in the landscape is still strong, and still felt by the Cornish people. A key recurring theme is the peril that Cornwall faces from modernisation and noise which threatens to change its character forever and remove the people from their natural capacity for magic. So, while this book is a love letter it is also a warning.

The Living Stones was written while Colquhoun was still a part-time resident. Two years later in 1959, with her move to the tiny village of Paul, she shifted from a cosy artist community to the ideological heartland of the Cornish revival. Paul is a small village between Newlyn and Mousehole near the Cornish coast. Most people might breeze past it, but it is historically noteworthy as a centre of interest for the Cornish language. Dolly Pentreath, who died in 1777, is buried in the church yard. According to legend, Dolly had the reputation of being the last native Cornish speaker, a story which has been well refuted by evidence of later speakers and shifts in understandings about the nature of the decline of Cornish. Yet Dolly's legend is nevertheless memorialised in Paul churchyard by a commemorative stone, put there by, among others, the philologist and Celtic language enthusiast Louis Lucien Bonaparte. The Boson family, who were native Cornish speakers working to preserve the language in the 17th and early 18th century, are also buried in Paul. In fact, that whole area at the tip of West Cornwall was of central interest to Cornish language revivalists, with some of the most significant collecting of Cornish language fragments having been undertaken in Newlyn in the 1880s by the antiquarian and science fiction writer W.S. Lach-Szyrma. So, in addition to being a destination for artists, writers and holiday makers, West Cornwall has had a reputation as the purest of Cornish lands, especially in the Cornish revival's earliest days. It was the place where Cornish customs and language clung to life. Although views on the distribution of authentic Cornish culture have changed, and most see it more evenly spread throughout the territory, West Cornwall is still somewhat fetishised as the most Cornish of all Cornish places. And it was here that Colquhoun eventually settled, as her own Celtic journey deepened.

The quest for the native wisdom of the Celts

From the early 1950s until the 1970s, Colquhoun joined a number of esoteric orders with a Celtic theme. The spiritual focus of the orders ran from Orthodox Christian to nominally Pagan. Each of these Celtic groups had a Perennialist world view and interpreted their Celticity as one strand of a universal wisdom tradition. Depending on the location or sometimes the 'race' of the member, the mysteries revealed would provide a means for culturally appropriate access to the 'wisdom current'. Yet in the early and mid-1950s, Colquhoun was still following the trail of her Golden Dawn Secret Chiefs, working with the O.T.O. and the Society of the Inner Light. Even with her clear early focus on Hermeticism, it is evident that Colquhoun had an attraction to nativist spirituality, and the Society of the Inner Light may have provided an attractive synthesis of these worlds. Although The Society of The Inner Light characterised its curriculum as being of the wider Western Esoteric Tradition, employing Hermetic and Kabbalistic material as the basis for its teachings, there was a heavy focus on Arthurian legend, British mythology and an explicitly nativist cultivation of a spiritually energised Britain. This was reflected in the headquarters of the Society being in Glastonbury, the heartland of British nativist spiritualities. This may have been a combination that would have worked well for Colquhoun philosophically, but as she was seen as unfit for full membership, she never accessed the Society's inner mysteries. And when that relationship fell apart, she moved in a different direction.

Around the early 1950s Colquhoun met Ross Nichols, Chairman of the Ancient Order of Druids, also known as the British Circle of the Universal Bond or the *An Druidh Uileach Braithreachas* (ADUB), which she would eventually join. Nichols was already established in occult circles, and had known Gerald Gardner from perhaps as early as the 1930s. Nichols and Colquhoun shared an interest in mythic and esoteric themes and in the late 1940s they had run in the same literary circles. They were both associated with the New Apocalypse literary circle, and both published in Antony Borrow's literary magazine *The Glass*. Given their mutual concern with archetype and myth, this would have been a good cultural fit for them both. They were often on the same bill during poetry readings, and Colquhoun noted doing poetry readings on the same stage as Nichols as early as 1952. When they met, she was traveling between Cornwall and Hampstead, and the wave of her joining esoteric orders was just starting, but she attended a ritual at Stonehenge with Nichols in 1957. By 1958 she had joined the ADUB, remaining a member for about a decade. Nichols may also have provided an entry point for her forays into Martinism.

Colquhoun's Druidic study notes from the mid-1960s show that the curriculum of the ADUB was not particularly 'Celtic'. It had a more Perennialist sensibility, and seems to have been an attempt to develop a synthesis of Indo-European spirituality. The driving idea was that the Druids were the inheritors of a Sanskrit-based traditional world view that had diffused throughout Europe. Later writings in the early 1970s by Thomas Maughan, who remained as head of the ADUB after Nichols' departure, characterise the ADUB as representing one branch of the ancient wisdom inheritance from Atlantis, similar in character and training to the mystery schools of Egypt, and focused on individual enlightenment. Like several Druid orders, they may be thought of in today's parlance as 'spiritual not religious' and there is no barrier to entrance from members of any religious tradition, since ADUB holds that Druidry reflects the light of all faiths. These seem to be the underlying principles of most of the orders Colquhoun was initiated into, and her convictions about this underlying wisdom tradition must have been quite strong. Much of the ADUB curriculum that Colquhoun followed involved meditation, chanting and direct experience, and her explorations of Druidry certainly inspired her poetry.

Colquhoun's involvement with the ADUB in the 1960s also intersected with her seemingly odd involvement with Celtic heterodox Christianity. Although many of her interests involved Christian iconography and symbolism, she considered Christianity 'boring' and generally referred to herself as an animist. So, what was the attraction of these groups and orders? She generally found her way into these orders through esoteric colleagues, but there is no doubt that some of the key tenets of these orders would have appealed on a number of levels. As we have seen, Colquhoun did employ Biblical and Christ metaphors to represent a perfected and transcended human state, but in these orders it is likely that she was seeking another type of relationship.

The overriding interest was probably Colquhoun's investment in the deep sacrality of the land of Britain, along with the idea that there were native Celtic wisdom traditions intersecting with wider ancient wisdom traditions, and that through initiation she could contribute to that current and be involved in something that would resonate with her sense of her own ethnicity. In other words, as a Celt, these traditions were in her blood. It is also worth noting that the cultural lines between what might be considered 'Pagan' and 'Christian' were more fluid in the occult subcultures of the 1950s, and that the categories can collapse in on one another, especially to someone with a Perennialist outlook. Esotericists such as Rudolf Steiner could read Jesus Christ, Archangel Michael, and Arthur all as incarnations of a Solar God, whose worship has continued in various guises, changing with the ages. However, as Joanne Pearson notes, there was also unexpected crossover with the early developing British Paganisms and heterodox Christianities. Aleister Crowley, Gerald Gardner and Ross Nichols were all involved at times with varying forms of heterodox Christianity. It may even have been, as in Colquhoun's case, that involvement and ordination in these Christian groups was not difficult, and people tended to collect initiations. But as Pearson notes, for most initiates these orders were professing the belief that the true Christianity of Britain was heavily influenced by the wisdom tradition of the Druids, and therefore represented authentic Celtic cultural values and spiritual practices. Additionally, much of the symbolism of Christianity in this framework was not considered particular or exceptional. It was another wisdom tradition, using mythology, that had a universal, interchangeable significance. This is not to imply that Colquhoun's, or any of these figures', involvement with Christian orders was not sincere; it's rather that they probably had a different understanding of Christian tradition and practice than conventional Christians.

In the early 1960s Colquhoun's Druidry and Hermeticism became more deeply enmeshed with esoteric Christianity. This period dovetailed with Colquhoun's relationship with Serge Hutin, her emerging relationships with Co-Masonry and Martinism, and her personal engagement with France and Brittany was also becoming more intense. Her relationship with Druidry took her to Brittany on several occasions, and in 1960, 1961 and 1962 she participated in the Breton *Goursez*. This is both the title of a cultural organisation and an annual event linked to the Welsh *Gorsedd* and the Cornish *Gorseth*. The Breton *Goursez*, like its counterparts, was founded to promote native Celtic Brythonic languages and cultures. The Welsh *Gorsedd* is seen as the parent organisation of the three, and it is customary for each organisation to receive members of the others at their yearly festivals. However, the Breton *Goursez* has also had a distinctive character with regard to its links with esoteric orders, which the Welsh and Cornish organisations have taken great pains to distance themselves from.

In the mid-20th Century the Breton *Goursez* began reciprocal visiting arrangements with members of the Ancient Order of Druids, and also fostered relationships with members of the Ancient Celtic Church, now known as the Holy Celtic Church International. The charismatic founder Jean-Pierre Danyel, also known as Tugdual, was a heterodox Christian who aligned himself with Breton ethnocentrism to promote a variety of Celtic nativist Orthodoxy. He believed this path would be well suited to Celts of the 20th century, and that this move would finally wean them away from Roman Catholicism. As the Ancient Order of Druids had a firm Christian membership, and many believed in the fiction of a smooth transition between the doctrines of the Druids and the early Christians of Britain, this set of organisational relationships would have made perfect sense. In 1960, on a visit to the Breton *Goursez*, Colquhoun was baptised in the Ancient Celtic Church. In 1961 she returned with Ross Nichols and Robert MacGregor Reid and was made a Deaconess.

Colquhoun's involvement with Druidry and her visits to Brittany intensified her interest in the growing Cornish movement, and in the preservation of Cornish language and culture. According to her own notes she even joined the Celtic Congress in 1963. However, her esoteric affiliations did not always sit comfortably with the aspirations of ethnic Celtic activists who frankly did not identify with esoteric Celtic spirituality. Unlike the Breton *Goursez*, the other ethnic (Welsh and Cornish) *Gorseddau* did not recognise 'English' Druids, and in fact were hostile to them. In the early 1960s the Breton *Goursez* came under censure from the Welsh organisation for their acknowledgement of esoteric Druidry, and in Cornwall the *Gorseth* has worked to distance itself from any association with contemporary Pagan Druidry. 'English' Druids were believed to be culturally appropriating Celtic tradition for ends that were not native, and which did not reflect the Christian identity of these primarily political bodies. It may be that any association with esoteric movements would have further marginalised these groups, and would have culturally muddied the intent of a body that was seeking greater legitimacy for minority cultures and languages.

Colquhoun was also interested in manifestations of Druidry closer to home, but her participation was limited to observation. She first attended the Cornish *Gorseth* in 1950 and later became acquainted with Hugh Miners and William Paynter, Cornish bards, historians and activists. They shared concerns with the preservation of Cornish culture, and in the case of Paynter Colquhoun shared an interest in researching Cornish witchcraft practices. Miners and Paynter, who was barded specifically for his research into Cornish witchcraft and folk magic traditions, wanted to have Colquhoun honored with a bardship for her services to Cornish culture, but her other esoteric affiliations prevented it. She made it very clear in *The Living Stones* that she recognised the distinction between ethnic Druidry and the esoteric Druidry in which she was involved, yet she had still had hoped for recognition from the Cornish *Gorseth* with a bardship. Sadly, she was never granted the privilege.

Despite her earlier friendship with Nichols, when he departed the order in 1964 to start the Order of Bards, Ovates and Druids, she appears not to have followed him. Letters to her from ADUB personnel in 1966 mention the split in somewhat acrimonious terms, and, given Colquhoun's frequently Pagan sensibilities, one wonders why she chose not to move in that direction. She appears to have moved on from institutional Druidry in 1968, seemingly having reached what she considered to be the end of the line with their teachings by sometime in the mid-1960s.

In 1965, while still pursuing her Druidry and membership in several other, non-Celtic, traditions, Colquhoun became a member of William Bernard Crow's Order of the Celtic Cross, which appears to have been a specific guild within Crow's Order of the Holy Wisdom. Her membership was the culmination of several decades of contact with Crow and interest in his spiritual work. Crow was an active occultist throughout the 20th century, and his interest in magical societies that focused on ideas of lineage, initiation and transmission intersected with Colquhoun's. The Order of the Celtic Cross was focused on heraldry and lineage, another deep interest of Colquhoun's; research into heraldic symbolism and her own coats of arms is evident in her archives and her poetry.

Colquhoun first encountered Crow in the early years of her esoteric enculturation in the 1920s at the Quest Society, of which they both were members. In 1934 Crow and her cousin Edward Garstin had co-founded The Institute of Cosmic Studies. She had sought membership in Crow's Order of the Holy Wisdom, which he founded in 1939, as early as 1952, and was finally made a member in 1959. The Order of the Holy Wisdom was not a strictly Celtic based organisation. It was exceptionally Perennialist in its outlook, explicitly Traditionalist, and sought to teach the 'Ancient Wisdom Religion', which was an attempt to reconstruct and synthesise a number of ancient wisdom schools, including that of Druidry. Even though the order was somewhat aligned with Orthodoxy and heterodox Catholicism, membership was not restricted to Christians. This would have appealed to Colquhoun's sensibilities and dovetailed nicely with her Druidry. In fact, unsurprisingly, Crow had also cultivated a relationship with the ADUB.

Crow was primarily a fringe Catholic, having become a priest in the Liberal Catholic Church in 1935. He corresponded with Aleister Crowley from 1944 to 1947, with each trying to get the other to support their organisation. It is likely that Crow's interest would have been chiefly in the promotion of the Ecclesia Gnostica Catholica, described as the ecclesiastical wing of the O.T.O., but it is not clear whether or not Crow was an initiated member of the O.T.O. Nevertheless, there is no doubt that Crow was steeped in the cultural milieu of the British occult scene in the first half of the 20th century, of which Colquhoun was also a part. Much of Crow's involvement in Orthodoxy involved various British nativist Orthodox orders which argued for a native, British Orthodox Christianity, partially derived from the teachings of the Druids, since he believed that the British were one of the original tribes of Israel. Much of this was an attempt to rewrite the story of British Christianity by circumventing Roman Catholicism and appealing directly to a relationship with Orthodoxy coloured by myths of British nativism. The various orders which he started or to which he belonged were excessively preoccupied with legitimate lines of transmission of the mysteries, which would have resonated with Colquhoun's need to anchor her own place in the Celtic world.

Although this seems like one small order among many that Colquhoun joined during this period, Crow's work and mission also reflects the way Colquhoun was synthesising and conceptualising her Celtic spiritual identity with other magical pursuits, and how she intersected with the various landscapes of Celtic spirituality as it was developing during the 1960s and 1970s. She was working through a more intensive period of focus on Christian mysteries, as filtered through both the Hermetic and the Celtic. It was a phase, but not a sustained one, and she eventually returned her focus to her spiritual home of the Golden Dawn, supplemented with Celtic mysticism.

I Saw Water

During her experimentation with various forms of Celtic Orthodoxy and her trips to Brittany, Colquhoun composed another novel, *I Saw Water*, originally titled *Unfaithfully Departed*, probably in reference to her ex-husband. Pieced together over a number of years, *I Saw Water* reflects a synthesis of Colquhoun's Celtic interests from the late 1950s through the mid-1960s. It also contains themes and features that we see in her other novels *Goose of Hermogenes* and *Destination Limbo*. In *I Saw Water* we can see the way in which she struggles with heterodox Christianity, incorporating it into her own alchemical sensibilities, providing an otherworldly Celtic setting for spiritual transformation. The novel was probably started in the 1950s while she was working as an illustrator for Peter Owen and concentrating much of her effort on writing full-length manuscripts. As she had luck in publishing her travel books *Crying of the Wind* and *Living Stones*, she started expanding into long-form Surrealist fiction. Like her other fictional works, *I Saw Water* was drawn from dream material generated years and even decades earlier, but she finally found the impetus to set it down in probably the late 1950s and into 1960–61. The manuscript went through a number of drafts over the years, and the recently published final version, edited and annotated by Richard Shillitoe, was taken from a completed typescript manuscript dating from 1967. She repeatedly tried to get earlier versions published in the 1960s but was unsuccessful; her literary innovations were difficult to target to any market. Although the novel had a broadly Hermetic structure based on the Sephiroth, the imagery and scenes come from her dreams, which results in a somewhat disjointed and hard-to-follow narrative.

The book is set on the island of Ménec, supposedly an island off the coast of Brittany, but also a reference to one of three massive stone alignments at Carnac. The newly arrived inhabitants have just died, and have arrived at the strange island as a stopping place prior to their next incarnation. While there, they still behave as though they are alive, which perhaps gives them an opportunity to address crucial issues before they are reborn into a new body. Their holding place on the island is the Ianua Vitae Convent, run by nuns who seem to have a strong connection to natural ritual and a more tenuous relationship to Catholicism.

In addition to the dream work, Colquhoun was using this novel to explore other personal situations, including the dissolution of her marriage, and her working relationship with dream researcher Alice Buck. She was exploring Christian themes outside the framing of the other esoteric orders with which she was associated, and *I Saw Water* was probably a result of those explorations. In addition to her friend Alice Buck's eventual retreat to a convent, one of Colquhoun's relatives, Elizabeth Colquhoun, was a sister in the Anglican convent at Burnham Abbey. As with most of her work, her commitment to the role and capacity of women is uncompromising, and despite the Catholic setting, the text shows a strong sense of resistance in its engagement with Christian themes. The island is populated by nuns, yet they seems to be more engaged with Pagan ritual and nature worship than Catholic rites. 'He then asked whether I had any perplexity or question regarding catholic doctrine? I answered now the only question worth asking was how to become enlightened and no one could tell one that.' Throughout her life, this was the one question that mattered most to Colquhoun.

A key theme of the text, which recurs tantalisingly yet incompletely in a number of Colquhoun's works, is parthenogenesis. We have seen Colquhoun's preoccupation with the unification of the genders as the key to both individual and societal enlightenment, but by the time we reach the Isle of Ménec, her view of the unification of genders seems to have been distilled to the capacity of women to reproduce asexually. She appears to have held beliefs about the ability of women to become receptive to divine conception if a state of spiritual purity was achieved. We can see her representing this visually with the small watercolour sketch she completed showing St. Anne tantrically transmitting the capacity to reproduce asexually to Mary. Only a few years later, during her cruise through Egypt, she wrote in her manuscript *The Blue Anoubis* of the Goddess Hatshepsut 'may it not rather enshrine a forgotten truth that of the conception of a semi-divine being during a trance wherein the inhabitants of a heaven-world may exercise their power? Such is the basis of all parthenogenic myth.'[55] In *I Saw Water* Colquhoun was probably drawing on ancient legends of the cults of the virgin priestesses who coupled with divine beings to produce semi-divine offspring. Although Colquhoun makes her priestesses nuns, she may have been extending the notion of a Catholic sisterhood into a wider context of sacred congregations of spiritually advanced priestesses.

The novel brings together a number of esoteric themes that had consumed Colquhoun personally for a couple of decades, and positions them firmly within a Celtic setting and framework. Although she had always focused on the natural world, we see here a blend of the Hermetic, the alchemical and the Pagan, perhaps a movement on Colquhoun's part towards integrating a nature-based spirituality at a time when it was also evolving within the wider milieu of British Paganism.

After the end of her formal association with Druidry in the late 1960s, Colquhoun moved on to other magical matters, yet her interest in Celtic subjects remained undiminished. A pointedly political poem, 'Living Boy', probably written in the late 1960s, is dedicated to the Breton sculptor Patrig (or Padraig) Ar Goarnig, the son of Breton activists Jean-Jacques Manrot-Le Goarnig and Mireille Manrot-Le Goarnig, who fought the French state in the late 1940s for the right to give their children Breton names. Initially intended to have been translated into Breton and sung to a traditional Breton tune, it was eventually published in *Osmazone* in 1983. In this fragment we can see how the poem supports the bold self-determination of the family and also, once again, returns to Colquhoun's common theme of preserving the wild and unspoiled Celtic landscape and character:

Rebel mother rebel son
Token to all who would be one

The boy who is most alive
In the centre of tumult makes no noise
Keeps to himself in spite of those
Who make newspaper and radio
Padrig Padrig don't cut your hair
Down to your haunches let it flare

The living boy is strong
As bull and horse he wrestles
For sport and always wins
To prove himself he crossed the sea

Padrig Padrig don't cut your mane
Down to your thighs, now let it gain

He comes from an early world
enfolded in Pagan stillness

Atlantean currents: Celticism

No telegraph or barber's shop
Machine or science Church or State.

Padrig, Padrig don't cut your locks
Let them ripple down to your hocks

Colquhoun was also gaining a reputation as a contributor to *Prediction* magazine. In 1970 she offered essays synthesising Celtic and Hermetic materials, a project she had been interested in for some time. She also published more straightforward pieces on Irish and Cornish landscape and places for the *Times Educational Supplement*. In 1971 she published an essay, 'Cornish Earth', in Denys Val Baker's *Cornish Review*, a collection of very localised phrases and lore that she had collected from elderly people she knew in West Cornwall, including her personal gardener and cleaner. This article, too, decries modernisation, even that of the farming industry and the spread of suburbia, which is still hard to imagine encroaching on the tiny hamlet of Paul, and suggests that these factors were diluting the pure folk wisdom of the Cornish.

Grimoire of the Entangled Thicket

By 1968 Colquhoun had started publishing poetry in Eric Ratcliffe's *Ore* magazine. In Ratcliffe's 2007 biography of Colquhoun he recalled that the two of them met when he was a Druid and she was a participant in Druidic ceremonies. Although he gives no date, it was probably in the late 1950s or early 1960s. He noted that he went to visit her some years later, probably around the mid-1970s, when she was a guest at Champney's Nature Cure Resort (now Champney's Spa) in Hertfordshire, a longstanding health resort started in the 1920s. Ratcliffe (1918–2009) was a scientist with a love of Celtic and Arthurian legend who published *Ore* from 1954 to 1995; a noteworthy achievement in itself. Ratcliffe and Colquhoun shared a love of the Celtic mysteries, and she would regularly publish Celtic themed poems in *Ore* until 1981. In 2007 Ratcliffe published a sort of biography/homage to Colquhoun with the title *Ithell Colquhoun: Pioneer Surrealist, Artist, Occultist, Writer and Poet*, in which he included a number of the poems that she placed with *Ore*.

In 1973 Ratcliffe published a small illustrated text of poems, *Grimoire of the Entangled Thicket*. The title is from *Hanes Talesin*, a sixteenth century Welsh text discussed in Graves' *White Goddess*. In 1972 Colquhoun had started a project to write 22 poems with accompanying images created a year earlier, reflecting the work she had been trying to achieve synthesising Graves' tree alphabet with the 22 paths of the Kabbalistic Tree of Life. This was part of a long-term interest for Colquhoun. For many years she had been experimenting with a synthesis of Celtic archetypes and symbolism with Kabbalistic principles, a project she would have considered as an extension of the Celtic Mystical System that Yeats and Mathers were building during their years together in the Golden Dawn. Colquhoun did some work with Yeats's correspondence and archives in Ireland. Her own archives contain copies of correspondence between Yeats and Annie Horniman and notes from Moina Mathers showing attempts to develop a 'Celtic Rosicrucian' type of order. Other papers show her own early graspings of a synthesis of Kabbalistic principles with Celtic spirituality, which also later inspired her interpretations of Graves' *White Goddess*. In 1966 she wrote a short and impenetrable essay called 'The Tree Alphabet and the Tree of Life' where she reinterprets the fanciful Druidic text *Barddas* in a Kabbalistic framework. *Barddas* was compiled in the 19th century from the writings of Iolo Morganwg/ Edward Williams, 18th century Welsh cultural activist and founder of the Welsh *Gorsedd*. The esoteric Biblical context of *Barddas* would have been compelling to Colquhoun.

It appears that she never completed the sequence, or that the remainder of the Tree Alphabet poems have been lost. The poems which do remain, and which were published by Ratcliffe, cover sections of the tree alphabet/calendar and work with a number of other correspondences that Graves provides in *The White Goddess*. Colquhoun's illustrations are visual elaborations on diagrams that Graves provides and show

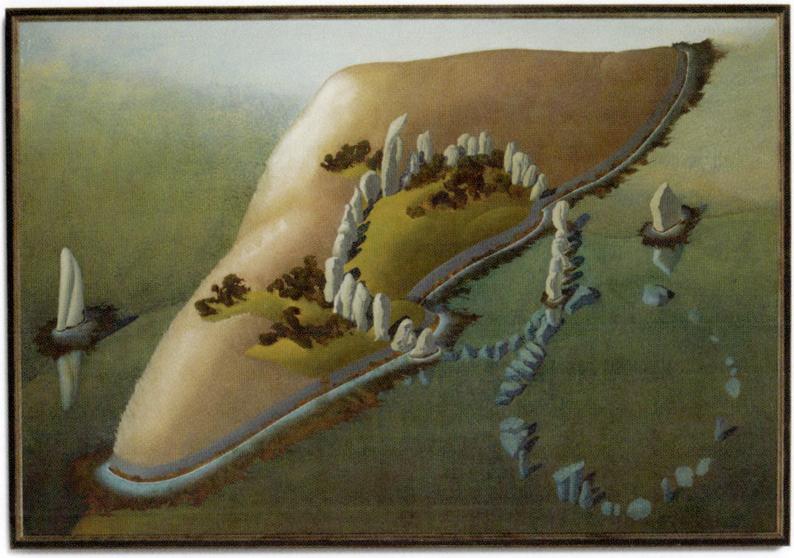

ABOVE
La Cathédrale Engloutie (1952)

her extensions of his theories into Kabbalistic synthesis. In one, which shows the letters placed on a dolmen, she included three-rayed spheres which not only suggest the spheres on the middle pillar of the Tree of Life and the three supernals, but also the rays of the Druidic Awen, suggesting paths of manifestation for divine inspiration. Colquhoun's Celtic interests were always most comfortable for her when grafted on to another aspect of Western esotericism, in this case the Kabbalah, indicating its universal and eternal relevance.

Colin Murray's Golden Section Order

By the mid-1970s Colquhoun became involved with Colin Murray's Golden Section Order, and remained an affiliate until quite late in her life. Her archives show she was receiving newsletters from 1975 until 1986. The Golden Section Order was a group devoted to developing a Pan-Celtic mystical tradition based in mythology and earth mysteries, but was also infused with the agenda of a Pan-Celtic nationalism. Murray lovingly hand coloured and illustrated the Order's newsletters and a magazine, the *New Celtic Review*, which were exquisite and

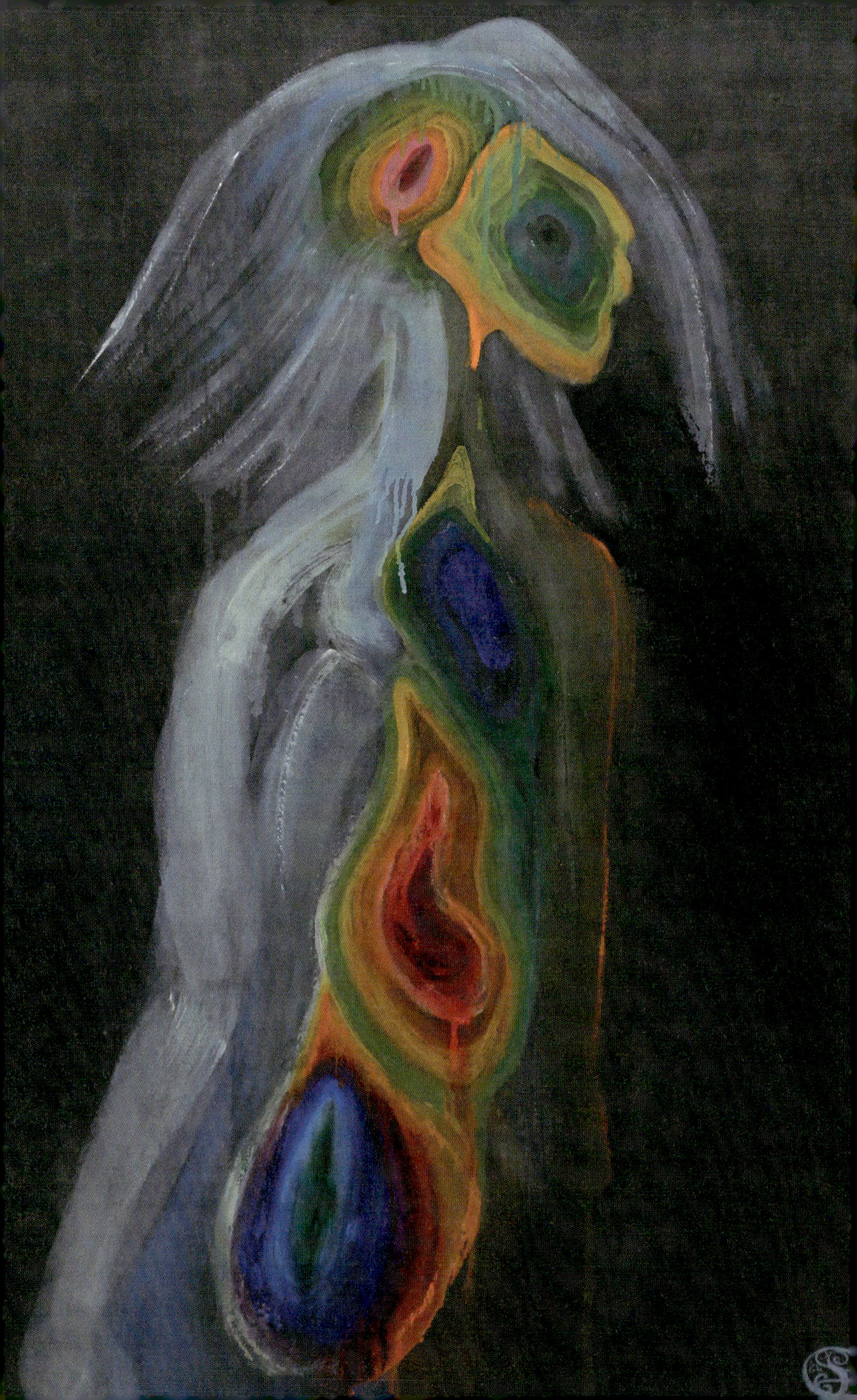

contained articles on Celtic mythologies and place lore, and also about language and music. Other members of the GSO included Patricia Villiers-Stuart, Stewart Farrar and Caitlin Matthews.

The Golden Section Order was a highly romantic enterprise. One aim was to re-Celtify England by highlighting its Pre-Christian Celtic past, and also through building connections and alliances with ethnic Celtic political movements. Murray himself was a 'Cardiac Celt' having come from the West Midlands, and had adopted a 'Celtic' identity through his spiritual pursuits. Like Colquhoun, he was highly influenced by Robert Graves and designed his own Celtic tree oracle divination deck. This was eventually published and released by his wife in 1988, but Colquhoun had a beautiful hand-copied and coloured version that Murray had sent her. The GSO also seemed to have a somewhat Pagan emphasis. Colquhoun noted that Murray held ceremonies at Imbolc, Beltane, Lughnasadh and Samhain as well as the solstices and equinoxes.

LEFT
Oil and Water Nymph (1964)

It is clear from Murray's correspondence with Colquhoun that he was trying to create a Celtic spiritual identity that would be compatible with nationalist politics, possibly inspired by Yeats's attempt to promote a non-Christian Celtic spirituality that would unite Ireland, but this vision was not to succeed. Ads in the back of the Golden Section Order newsletter promoted various political ventures, including the enterprises of some Cornish cultural activists and nationalists such as the nationalist newsletter *An Baner Kernewek*. In fact, James Whetter, the leader of the Cornish Nationalist Party (a separate party from *Mebyon Kernow*), was clearly involved with the Golden Section Order at some stage, and a letter to Colquhoun from Whetter in 1978 discussed the possibility of her contributing to his newsletter.

Colquhoun was clearly inspired by the re-Celtification of Britain project undertaken by her compatriots in the GSO. Her archives show a 1976 architectural design for a monument to commemorate the Queen's Jubilee in 1977. The monument, rich with symbolism, represented a huge vulva with a hexagram and Celtic cross in the centre intended to be placed on a hilltop in London. It was a celebration of the Goddess, of free speech and the union of the Old Religion and the New. It is unclear if these plans were ever submitted to a competition, but the project never seems to have progressed beyond the draft stage.

It was also in 1976 that Colquhoun seems to have been involved in putting together a Golden Section Equinox Ceremony with a distinctively Cornish flavour. She possessed a draft ritual banner and script for the Autumnal Equinox in the style of the Golden Section Order, laying out each part of the ritual. It is unclear where this ritual was held, but the script says that the officiants were hailing from London, Paul and Helston. It's likely that Colquhoun's companions in this were Beryl and Archie Mercer of Helston, and James Whetter's influence may have also shaped the project. The Mercers were significant contributors to early British fantasy fandom, and Beryl had a longstanding interest in the occult, even reading drafts of *The Sword of Wisdom*. Portions of the ritual script were in the Cornish language, using the opening prayer from the Cornish *Gorseth*, and incorporating a poem in Cornish by Cornish Revivalist poet Edwin Chirgwin. Another section included remembrances for Dolly Pentreath, early Cornish language activist Henry Jenner, antiquarian William Borlase and François Taldir-Jaffrennou, a Grand Druid of the Breton *Goursez*. This banner reflected the aesthetic sensibilities of Cornish cultural activists, and shows the co-impact of Celtic spirituality and Celtic ethno-nationalism in helping to create emblems of cultural difference. While Colquhoun was clearly lending support and talents to this ritual, it seems to have been a relatively isolated incident of an expression of nationalist sentiment. At times Murray seemed rather frustrated that more Celtic activists were not getting the point. A 1977 note to Colquhoun states that he had wished to 'propagandise'

RIGHT

Autumn Equinox ceremony

designed for the Golden Section Order Society.

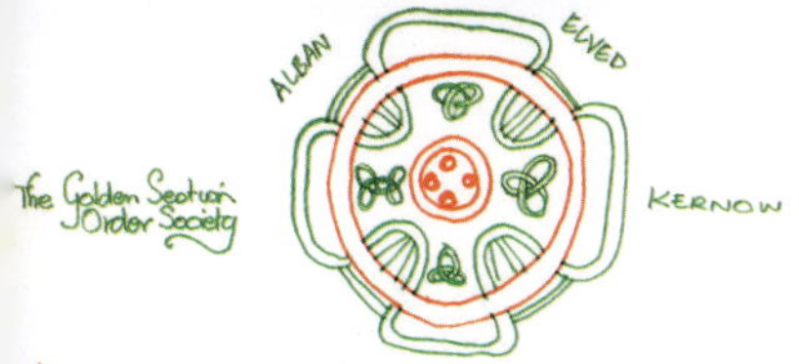

Celtic Era 4349

1
A Ceremonial for The Autumnal Equinox

It is Ambaktos - Intercalcaire, The 13th Month of The Lunar Calendar or Ruis, by The Beth Luis Nuin. The 10th Day of Ruis - Elder

We have come from Lugdunum, or Caer Troia - as it was known, from Helston or Henilston and Paul - both in Cornwall.

2 The Fourfold Hymnal of The Procession - from The Carmina Gaedelica.

Valiant Myrddin! of Pentonville Mount, who subdued the darkness - Praise the Triune, Praise Annis, Praise Brigid, Praise Morrigan. Spread thy wings over us, shield us all, shield us all. White Goddess beloved, Mother to Earth, Shield us all, Oh Shield us. Pure Principal Divine. And Brigid the Beauteous, Shepardess of the flock - Safeguard thou our Cattle, Surround us together, Surround us together. And Columba, beneficent, benign: in the name, in the hour and in the deed, through The Three in one - Through Triune - Encompass though ourselves - Shield our progression - Encompass thou ourselves - Shield our procession - Encompass thou ourselves.

O Lugh, O Dagda, O Bendigeidvran -

Be the Triune with us Day and Night, on The Machair Plain or the Mountain Ridge: Be The Triune with us and the arm around our head.

Be The Triune with us and the arm around our head.

O Lugh! O Dagda! O Bran!

3 The Sacred Grove

We circle thrice The Sacred Grove, Deasil.

4 The Raising of The Four Quarters.

In the North - Earth : The Lady Ceridwen and her Cauldron.

In the South - Fire : The fire of Lugh

In the East - Air : The Prophecies of Triple Brigid

In the West - Water : Manawyddan and his bag of Sacred Ogham

5 Introduction To The Grove

The members and friends present are introduced to the Spirit of Grove, in Turn.

6 The Grove is raised

(SOUTH)
We bring the Autumn fire to Earth in Kernow.

(NORTH)
Let The Land bear fruit and give forth.

(WEST)
May the four Corners of the Cubic Stone be struck with Ogham.

o Beth o Luis o Fearn o Saille o

(EAST)
Fair Brigid Divines the way into the circle of the ... round.

... of the ...

7 Now is The Golden Circle balanced in our midst. Shall the place of inspiration record our compound memori

Of Time past, - the present of our future selves.

We remember:

Dolly Pentreath : who lies close by at Mousehole.
Henry Jenner : first Grand Bard of the Kernow
William Borlase : rector of Ludgvan Gorsedd
Taldir Jaffrennou : father of the Breton Gorsedd.

8 Now Shall we circle Deasil but thrice
Let The Quarters return to their rightfull aspects

9 The Call of The Gorsedd Hymnal

RO, A DEW DHA WYTH — Grant of God thy protection
HAG YN GWYTH, NERTH — and in thy protection strength
HAG YN NERTH, SKYANS — and in thy strength : wisdom
HAG YN GOTHVOS AN EWN, Y GARA, — and in the wisdom : knowledge
HAG 'A GARA, CARA PUP BEWRAM — and in the knowledge : the
HAG YN PUP BEWRAM CARA DEW — Knowledge of Justice,
DEW HA PUP : OLL DADAR — and in Justice the Love of it,
and in the Love of it
The Love of all existences
and in the love of all existences - the love of God and all Goodness.

10 The Closing - Poem by Edwin CHIRGWIN.

NY ALLAV VY LEVEREL, OLL A-DHETH - I cannot tell of all things that came
AJY OW HELON OMNA YN ON SAF - into my heart as I was standing here
PASS ES ON-MERKEL DETH PUR SPERE YN HAF - while the summer day
HA GAWAS WAR Y FORTH AN HOWL DH'Y VETH - was quietly dying
A-UGH AN BRON Y-TETH YN HEW AN LOR
HA POWES WHEK WOR AN AN HYS A-GOTH - and the sun had gone
YRA G'N EBRON HANETH STEVENS - GOTH - upon the road that leads him to his grave.
HA GOLON - LOR A GRAM A HES AN DOR
HEM YU AN UR HAG OW A WHYLA CRES - Above, the hill, slowly the moon rises
A-UGH OWN LEN COMOLOW MUNYS A - and sweet repose falls upon the earth.
RAG TEWLEL WAR KEN GRGROW AGA SKES
HA CODHA WOR AN GWELYOW YN GLAR DA - In the sky bright there is a shooting star and
MIS OT! GOTH CUF GORTHEYER PLAS A-RE - all along the ground
HA GAMS GONGREK COTH Y-WHYLAF TRE. - the moonlight creeps.

This is the place where all things seek to peace
Over my head the small clouds move
To cast their shadow over other lands
And fall in good rain upon the open fields
But Lo! evening giving way to kindly dew - with the old when I seek a home.

prominent Cornish cultural activist Richard Jenkin with 'the actual Celtik [sic] mysteries' but knew he would probably not be successful. Unfortunately, this particular type of Pan-Celtic organizing platform proved not to be an enduring one for Celtic political activity. The Celtic League has found much more success in that arena, and various Celtic nationalisms have diverged entirely from the Pan-Celtic spirituality of the 1970s. Yet it was probably as part of this spiritual community and milieu that Colquhoun came to join the Fellowship of Isis in 1977, which shared a number of members with the GSO including Colin Murray, Caitlin Matthews, and her old friend Ross Nichols.

The Fellowship of Isis, founded in 1976, is an organisation which has been devoted since its inception to honouring the Goddess in all her multiplicity of forms. The Fellowship, also simply known as FOI, has been wonderfully enduring with branches and members all over the world. It was founded by Olivia Durdin Robertson and her brother Lawrence Durdin Robertson in 1976, at the Vernal Equinox. It is housed in Ireland at Clonegal Castle, also known as Huntington Castle, situated between Dublin and Wexford. The Robertson siblings hailed from a minor aristocratic family, were born and raised in England, and eventually inherited the family castle which had belonged to the Esmonde Baronets, members of the Anglo-Irish peerage. The siblings had long had an interest in the esoteric and the spiritual, with Olivia having had psychic experiences from an early age. The pair were initiated as Druids by Ross Nichols and had a Druid grove, the Grove of Eithne, on their grounds from 1963. In 1976 Olivia and Lawrence officially started initiating Priestesses into the FOI. While FOI is arguably Pagan in character, the organisation considers itself open to people of all faiths who want to acknowledge the Divine Feminine. The spiritual flexibility of the organisation, with its focus on tolerance, celebrating joy and beauty, and a lack of dogma, must be a factor in its continuing success. No vows are required, and all activities and devotionals are optional.

Colquhoun joined the Fellowship in 1977 but had been acquainted with Olivia and Lawrence for quite some time. FOI contained a number of people in Colquhoun's spiritual network, and their website states that Colquhoun's partner in the Temple of the Pyramid and Sphinx, Tamara Bourkhoun, had been active in the spiritual community that the Robertsons had from the early 1960s. The emphasis of the organisation was in alignment with many aspects of Colquhoun's spirituality, especially the relationship between the Celtic and the Perennial. The Robertsons dedicated the FOI to Isis in name, as emblematic of the universal Mother Goddess, but the lineage they give to their Priest and Priestesshood, which they describe as 'hereditary', provides an extraordinary genealogy of Isis as the progenitrix of the Scots, commingling Celt and Egyptian in a way that may have enticed Colquhoun's sensibilities. The Robertsons believed that Isis was the mother of Princess Scotia, who left Egypt for Scotland, and whose son, Gaelglas, named the race of the Gaels. The Robertsons believed themselves to have been descended from Scotia, and therefore heirs to a line of Celtic/Egyptian priesthood. While this may sound like a rather implausible mythic genealogy, giving Celts an Egyptian origin was a time-honored tradition of British and Irish antiquarians, going back centuries. Antiquarians portrayed Druids as wearing headdresses similar to the Pharaonic nemyss as a way of suggesting that the origins of Druidic spiritual traditions may have been in the wisdom of Egypt. Lawrence and Olivia were also dedicated to promoting native Irish deities and renamed the abbey on site The Temple of Dana, where they held rituals using the Irish language.

One can become initiated as a Priestess in the FOI by remote attunement, and Colquhoun was probably made a priestess in this way. There is a record of the offerings she made to the Goddess on this occasion, although it is not clear how active she may have been in the spiritual workings of the Fellowship. Although Colquhoun had incorporated ideas of the Divine Feminine into her work and writings, and copies of rituals and entreaties to Goddesses exist among her archives, FOI offered her an opportunity to acknowledge her interest in the Goddess in an environment that was forward thinking, yet not overly politically challenging, although any celebration and recognition of the Divine Feminine is ultimately political. Although Colquhoun had always fought for the acknowledgment that there was a Divine Female counterpart to the Divine Male, it was really only at this moment in history that a Goddess-focused organisation could emerge that would reflect her sensibilities. Further, FOI had solid roots in 'Celtic' spirituality, yet it was celebratory and without explicit aims regarding matters of Celtic sovereignty.

Although Colquhoun was deeply sympathetic to Cornish and other Celtic political aims, her mission was clearly located in spiritual Celtic identities, which is where she chose to dedicate most of her time and energy. However, there are deep strains of cultural preservation that run through all of her writing on Celtic subjects, even if many ethnic Cornish might have viewed her as an outsider. It's clear that Colquhoun loved Cornwall, and believed in some sort of self-determination for Celtic peoples; however, we can see from her life and preoccupations that her interests were firmly in opposition to her urban experiences, and what she called 'the claustrophobic fright of cities'. Colquhoun's Celts were inexorably tied to sacred landscapes. Celtic identity was essentially pre-Christian, and could be accessed by connection to the land, whereas progress and modernisation were causing the atrophying of the Celtic spirit. Yet Colquhoun's attitude toward Cornwall, even if tinged with romanticism, still showed an unwavering commitment to a uniquely Cornish future, even if it's possible that her vision of what that meant would have been incompatible with the Cornish future that many Cornish people would want for themselves today.

By 1983 many of Colquhoun's creative efforts were winding down. Some of her final Celtic-themed publications were in the Goddess-focused 'zine *Wood and Water*, which merged British Pagan sensibilities with environmental preservation efforts, reporting regularly on the actions at Greenham Common. It may well be that this was a political direction she would have endorsed.

Atlantean currents: Celticism

Like her artistic output, it is impossible to extricate Colquhoun's Celticism from the other currents of her life. They were woven together, each a strand of a complex world view involving spiritual purity and practice, other dimensions, and communication with the beings who inhabit them. Colquhoun as artist was inseparable from Colquhoun as mystic and seer, translating between worlds. It is perhaps primarily through an exploration of her occult influences that we can best see the web of philosophies and influences that shaped her work.

'A stream of power, set in motion':

V – Occultism

NEXT PAGE The Bird of Hermes from the Ripley Scroll. 'In the sea without lees standeth the bird of Hermes. Eating his wings variable, and maketh himself yet full stable.'

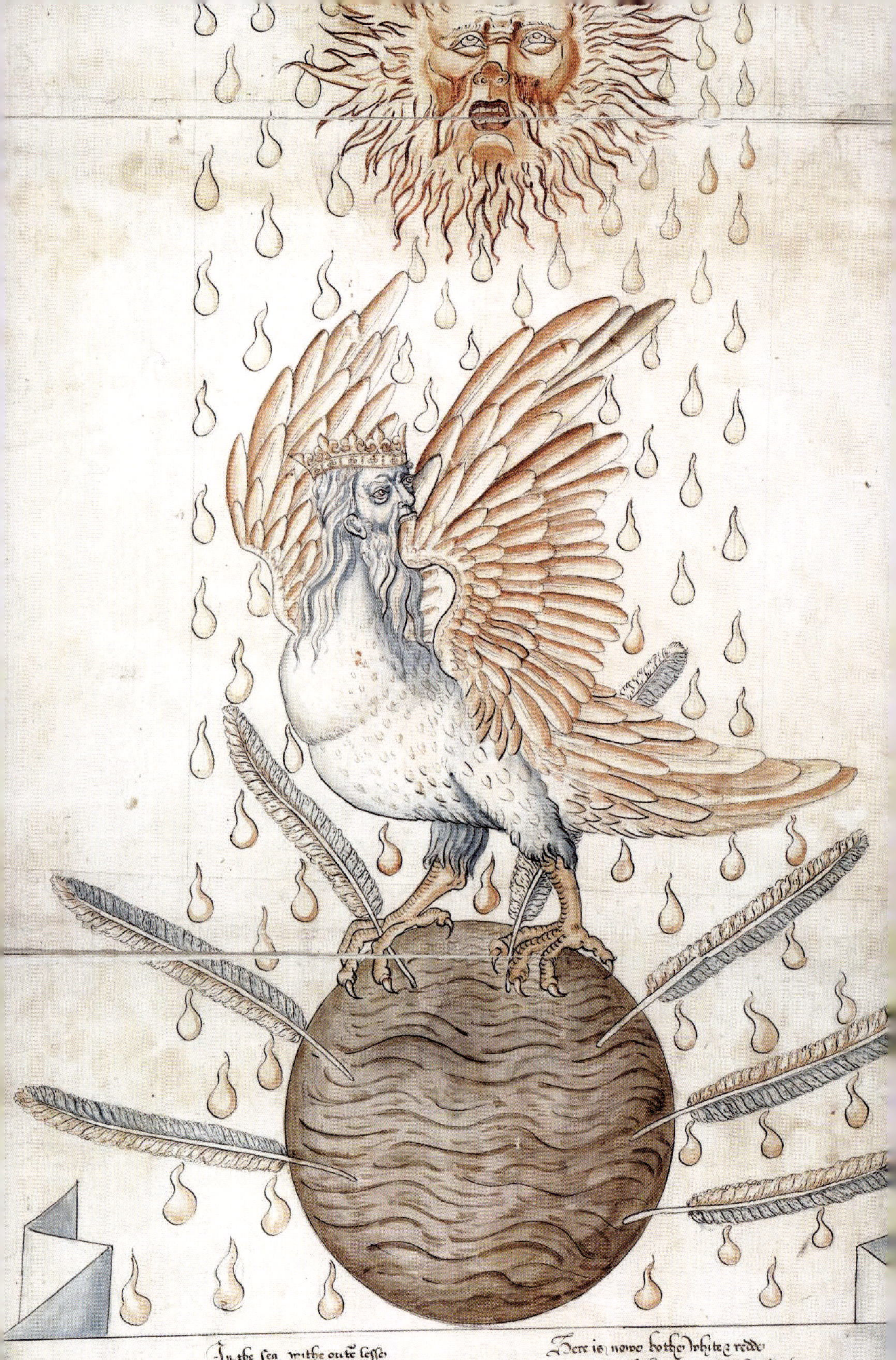

In the sea withe oute lesse
standeth the byrde of Hermes
Eatinge his wynge variable
And maketh him selfe full stable
When all his fethers by him from gonne

Here is nowe bothe white & redde
and also the stone to quicken ye deade
All and some wthouten fable
bothe harde & softe & maliable
Understand nowe well & righte

V

To me, a sigil does not begin to live until it is represented in colour.

— Ithell Colquhoun, 'Colour and the Two Sigils' (1979)

It is hard to imagine what Ithell Colquhoun's everyday visual experience of the universe was like. Her colourful and abstract tarot deck, created in 1977, was laden with magical correspondences drawn from the world of the Kabbalah. Part of the narrative of the deck, inasmuch as there is one, is that each colour is united with many other principles, numbers, deities, gems, zodiac signs. Each colour, each shape that Colquhoun would have encountered in her daily life, would have pointed to so many other things in a rich tapestry of correspondences. This is a sensitivity that Colquhoun had cultivated since her youth, and it is staggering to imagine the layered complexity of her visual and embodied experience by the end of her life. Study of the occult was the key to that life. It was her first love and passion, and it sustained her through the hardest times of illness and the fear of poverty. What constitutes the occult is imperfectly defined, so perhaps it is best to ask what Colquhoun was seeking that 'mainstream religions' could not provide.

The middle part of the twentieth century was a dynamic and fertile time for the occult in Britain, one which in many ways set the stage for the development of occult subcultures into the twenty-first century. However, historical overviews of this period are rare. The 'Occult Revival' from the 1880s to the 1920s gets a lot of attention, as does the flowering of occult movements that emerged during the late

1960s, but from 1920 to 1970 there was also a great deal of cultural dynamism as the occult milieu reformed after the devastation of two world wars. Magic was both engaging with modernity and rejecting it, simultaneously. We can see an embrace of the language of scientific principles in the magical theories of Aleister Crowley. There was an increase in interest in the fourth dimension, space travel and aliens, all of which easily share the same conceptual space as ancient wisdom from Atlantis. During this time the occult scene in Britain was reconfiguring itself, with the decline of Theosophy and the fracturing of the Golden Dawn. We see the emergence of Wicca and witchcraft, Druidry moves out of its previous role as simply a 'friendly society' and develops a greater presence as a spiritual movement, the O.T.O. gains a higher profile and splinters, then in the later 1960s we see the emergence of Satanism, and the earth mysteries movement coalesces around more esoteric principles involving electromagnetic currents.

Colquhoun's relationship with the occult and the esoteric was lifelong, and her art and writings constitute the working record of a dedicated practitioner and theorist. Although Colquhoun clearly showed Hermetic and alchemical influences in her art from a very early age, her involvement in occult organisations really begins in the 1950s, after her divorce from Toni del Renzio in 1947. Until this time, Colquhoun was much more integrated into both Modernist and Surrealist art and literature communities in London, but by the 1950s her social focus had started to shift. Not only did she begin joining occult and magical organisations, but her investigations into witchcraft began in earnest, and by the end of that decade she had moved permanently to the west of Cornwall. So many of the themes which captivated her were woven throughout the entire tapestry of her life and art, which makes a truly linear narrative difficult. For instance, we can chart her engagement with an esoteric theory, such as the fourth dimension, and note how she experiments with it in different artistic and magical contexts from the 1940s to the 1970s. Her work in esoteric colour theory, her love of the Golden Dawn, the androgyne and the sacred feminine all reemerge as themes she develops throughout the span of her career, interweaving with other interests and her own history.

Colquhoun herself emerges as a nexus of all of the major occult currents of the 20th century. She was very firmly entrenched in the Western esoteric tradition, but was also well read in Asian philosophies and practices, including Buddhism, Tantra and yoga. Kabballah and alchemy were probably the most consistent references throughout her body of work, followed by her interest in Druidry and nature religion. She was an initiate of a wide variety of different orders representing Hermetic and Pagan traditions, including the O.T.O., Co-Masonry, Martinism, British Circle of the Universal Bond (also known as ADUB), the Golden Section Society, and in later years the Fellowship of Isis. Although she was unsuccessful in her attempts to become an initiate of the Golden Dawn at an early stage, the Golden Dawn system of magic was clearly one of her guiding principles, and she wrote the influential account of the Golden Dawn magicians, *The Sword of Wisdom*, which was published in 1975. She was also a key member of a Golden Dawn-type organisation, The Order of the Pyramid and Sphinx, founded by Tamara Bourkhoun in the 1960s with a heavy emphasis on Enochian magic.[56] She was also affiliated briefly with Dion Fortune's group, the Society for Inner Light, but the organisation did not suit her and she failed to meet the criteria for full initiation. She had deep interests in and knowledge of both traditional and contemporary witchcraft, met with Gerald Gardner more than once, yet did not become a member of any Wiccan organisation. Although she was not a spiritualist, she had knowledge of and correspondence with folk healers around Britain and Ireland and made extensive use of remote healing services throughout her life.

Despite what seems like an eclectic mix of spiritual pursuits, there are clear themes which emerge. In general, Colquhoun was interested in groups which espoused a Perennialist view of a universal wisdom tradition, reliant on a heavily ordered universe. She was drawn to initiatic schools with some sort of Hermetic basis. She clearly believed that there was an esoteric current, even if there were many paths of its expression.

Colquhoun chronicled many of her early occult meanderings in *The Sword of Wisdom*, and we can see a woman who was really looking not only for community, but education and ultimately enlightenment. When it came to esoteric topics, Colquhoun was always hungry for more. Her accounts show that even as a young woman she knew her own mind and was forceful with her opinions. This would not make her well suited to magical organisations that required passive members, who would not question leadership or appear too bold. She learned this lesson early on with her attempts at joining the Golden Dawn. It may have been a function of her strong will and enquiring mind that she sought membership in so many magical orders: her involvements are somewhat staggering, and her affiliations with several groups didn't materialise well or were short lived.

Yet the full picture of her involvements in esoteric orders is still hard to piece together despite a relative bounty of letters, books, and artistic experiments. When Colquhoun was in London, much of the occult world of the time would have been on her doorstep, and that would have continued to be the case as she travelled back and forth between London and Lamorna until the late 1950s. However, when she fully relocated to Cornwall in the late 1950s, she lived in more isolated circumstances yet kept up her affiliations and experimented with a number of different orders. Was most of her practice conducted as a solitary magician? Did she travel to participate in group ritual? Did she pour out the teachings from her magical groups into her art and writing? It is important to keep in mind, though, that just because someone was in a particular group or society, it does not imply that they were totally dedicated to the curriculum. It was common for people to join an order just to get a foot in the door, and then to abandon it for other societies which held more interest. People regularly joined multiple orders, which created an interconnected occult community. But although some of Colquhoun's initiations and involvements may have been somewhat ephemeral, many were not. She was a dedicated student within a number of initiated orders, and also supported that work with her own research.

Importantly, however, Colquhoun's participation in the occult milieu of her day was not just about enlightenment or her desire to recapture the wisdom of the ancients. Her occultism reinforced her position on the margins, and is charged with the power of the outsider. Being a woman artist established her firmly in that category, but her occult convictions required that she embrace it. Scholars of the occult frequently refer to the idea of 'rejected knowledge', meaning that central to our understanding of what constitutes the core of an esoteric worldview or curriculum is the idea that the knowledge of the occultist is that which has been discarded by mainstream or, more disparagingly, more enlightened society.[57] This suggests an inherent lack of rationality in the occult practitioner, a condition which puts them at odds with a modern, secular worldview. But it isn't quite that black and white, because no culture has ever been so neatly divided into rational and irrational. No society is ever fully disenchanted, regardless of how many philosophers wish to condemn us all to dark, perpetual alienation. It may well be that the occultist is the one doing the rejecting, and finding alternative structures in which to shape their own personal power and agency. In this view, the occultist is not the possessor of a superstitious or gullible mind, she is a creative actor commenting on and rejecting power structures and working to shape her own reality with a different set of tools and rules.

How can we understand what drove Colquhoun and motivated her overwhelming commitment to the occult? What was she looking for in her relentless searching? It could almost appear to anyone not familiar with the incredible depth of her work that she was a dilettante, hopping from group to group, gaining initiation and then dropping the curriculum when it did not suit her. This could not be further from the truth. Colquhoun was knowledgeable and challenging, and when it came to the viability of an occult curriculum she did not defer to supposed superiors. The stakes were too high. She asked a lot of questions and, when she felt she had come to the end of a group's usefulness for her, she would bid them farewell, even after many years of engagement.

She was involved in so many different types of groups that at a glance it is hard to find the common thread. Was she into Goddess spirituality? Was she an esoteric Christian? Monotheist? Polytheist? The answer is probably a little bit of yes to all of them. Colquhoun most frequently identified as an animist, and this perspective is apparent in many aspects of her work. She believed that the earth was fully alive and that everything was imbued with spirit. As we shall see, for Colquhoun, the ultimate nature of divinity was formless and genderless, but not Other. Godhood was within our grasp. Her mission was theurgic. She wanted to experience and unite with the divine, and all of her magic was designed to facilitate that process.

Colquhoun could best be described as a Perennialist.[58] Perennialism is a spiritual philosophy emerging from Renaissance Neoplatonism, suggesting that all the great spiritual paths and religions reveal the same universal wisdom, and that it is the ultimate goal of humanity to return to and merge with the one divine source of all things. All teachings which contain this truth will point to it, and as a result Perennialists tend to embrace a very ordered cosmos based on essential (and sometimes essentialist) truths and principles. Under the influence of Perennialism we see the tendency to focus on the commonalities of different religions, frequently without consideration of the contexts from which they emerged. Practices, pantheons, deities, and concepts get recombined and conflated into not always correct or comfortable categories. Various mythologies are approached using structural analysis to try to tease out universal stories and frameworks. In more recent times, Joseph Campbell has been the great populariser of this approach. Campbell's powerful cross-cultural analysis of myth provided for his many admirers a set of grand stories that speak to the common experience of humanity. It emphasises that which is universal and provides a compelling argument that at the root of it all, we are all the same. This is frequently the emotional and even logical centre of Perennialism, and the sentiment is, indeed, beautiful. It is also deeply flawed because, in fact, we are not all the same.

Perennialism was part of the wider project of putting together an ordered, categorised universe, with predictable rules and a Grand Narrative. This is why the Kabballah has worked so well as an organizing schematic within Western occult traditions which have Perennialism at their core, and partially why Colquhoun resonated with it so deeply. This originally very Jewish system of mysticism became a series of open conceptual spaces into which almost anything could fit – deities, colours, tarot cards, elements, planets, philosophies. Flexible and resilient, it became the perfect system to support the continuing development of Western Esotericism and its contact with other esoteric systems, particularly those of India. Although historically a number of Hindu, Buddhist and some Islamic philosophers have also recast these religions as transmitting the 'universal current', Perennialism still tends to skew very Western in its construction, erasing uncomfortable cultural differences and focusing on salvation, transcendence and anti-materialism. Embedded within the idea that all religions reflect a single ancient wisdom tradition, is that the original divine state of humanity was in the Golden Age of the past, and that spiritual traditions have only degraded over time. It is the continuing story of The Fall, and the desire to return to a Golden Age.

Of course, much of the development of the Western occult tradition was refracted through Christianity, and Colquhoun was involved with a variety of groups and orders which were either heterodox Christian, or which had notions of 'The Christ' as a focus of practice and contemplation. So how Christian did this make Colquhoun? It is a hard question, and it's possible that the answer may not be consistent over her life. Ultimately, she seemed more invested in the idea of a 'Christ' than devotion surrounding Jesus in any conventional Christian sense. Her art and writing often dealt with Christian or Biblical themes, such as saints and various crosses, but there is little to suggest a personal devotional relationship with Jesus. The interplay of esoteric Christianity with occultism and occult movements as they were developing in the 19th and 20th centuries is messy. The Perennialist thrust of Theosophy casts Jesus as one master teacher among many, and sees the truths of Christianity as universal truths to be uncovered in all religions from the dawn of time. The basic idea is something like this: 'Christ' is the title of an office or station of a great and enlightened teacher who represents the descent of the divine into the material world. It is through Christ that people are brought into 'The Light' and can ascend to their own divinity. Thus, in some occult traditions which use Jesus as a significant figure, he is seen as one of a number of solar deity figures who die and are reborn, such as Osiris, Tammuz, and even King Arthur. This solar deity focus is also broadly true of the Golden Dawn, and we see it in Theosophy and the teachings of Rudolf Steiner.[59]

In this view of the spiritual role of Jesus, the crucifixion becomes a more generalised tale of sacrifice. Theosophist Annie Besant characterises Christ's death and resurrection as potential experiences for any initiate seeking to become a Christ:

> Every man is a potential Christ, and the unfolding of the Christ-life in a man follows the outline of the Gospel story in its striking incidents, which we have seen to be universal, and not particular.
>
> There are five great Initiations in the life of a Christ, each one marking a stage in the unfolding of the Life of Love. They are given now, as of old, and the last marks the final triumph of the Man who has developed into Divinity, who has transcended humanity, and has become a Saviour of the world.[60]

This is a crucial distinction between esoteric Christianity as it has developed in an occult context, and any sort of conventional Christian belief or practice. Most forms of Christianity hold that God and Christ are wholly Other to humankind. The salvation offered by the crucifixion and resurrection allow for being in the eternal presence of God, but not for becoming a deity oneself. In fact, this would be a heretical notion. While Christian mystics may occasionally, and controversially, commune directly with God, they are not merging with the Godhead. The way in which occult orders such as the Golden Dawn re-envisioned Christianity was as a part of a continuation and extension of a much older and primordial religious tradition, In short, they extend the pedigree of Christianity back in time to the ancients.

Occult Christianity fundamentally changes its central tenets, and this is crucial in considering the way in which Colquhoun was working with, and inspired by, Biblical and Christian material in her art and writing. She was also a member of several orders that were heterodox Christian, yet which were orthodox in flavour. Orthodoxy is also a valued principle within Perennialism, since it suggests a tradition which is closer to the original source religion. It is likely that Colquhoun's involvement with orthodoxy reflects her interest in localised reflections of the source.

Further, in many occult traditions, Jesus was considered an initiate of the mysteries. This sort of enlightenment wasn't meant for just anyone, and so magic was taught and used primarily within a curriculum designed for spiritual ascendance and moral perfection. The role of the initiate preparing herself for the hard road to enlightenment becomes a crucial part of occult culture, as opposed to people who might be using similar practices and texts in a solely magical context. In other words, using tarot cards to figure out how to get out of a messy relationship is considered a more debased usage, by some occultists, than using tarot cards to contemplate the nature of the absolute. The magical orders Colquhoun joined all shared a curriculum designed toward anti-materialist ends. Developing physical, moral and spiritual purity and cultivating attunement with the universe all tended to be important practices in the orders Colquhoun joined.

Many of the esoteric themes and orders which shaped Colquhoun's life and art are not easily approached in a strict chronological order, so I will approach her interests thematically, pointing out the touchstones of her life's journey and work as we go.

Early years

Colquhoun had a very early interest in the occult and in alchemy. Early notebooks from her days at Cheltenham Ladies College show an obsession with correspondences, containing notes on the zodiac, correspondences with perfumes, and symbols related to plants and birds and planets. Her own writings about her early life suggest the perfect conditions for the cultivation of an occult sensibility (although, naturally, she wants the reader to see how suited she was for these pursuits). She writes frankly about her belief in the power of menstruation as a token of women's psychic ability, and an early fascination with sex. A recurrent theme in a number of her writings is her belief that despite her British heritage, her birth in northern India marked her and made her spiritually predisposed to that place, and that her move back to England deprived her of direct access to the spiritual traditions of India to which she believed she was authentically heir. In this passage from the section titled 'Faith', from her unpublished autobiography *Until Twelve*, she expresses a sense of longing for her spiritual home while also providing a key to the ways in which she understood a common framework for disparate spiritual ideas and symbols:

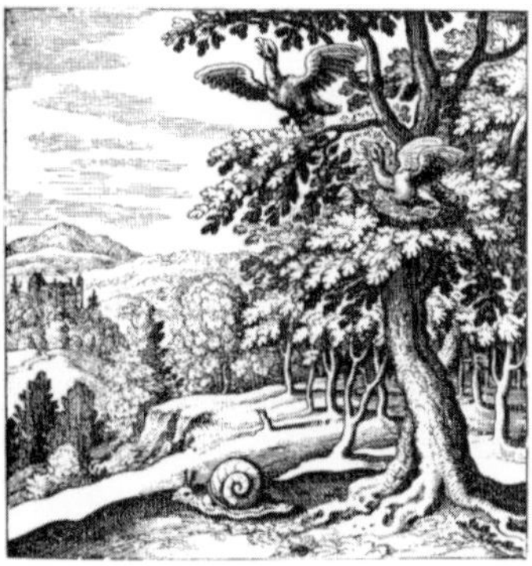

ABOVE *Book of Lambspring* Figure 8, 'Here are two birds great and strong – the body and the spirit. One devours the other.'

> If I say that at 10 years old I imagined Christ as a hermaphrodite I shall not be believed. Yet it was so. Uncared for by my distant parents, and needing shelter, I fused the red hearted Jesus with the blue cloaked Mary and made a god with breasts. I did not know the word El-Shaddai, nor any word to express this image.

> I simply made the image and worshipped it. But five years earlier I had placed a tomato of monster size and ripeness as the centre-piece in a Palestine exhibition, for I knew it to be full of Christ's blood. I found this saving juice in the exuberant fruit of the earth rather than in the veins of a sufferer; I chose the green tree rather than the dry. Already, it seems, I had embraced Hinduism; but why was I not born a Brahmin? Why was no caste mark impressed upon my subtle body? Where am I, between east and west? A lost soul indeed. Is there an alternative to the back-parlour meeting, the stiff little book in tawny dustjacket about the wisdom of the east? What I need, and cannot have, are fireworks, carnival, gay gods embracing, coloured powder thrown at everyone, ritual dance and above all the balsamic microtone rhythms compared to which all others are crude… Or do I have to found a new religion, beside all my other work? May I rest at least in the animism which has been revealed in part.[61]

She was certainly precocious and dedicated to an unconventional spirituality very early on. The value of the Divine Feminine is asserted very early for her in this tale, or at least she wants us to believe that she always, instinctively and even as a child, recognised that the natural state of the divine is the fusion of male and female.

By the time Colquhoun was 20 she was already familiar with alchemy and alchemical texts, and had evidently taken an interest in the 15th century English alchemical text known as 'The Ripley Scroll', which was to inform a number of her alchemically based projects. In 1926, while attending Cheltenham School of Art, she wrote, acted in and designed the set for a play, *The Bird of Hermes*, an alchemical allegory exploring the symbolism of the twin as non-integrated self which appears as a recurring theme in her work. It is very likely that *The Bird of Hermes* seeded the foundational themes for Colquhoun's 1961 Surrealist novel *Goose of Hermogenes*, which she probably started drafting as early as the 1930s.

The Bird of Hermes is short and it's not clear whether or not it was staged as part of her school work, although it probably was. To a modern audience it would seem to lack plot, and is laden with symbolism. Yet this is perfectly consistent with the late nineteenth-century occult theatre of Florence Farr and the Mathers' Rites of Isis in Paris, which would have been designed to impart occult teachings directly to the audience without their fully needing to apprehend the entirety of the plot or characters. One wonders if perhaps Colquhoun was already conversant with this type of theatre even at this young age. A stage direction reads: 'Words are to be intoned and movement needs to be deliberate. Subdued strokes on a gong.'[62]

The main characters in *Bird of Hermes* are 'The Fair-Haired Girl', 'The Dark-Haired Girl', 'The Phoenix' and 'Hermes'. The stage directions state that this is to be formally acted by mummers or puppets, and that the actors need to wear masks or heavy make-up and wigs. We can already see the importance of colour symbolism in Colquhoun's work, as she carefully details each colour to be used in the costumes and props. The Fair-Haired Girl and the Dark-Haired Girl dance with Hermes and the Phoenix at various intervals, and finally the Fair-Haired Girl and the Phoenix are consumed in flames after he shares secret wisdom with her. Dance was an essential element in this short production, and even the dances were imbued with magical intent, as Colquhoun's stage directions imply that the dancers were creating sigils on the ground with their movements. This performance was not merely a spectacle of an allegory; the players were invoking beings with their feet.

It is interesting to see the degree to which Colquhoun was already so immersed in occult thought, practice and symbolism at the age of 20, and the ways in which the beginning of her formal arts education was being put into the service of her esoteric pursuits.

The Quest Society

By 1928 Colquhoun had moved to London to start her formal art education at the Slade, and finally found the opportunity to participate in an esoteric community with like-minded people. Almost immediately she joined George Mead's Quest Society and became its youngest member. Mead was a well-heeled, Cambridge-educated, former Theosophist who had once served as Helena Blavatsky's personal secretary. He was a respected essayist and author in his own right, having written widely on various aspects of esotericism and Gnosticism. He founded the Quest Society with a significant number of former Theosophists who left when Charles Leadbeater was reinstated into the Society, having been previously dismissed for instructing young boys in masturbation. He founded it in 1909 and it ran until 1931 and boasted a fairly healthy membership, probably over 150. It also produced a publication, *The Quest: A Quarterly Review,* which included contributions by Gershom Scholem, A.E. Waite, W.B. Yeats, T.W. Rolleston and Jessie Weston among many others. The Quest Society included many notable members, some of whom were to be in Colquhoun's magical circles for decades. Members included Moses Gaster, whose daughter was with her at the Slade, Hugh Schonfield, author of *The Passover Plot*, William Bernard Crow, Margaret Woods, Ezra Pound, Gerard Heym and Edward Garstin. Meetings consisted of lectures and sometimes spirited rebuttals. Colquhoun's notes for *The Sword of Wisdom* say that 'The Quest Society met in two large studios at Clareville Grove, situated between the stations of Gloucester Road and South Kensington' and that the building took a beating during The Blitz. It was sizable enough to have both a lecture hall and a lending library. She also noted that the wife of George Bernard Shaw, activist and heiress Charlotte Payne-Townshend, helped to subsidise the rent. She wrote of Mead himself in *The Sword of Wisdom* that he 'looked like a florid version of the Paul Verlaine statue in the Luxembourg Gardens.' Despite the parade of luminaries, precocious Colquhoun did not stay on the sidelines, and used this opportunity to present some of her earliest writings on esoteric philosophy.

It was through The Quest Society that she met her distant cousin Edward Garstin, who had served as secretary to the Society for two years and became known for his writings on alchemy in the 1930s. In a 1979 essay recalling his life, Colquhoun admits that she was never clear on the exact family connection.[63] She wrote in *Sword of Wisdom* that she had heard of a cousin, 'Eddie' Garstin, as a child, and was pleasantly surprised to make his acquaintance in such an unusual community of like minds. Garstin had a keen occult mind and was a student of the mysteries from a very early age, yet like many occultists he had trouble managing his material circumstances. She recalled that he had poor luck and poor health. His wife had cleaned him out financially and then disappeared during his service in WWI, and he fared little better with his second wife. Colquhoun noted that he never seemed to be able to hold on to decent employment and spent much of his later life in poverty, tragically dying by suicide in the 1950s.

Yet when Colquhoun was at the Slade, Garstin took her under his wing and served as her initial mentor in the occult world. The impact of meeting and befriending Garstin on Colquhoun's occult interests cannot be overstated. He was clearly a sympathetic and encouraging mentor, providing her with hard-to-find manuscripts on Kaballah and alchemy. He wrote two books, *Theurgy or the Hermetic Practice: A Treatise on Spiritual Alchemy* (1930) and *The Secret Fire* (1932), a book more focused on alchemical symbolism. In *The Sword of Wisdom*, Colquhoun recounts her visits to Garstin and the access she had to alchemical manuscripts in his library. She also tells of the practical alchemists Garstin used to visit and the alchemical experiments he witnessed. Garstin was also the Cancellarius (secretary) of the Alpha and Omega Lodge, which was one of the remaining fragmented orders of the original Hermetic Order of the Golden Dawn, founded by Moina Mathers after the death of her husband, Samuel 'MacGregor' Mathers. Garstin introduced Colquhoun to the Golden Dawn, thinking that her interest in art and colour would make her well suited to this type of magical work. This connection ignited her lifelong obsession with the Golden Dawn.

Around 1930, The Quest Society became financially insolvent. Garstin tried to pick up the pieces by starting The Search Society, which Colquhoun duly joined, and it was during this time that she started to make her own early contributions to esoteric thought in this community. Colquhoun noted that The Search Society failed to gain the membership of The Quest Society, but (W.B.) Crow, who, as we have seen, remained in Colquhoun's own esoteric circles for several decades, was a supporter of the new group. She had her first publication in 1930, 'The Prose of Alchemy' in *The Quest*, vol 21 no 3. Also, around 1930, when she was only 24, she delivered a paper to The Search Society called 'The Connection Between Mysticism and Blasphemy'. This is a rather sophisticated consideration of blasphemy and taboo, and it's worth considering in some detail because it is likely, given Colquhoun's penchant for shock and disruption throughout her life and artistic career, that these views coloured many of the creative and life decisions that she made.

In this densely packed and theoretical essay, the young Colquhoun wrote about the role of both mysticism and blasphemy in rejecting authority, and therefore giving one access to the immanent divine:

> Thus, though the blasphemer may be said to lower the divine, while the mystic raises himself to meet his Lord, yet in fact both perform the same process, that of bringing the divine and the human into contact. Since any vehicle cannot be unworthy of divinity, the doctrine of the Incarnate God and the whole train of sacramental teaching that follows in its wake is in this sense blasphemous... Another striking characteristic which both share is a fundamental nihilism. Their core is self-devastation, the breaking and defiling of the highest attained, since even the highest is low. Both turn to the East as symbol of the identity of hope and annihilation...There arises the strong conviction that all sense impressions, all thought activities, all known forms of being are poor, futile, worthless and without dignity or consequence. The 'rotten rags of memory' which recall by travesty some more exalted life.[64]

Although much later in life Colquhoun followed a Theurgic path which grew more oriented toward transcendence, this shows that even early on she was interested in the possibilities of the sacrilegious to transform and uplift. Everything has the potential to be holy. This passage also suggests an interest in Tantric practices of embracing that which is taboo and defiled to erase the boundaries between sacred and profane. Recall that Colquhoun felt a connection to the religions of Northern India, and an interest in Tantra emerges in her work quite early on. Was she perhaps already integrating these ideas into her own conceptions of the sacred?

Colquhoun believed that through blasphemy, debasement and the destruction of the category of the sacred one can reach an experience where nothing can be destroyed any longer. She states 'Where there is nothing, there is God.' 'And if all can be destroyed, why, let there be destruction.' As we have seen in her art and life, time and again, there is a recurring theme of breaking boundaries, challenging convention and exploring themes that most women of her era would not even dare to approach. Perhaps her embrace of taboo in a spiritual context was an attempt to induce in herself and her viewer an experience where that which has been categorised as base is elevated, and the audience given access to a space where they can experience the potential of divine creative energy. This is perhaps most evident in her early and more representational Surrealism, where she combines sex and decay, themes which also emerge in her writing. But it may also explain why, even later in her short stories, she writes in such a detailed manner of eating human flesh, incest, and the beauties of excrement. From 'Images of Joy':

> Presently, I heard a step and a peasant came along who thought he was alone and let down his pants and had a good shit. It was done in a minute with complete simplicity; he pulled them up again, not wiping his arse hole with so much as a leaf, fastened his belt and walked away.
>
> I went forward to look at what he had done; It was beautiful. Three concentric rings of golden brown, decorated like a cake

> with olive-stones and shreds of tomato peel. The topmost ring ended in a little point aiming at the sky. I think the whole lot must have come away clean without leaving a trace.[65]

There is little doubt that Colquhoun intended to shock, but also to present to her readers the potential for a moment of transcendence.

What is truly striking about these early musings on blasphemy is not only their theoretical sophistication, but that she grabbed on to this concept at such an early stage in her own life and used it to resist conformity and restriction, challenging not only her audiences but also herself. When we consider the bold and edgy moves that Colquhoun made, the explicit sexual imagery in her art, and the references to incest and excrement in her writings, the initial tendency is to put a feminist frame on all this and look at the way she defied conventions that would have restricted her as a woman. This is certainly true and useful, but there may be more to it. It may be that Colquhoun from her earliest days was breaking boundaries and embracing taboo as a spiritual exercise, helping to move herself and her audience towards liberation, which also became a theme in her work.

It was probably around 1928 or 1929 that Colquhoun first encountered the Golden Dawn. As she recounts in *The Sword of Wisdom*, Garstin, who had been hinting of a secret group to which he belonged, took Colquhoun to meet a couple of Order members in the hopes that she might be accepted for membership. After a short interview with a 'Mrs. Weir' (an alias Colquhoun gave her), she filled out an application, but was rejected. Colquhoun and Garstin were obviously both disappointed. Colquhoun believed that although the 'Secret Chiefs' may have deemed her not yet ready, she may have appeared too knowledgeable, and 'that' Mrs. Weir had conflicts with other women.

> Aside from possible Secret Chiefs the obvious explanation is the Mrs. Weir did not take to me – no doubt I was naïve and my attempts at intellectual honesty may have seemed

> to her misplaced. A woman of her age can find it difficult to accept someone much younger, especially another woman.[66]

Colquhoun was, indeed, young, and she came across as arrogant in the meeting. She knew it. Still, she wanted to give Mrs. Weir the benefit of the doubt. And she believed that after her initial encounter with Mrs. Weir she had been astrally contacted several times by the current of the Order's Secret Chiefs, and this was prompting her to connect with an Order that would initiate her into that tradition. However, she was not going to pursue this astral calling for over a decade as she focused more intensely on her life and career as an artist, and left her occult life in London behind to adventure abroad. Garstin's Search Society rather rapidly folded, and with the relationship between them somewhat strained, Colquhoun left and they lost touch. However, his influence on her was significant and abiding, as we shall see.

In *Sword of Wisdom* she writes that she picked up the occult thread again in around 1936 or 1937 after reestablishing herself in London. She recounts a punishingly austere weekend at Meredith Starr's nature retreat, at Frogmore Hall in Hertfordshire. It was also around this time that she completed an odd little watercolour of Allan Bennett, former Golden Dawn member and mentor of Aleister Crowley, as a Buddhist monk. Much of her life at this time was focused on trying to establish herself as a working artist, and the fetishisation of the occult by many Surrealist artists would have suggested that her own occult preoccupations might find her a comfortable artistic home within the movement. The perfect segue was alchemy.

Alchemy

'Between Lives'
In the eggshell
In the casket
Bird unborn
I lie in albuminous white

I sink
I swim
In the silken element
Formless germ
In our body's shell

I would grow
I would fly
Released into knowledge
I would still return to
The dovecot of your heart

Alchemy dominated Colquhoun's earliest art and writings, and it is easy to see what the attraction would have been for a budding artist and serious young occultist. The beautiful and strange iconography would have been seductive, and it provided a symbolic system to explore ideas about the transformative potential of magic. From the late 1930s and her real entwinement with Surrealist culture until about 1943, just after her marriage, Colquhoun's paintings and writings are filled with references to alchemical texts, iconography and processes. She was already familiar with alchemical texts and images such as The Ripley Scroll well before she met Edward Garstin, but her cousin's writings further inspired and illuminated her own understanding and application of alchemical imagery and became an important early influence. Garstin's book *The Secret Fire* contains a blend of Indian Tantric, alchemical, and Kabbalistic symbolism, and it's likely that this particular synthesis was an inspiration for Colquhoun's own artistic alchemical experiments from the period of her entry into the Quest Society through to the mid-1940s. It is also likely that Colquhoun used A.E. Waite's edition of *The Hermetic Museum*, published in 1896. The original text, published in Frankfurt in 1678 by engraver Lucas Jennis, was a collection of shorter writings on alchemy centred around the idea that the inner secrets of alchemy were primarily to be transmitted to an elite body of adepts. This collection contained a number of pieces that Colquhoun drew upon for later works such as *The Goose of Hermogenes*, including *The Book of Lambspring* and the *Twelve Keys of Basil Valentine*. Sections of *The Golden Tract Concerning the Philosopher's Stone* also seem to have influenced some of her alchemical poetry and paintings.

An equally profound influence on Colquhoun's interest in alchemy was the work of W.B. Yeats, who also provided inspiration for her ideas about social reform. Many are familiar with Yeats's deep involvement in the Golden Dawn and with Celtic revival activities in Ireland, but as a working magician his imagery was steeped in alchemical symbolism. The alchemical marriage and the hermaphrodite are prevalent images within Yeats's wider corpus. Yeats and Colquhoun met briefly in 1937, and by that time he was experiencing a renewed and active sexuality, which, combined with his alchemical interests, may have also influenced Colquhoun's visual and artistic explorations concerning sacred sex and its revolutionary potential both for the individual and as a metaphor for an enlightened society. Yet even her apparent revolutionary streak was oddly backward looking. In most ways Colquhoun's sensibilities turned toward what could be labelled as Traditionalist. Although she was invested in the ways in which the occult could inspire personal and societal transformation, she was convinced that society was degraded and that humanity needs to return to its original state. We need to, literally, return to Eden, and Colquhoun

RIGHT Figures attempting a hexagram (c. 1940–1941)

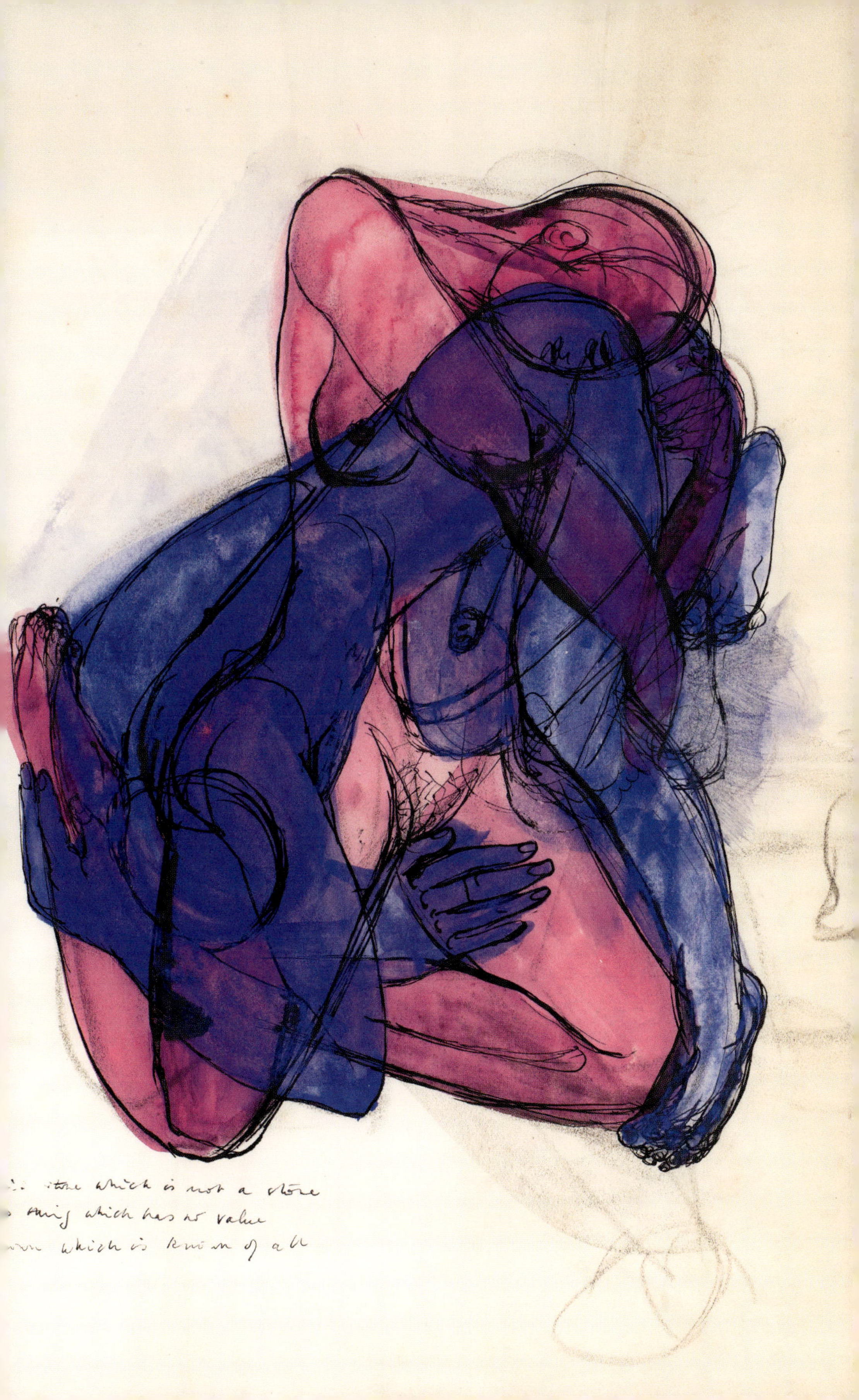
stone which is not a stone
thing which has no value
which is known of all

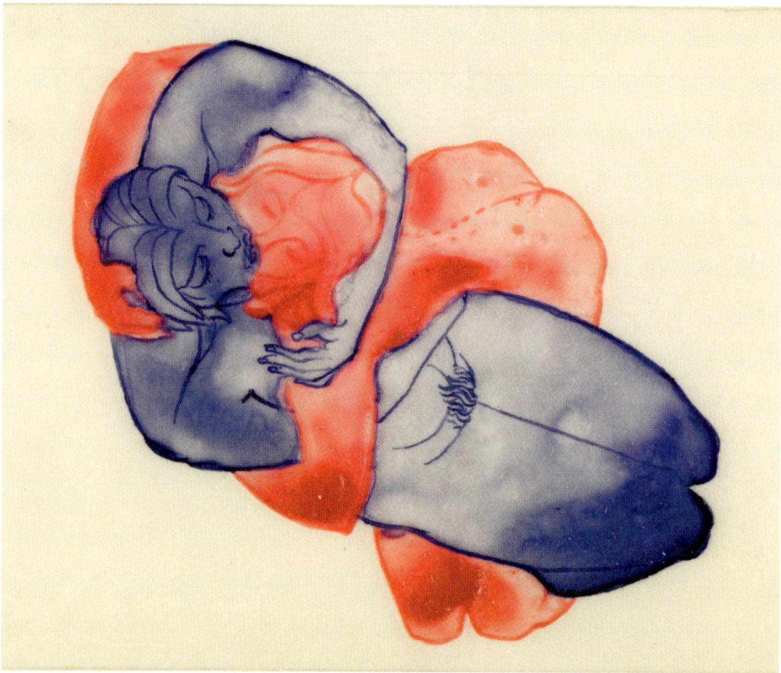

ABOVE
Two Women (c. 1940–1941)

felt that an embrace of alchemical principles could provide the best guide to broader transformation. She was not only interested in the metaphor of alchemy to provide a map for personal enlightenment and integration, she wanted to promote something bigger. Importantly, though, these ideas for Colquhoun always remained in the realm of the mythic. She never suggested an actual political programme.

The images and ideas of alchemy probably reinforced for Colquhoun the 'rightness' of her involvement in Surrealism. The rich symbolism and strangeness of medieval and Renaissance alchemical art provided an excellent repository for Surrealists to draw upon, helping to reinforce the dreamlike archetypal impact of their work. Colquhoun was certainly aware of Surrealist uses of alchemical imagery, and no doubt saw her own work as complementary. She had already been playing with alchemical symbolism for nearly a decade by the time she entered the culture of Surrealism. Unlike some Surrealists, such as Leonora Carrington or Remedios Varo, Colquhoun generally did not employ overt representational alchemical symbolism in her paintings; it was more a feature of her writing, although she did paint about alchemical themes. By the mid-1940s her alchemically inspired artistic production begins to wane. In 1946 Surrealist poet David Gascoyne wrote to Colquhoun hoping to persuade her to write a piece for *Horizon* magazine. Gascoyne wanted to show that the First Surrealist Manifesto and the philosophic Great Work were, in fact, working towards the same end, and thought Colquhoun could be helpful. He wrote that her 1930 article 'The Prose of Alchemy' was 'one of the best, most stimulating short introductions to the subject of Alchemy considered as imaginative literature, i.e. a special department of poetry, that exists in English, I think.'[67]

Since Colquhoun was also driven by the idea of a deeply structured cosmos, alchemy possessed a visual elegance and sophistication that must have been compelling to an intellect that sought the secrets of how the parts of the universe fit together, and how she could manoeuvre within it. From her earliest explorations in *Bird of Hermes*, Colquhoun shows her fixation on integration of the self. In her earliest and most intense studies this takes the form of integration of gender, with the ultimate goal of transcending it. Colquhoun's ideas about gender were synthesised from a variety of sources, but she uses the metaphor of alchemy to characterise the process by which one can move through states of spiritual refinement to achieve the Philosopher's Stone, characterised in part by the unification of the genders.

The Divine Androgyne

The Divine Androgyne was an artistic and spiritual preoccupation of Colquhoun's from 1940 to around 1943, but her wider interest in this theme persisted through the late 1940s. She mingled esoteric Christianity, Theosophy, Kabballah, and alchemy, in support of her belief that the union of the male and female, on both a physical and etheric level, was an essential precondition of returning to the divine state which is our birthright. She also believed that society needed to embrace 'the feminine', and that transcending gender entirely would create the conditions for enlightenment, genuine liberty and freedom. During these years she worked on a number of quite remarkable paintings and writings around this theme, including a private series of sex magic paintings, poems, the *Diagrams of Love* series and her essay 'The Water Stone of the Wise'. Although the androgyne was a persistent theme among Surrealists, it is likely that Colquhoun's interest in this theme was supported by other Surrealist explorations, not driven by them, since this was an interest prior to her involvement with Surrealism.

Colquhoun's ideas about the radical potential of the Divine Androgyne come from a number of systems and texts, most notably Kabballah and alchemy, but also Tantra. It is likely that the primary inspiration for her interest in the Divine Androgyne comes from Samuel 'MacGregor' Mathers' 1887 translation of sections of Christian Knorr von Rosenroth's 17th century text *Kabbala Denudata*, which resulted in *The Kabballah Unveiled*. Several chapters here comment on the importance of the unification of the male and female to achieve wholeness and spiritual completion, replicating the conjoined souls of Adam and Eve prior to the Fall:

> So also here. When the Male is joined with the Female, they both constitute one complete body, and all the Universe is in a state of happiness, because all things receive blessing from Their perfect body. And this is an Arcanum. And hence that which is not both Male and Female together is called half a body. Now, no blessing can rest upon a mutilated and defective being, but only upon a perfect place and upon a perfect being, and not at all in an incomplete being. And a semi-complete being cannot live forever, neither can it receive blessing for ever.[68]

This is a clear directive for the balance of the universe, and Colquhoun took it as such, exploring this mystery from a number of different angles. She found echoes of it in alchemy through the *Hieros Gamos*, the sacred marriage of the King and Queen (sometimes brother and sister), represented in the stage of *conjunctio* which results in the Divine Androgyne, the union of spirit and matter, the Great Work. This body of work was a further articulation of Colquhoun's insistence on the importance of women in the role of spiritual attainment, and probably helped her shape theories of the Divine Feminine and how she operated with respect to the primordial ungendered source.

Given Colquhoun's spiritual relationship with India, she was also very likely working to integrate Tantric teachings into her work with alchemy and Kabballah. Tantra was being popularised in early twentieth century esoteric circles by the works of Arthur Avalon, born John Woodroffe. Avalon's works helped to bring what would have been a radical set of practices and ideas to English speaking audiences, and Colquhoun would have resonated with ideas of non-duality and the importance of the female Shakti as the source of divine power. That she would have found echoes of these ideas in alchemy and Kabballah would have provided deep confirmation for her. And Avalon's works were being read by and incorporated into the work of her cousin, Edward Garstin, who inspired so much of Colquhoun's own theorising.

Around 1941–1942, prior to her marriage to Toni del Renzio, Colquhoun created a tremendous body of veiled and yet explicit visual work focused on the principles of sacred sexual union and which represent a fusion of Kabbalistic, Tantric and alchemical symbols. Her explicitly erotic pieces have the polished representational Surrealism we see in paintings such as *The Pine Family*, which also explores the theme of the hermaphrodite, but the explicitly sexual nature of most of these works suggest that they were not meant to be publicly displayed. Colquhoun explored the world of alchemical erotica like a woman obsessed. Her archives include many, many sketches and watercolours of men and women, women and women and humans and angels in various positions and couplings, most of them looking quite awkward. Frequently the men were blue and the women were red, but occasionally the figures were combinations of green and yellow or other colours. One sketch that was clearly meant as a colour key features a central abstraction of a stick figure couple in a *yab yum* pose in blue and red. Then, flanking the primary figure, there is another series of stick figures in different opposing colours, representing different, possibly Kabbalistic, colour schematics.

RIGHT

Diagrams of Love: The Bird or the Egg (c. 1940)

The striking feature of many of these pieces is how explicit they are. Fingers, mouths and phalluses are engaged in penetration and reception in incredible detail. Many of the tighter and more finished pieces of this series are quite small, about the size of a playing card, featuring most frequently a male figure (blue) and a female figure (red) engaging in a variety of sexual acts, including intercourse, oral and manual sex. Some of these paintings and sketches are stylistically inspired by Japanese erotica. Given her early interest in Japanese graphics, it is likely that she was using Japanese erotica as a template for her own work, but some sketches found alongside more finished pieces indicate that she was probably also using life models for these particular compositions. A number of the sketches have a man and woman standing side by side, one wearing blue briefs, and the other wearing red. Successive sketches show two life models in more and more intimate arrangements, which, given the literally hundreds of life sketches among her collection, suggests that she was not afraid to use live humans for this project. What is notable is the visual concentration in several pieces on the act of penetration, and also the focus on the erect penis. Clearly Colquhoun had an interest in both the symbolic and direct representation of genitalia in a state of arousal, and she was not afraid of placing the man in the position of visual object.

The positions of the couples in these sketches seem to have been taken from a number of sources, and Colquhoun had even made a sketch sheet of sexual positions as a guideline. Some pieces feature the couple in the Tantric *yab yum* position where the couple is face to face, but other positions may have been more fanciful and may represent an attempt

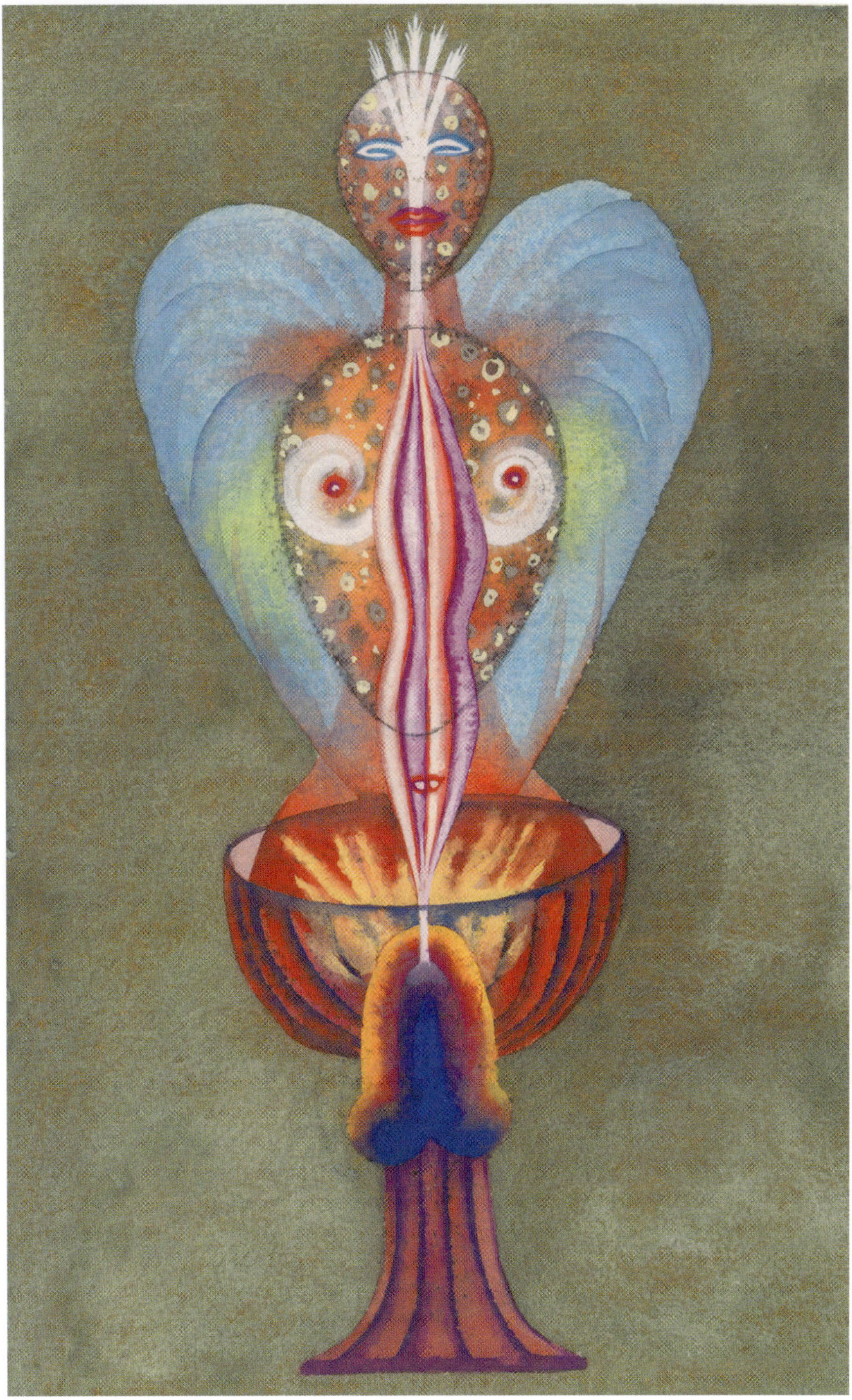

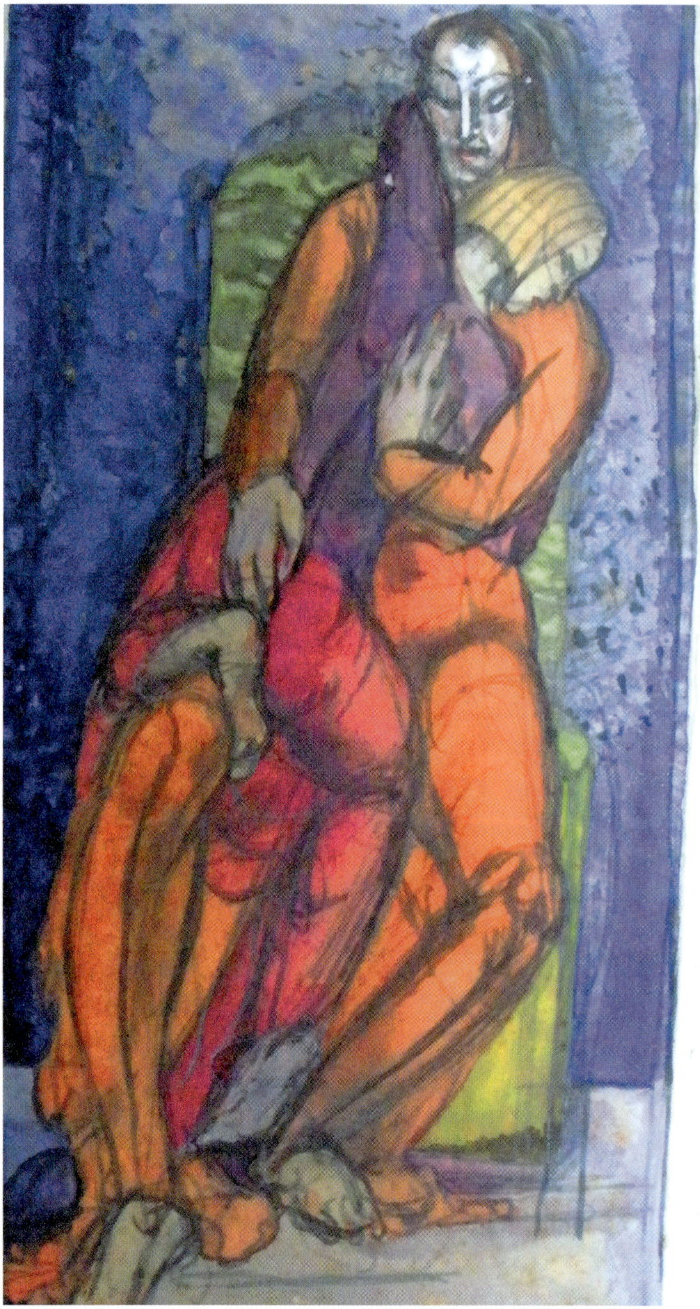

to fit sexual positions into specific magical forms. Most notably, she was focused on getting bodies to form a hexagram, which is an expression of the union of opposites, of male and female, and of elemental fire and water. It is possible that Colquhoun might have been familiar with Crowley's *Book of Lies* and was visually emulating Chapter 69:

This is the Holy Hexagram.
Plunge from the height, O God, and interlock with
Man!
Plunge from the height, O Man, and interlock with Beast!
The Red Triangle is the descending tongue of grace;
The Blue Triangle is the ascending tongue of
prayer.
This Interchange, the Double Gift of Tongues, the
Word of Double Power—ABRAHADABRA!—is
the sign of the GREAT WORK, for the GREAT
WORK is accomplished in Silence. And behold is
not that Word equal to Cheth, that is Cancer whose Sigil is [cancer]?
This Work also eats up itself, accomplishes its own
end, nourishes the worker, leaves no seed, is perfect in itself.
Little children, love one another![69]

It is worth noting that while Colquhoun clearly references polarity, not all the images are men and women. In some sketches one participant is an angel, and in another both are women.

Since Colquhoun seems never to have written about these experiments in any theoretical way, they are left to the viewer to decode. However, there are a number of clues to the nature of this remarkable magical project, which is astonishing on several grounds. It is remarkable that she produced so much material on this theme. This was not just a genteel thought experiment. Colquhoun would have been quite aware of the taboo surrounding this body of material, yet it was clearly important enough to keep this intensive exploration

LEFT
Virgin on the Knees of Saint Anne (ud)

going, knowing it would only ever be seen by a select few. This work was never meant for exhibition, it was a private exploration. But was this only a theoretical exploration , or was she interested in engaging in sex magical techniques?

Colquhoun's visual construction of this series was remarkably consistent: male figures are in a brilliant cerulean blue and females are in a violet red or scarlet. This scheme is idiosyncratic and a deviation from standard gendered western esoteric colour schemes. Generally, the 'masculine' energies are represented in red, the symbolic colour of elemental fire and the active principle, and the 'feminine' energies are blue, the colour associated with elemental water and receptiveness. And although Colquhoun uses the metaphor of alchemical conjunction, this is not an alchemical colour scheme. Richard Shillitoe claims that her choices suggest gender inversion, yet these are not the iconic primary hues of red and blue that one might see reflected in, for instance, a Golden Dawn or Masonic hexagram which might represent union of opposites through red and blue, often on a cross of yellow or gold flanked by white. Colquhoun does use these colours, red, blue, yellow and white to point to ideas of gendered spiritual perfection and transcendence (we see them in the 1939 architectural piece from the *Mediteranée* series *Rivières Tièdes*, and again in her esoteric landscape studies from the early 1940s) yet in her sex magic series Colquhoun's polarities sit elsewhere on the colour wheel and she is clearly trying to say something different about what these colours represent. The actual colour choices she makes here are odd. In some later pieces she attributes them to the king scale of the Kabballah, which would be 'pure soft blue' for Chokmah and 'Crimson' for Binah, yet Colquhoun's sexual imagery does not use these exact hues. In her poem 'Union Pacific' Colquhoun specifically refers to the colours 'scarlet' and 'cerulean' as representative of the two polarities which will mingle and ultimately be transcended for the perfected union. This poem is the clearest example of the fullness of her visual conception of the androgyne, replete with alchemical symbolism, as this selection from the poem indicates:

Why then exists division
Philosophers have asked
Division is life's substance
And may not here be masked
But though divided each can be
A chrysalis encasqued

That opens to a dragonfly
Sunning a scarlet hue
To call another of its kind
But of cerulean blue.
Or if it be cerulean
Follow a scarlet hue

And head-to-tail ecstatic float
Continuously one
Lyrical creatures to enjoy
So long a union
That they become a new being
Scarlet-cerulean.

These the self-same colours
The alchemists have shown
Lying in the alembic
Thalamus and throne
And have called them the opal
The stone that's not a stone[70]

There is also a sketch labelled 'Union Pacific', featuring a couple locked in an intimate embrace, which may have been meant to accompany this poem.

When we consider the entirety of Colquhoun's work these appear to be the colours that she consistently selected to represent polarity and union, and she repeats them in a variety of contexts. Intriguingly, scarlet and cerulean are specifically named in Exodus 28:16 as two of the colours which will be used in constructing the priestly garment, the *ephod*. Was Colquhoun representing the component colours of the purple Robe of Light?

Colquhoun's final goal may well be characterised by the notion of the *Lumen Vestimenti*, the Robe of Light, characterised by Welsh alchemist Thomas Vaughan as 'the very first receptacle of the influences and derivations of the supernatural world'. It is the body of light, the divine spark that elevates the material and degraded, and returns it to union with the Godhead, the pure and undifferentiated light. This was Colquhoun's Philosopher's Stone. While the Philosopher's Stone has been equated with many substances and concepts through the ages, including the idea that it confers immortality, Colquhoun took the Philosopher's Stone to refer to a particular enlightened state, one where humanity is connected with its true divine nature, which, for Colquhoun, required a transcendence of gender, and this was to be achieved through the alchemical state of conjunction.

A number of alchemical theorists have conflated the Robe of Glory, the *Lumen Vestimenti* and the Philosopher's Stone; however, many of the writers who would have informed Colquhoun wrote of the Philosopher's Stone as Jesus. Most likely, Colquhoun's own inspiration was taken from her cousin Edward Garstin's alchemical text *The Secret Fire*, which was primarily an exposition on the nature and symbolism of fire as the link from the human to the divine. Garstin synthesised a number of approaches, including Classical, Kabbalistic and alchemical and Tantric, all of which are apparent in Colquhoun's own project.

Garstin quotes from Mead's translation of *The Hymn of the Robe of Glory*, also known as *Hymn of the Pearl*, from the apocryphal Acts of Thomas. This piece echoes Colquhoun's own sentiments that we forget our true, divine character, but in the act of donning the purple robe, it is remembered. Garstin examines the mystical nature of the colour purple as the mixture of red and blue, which he attributes to the union of the mixing of elemental water and fire. Despite all of Garstin's warnings and hesitations concerning entering into an actual sexual magic practice, it is very clear from his writings that this is precisely what he is suggesting, and this quite clearly aligned with Colquhoun's magical vision.[71] Garstin's *Secret Fire* also draws heavily on Paul Foster Case's 1931 *Hermetic Alchemy: Science and Practice*. Case's alchemy is physical and practical, characterised as a system of purifying the physical instrument to allow for energy exchange and permutation. Although it is an awkward synthesis for the modern reader, Case maps alchemy onto yoga and maintains that command of the body and mind will also allow for command of material and immaterial reality.

Some of Colquhoun's visual explorations on this theme were still sexual but less recognisably explicit and may have been intended as series that would illustrate accompanying texts. It is possible, based on the progression of these figures, that the more explicit works in this collection preceded the *Alchemical Figures* and the *Diagrams of Love* series and were used to explore the physicality of energy movements between two people which she would later abstract. In one case, we see a sequence of drawings where a man is lying directly on top of a woman and we see him penetrating her and we see the streams of energy in their connection. In a subsequent drawing, Colquhoun removes the limbs and other details, but we can still see the penetration, the spinal column, and the energy flow. The result becomes *Diagrams of Love: Androgyne II*. The *Diagrams of Love* and *Alchemical Figures* series both use Kabbalistic scarlet/cerulean colour themes and feature interesting merging and unions of figures into a third. Titles of pieces in this series include *The Opal I and II* and *The Homunculus I and II*. The *Diagrams of Love* series, which spans from 1940–42, is not nearly as figurative or clearly representational and in many ways presents interpretative challenges. The subtitles of this series include *Christian Marriage I and II*, *Monogamy I and II*, *The Tree of Veins*, *Heart of Corn*, *The King and Centre*, *The Tree of Veins I and II*, *The Comet*, *The Concealed Mouth*, *Fruit, Fire and Water*, and *The Androgyne*. Both the *Diagrams of Love* and *Alchemical Figures* series feature very abstracted images with recurring connected eyes, lips and blue and red geometric features, suggesting that she may have been abstracting the energy 'gates' which were the points of contact. The *Homunculus* pieces, which are weird, almost bloated-looking sketches meant to portray a proto-human, also include compass directions of North, South, East and West. In several cases, it seems as though these pieces were conceptually significant, yet were never developed into mature works. It is very possible that these were mainly intended as diagrammatic. *Heart of Corn* does exist in several versions and in a more finished stage and was intended to be sold. In this series *Christian Marriage* almost certainly refers to the *Hieros Gamos* featured in the 17th century Rosicrucian text *The Chymical Wedding of Christian Rosenkreutz*.

Also evident in these paintings, supported by the poems, is the notion of points of contact within the body that will be most conducive to energy flow between the pair of lovers, and again, Colquhoun is informed by a variety of texts and sources that would have been floating around esoteric circles at the time. Mathers' *Kabballah Unveiled* provides the image source for the thirteen streams of magnificent oil which flow down from the beard of Macroprosopus and illuminate all things which are inferior. Colquhoun's 1940 painting, the *13 Streams of Magnificent Oil*, demonstrates the openings of the body through which the divine might enter, and Colquhoun utilises the theme of openings in the body as points of energy exchange and flow in a variety of paintings and even some of her poetry. She expands on this in an essay, 'Openings of the Body', published in 1970, but which reflects much earlier engagement with the topic. Here she theorises that the Theosophical concept of openings or energy gates in the body may allow for the transfer of divine energy, yet does not equate them with chakras. As women have one more opening than men, this indicates that women are 'more highly evolved and more specialised'.[72] In a number of erotic watercolour sketches, these entry points are indicated by red dots where the bodies need to be in some way touching, such as at the nipples. Also evident in some of these works are the streams of energy, probably indicating Kundalini and other flows of energy, throughout the body that would be occurring during sexual union. Colquhoun completed a number of pieces from the late 1930s that suggest interest and experimentation with energy flows and energy auras in and around the body, and much of her erotic work seems to be concentrated on the ways in which sexual union could create and enhance one's own body of light.

What did this project or set of projects suggest in any practical sense? Although Colquhoun used sexual imagery in her work for much of her life, this sequence was the only one which suggested sexuality as part of a sustained magical operation. What is notably different in this work from other sex magic theories and practices, certainly those in Crowley-inspired magical traditions, is that the woman is presented as having equal energy to the man and is not the passive recipient of his energy. In fact, success in Colquhoun's operations appears to be predicated upon the efficacy of the partners to manifest the perfection of the particular polarised currents and then to unify them in order to transcend any particular polarity. This project was solely in service of the creation of a better, more divine being. In Colquhoun's view, alchemical conjunction is not merely about the *Hieros Gamos*, the union of opposites through the sacred marriage, but it is about the power of transcending the limitations of gender. Unlike later notions of the 'magical child' promoted by Crowley, the union of opposites produces a new being out of the conjunction, not a distinctive third. The process is about transformation, not generation.

Although Colquhoun was concerned with self-perfection and the notion of spiritual attainment and enlightenment on the personal level, it is also clear that for her, overcoming the restrictions of gender and the repression of the female was key to the enlightenment of society as a whole. To be clear, Colquhoun did not reject all stereotypical notions of gender essentialism; she certainly embraced them in her work, and particularly where female symbolism is concerned, she portrayed them as empowering. However, she certainly rejected notions of female submission or the suggestion that women were in any way inferior.

Another question concerning this work is the degree to which another physical partner was even required. Given the explicit nature of many of these images, it is clear that Colquhoun was certainly interested in enacting these sexual manoeuvres on a physical plane, or at least in exploring their potential. What is less clear, however, is whether or not she felt the sexual act between a man and woman was physically necessary in order to achieve this enlightenment, or whether the individual, through training and the necessary spiritual work, could find this on her own. It is possible that the other partner could be an astral entity, or even represent the Holy Guardian Angel. It is difficult to know what Colquhoun believed were the ideal circumstances under which one would attain to this level. It seems that she believed that one could do this work with a partner, but she also probably believed that engaging with your *anima* or *animus* would serve just as well, and may even be more ideal.

It is also evident that Colquhoun experimented with the idea that the energy polarities did not have to be expressed by opposite genders. Some of these pieces are homoerotic, which suggests that the intended outcome can be achieved without the opposite currents being embedded into physical sexes. Only the energetic currents need to be opposed, not the bodies themselves. This would have been quite a radical suggestion in the early 1940s, certainly as one considering aspects of erotic or sexual magic regarding women. Crowley had done extensive homoerotic magical experiments with other men, but the degree to which lesbian sexuality would have been seen as magically effective or produce spiritual enlightenment is not well addressed. It is unclear what, if anything, Colquhoun knew of Crowley's sexual work when she was producing this set of imagery.

Colquhoun had at least a passing interest in the spiritual dynamics of lesbian sexuality and had at least experienced sexual and romantic attractions to women, so it makes sense that she would theorise about lesbian energetics. She also had encountered a variety of masculine of centre women over the course of her life in the various artistic circles in which she ran, and they may have embodied the androgyne for her in some way. Later in life, however, Colquhoun rejected the lesbian union as a way to secure ultimate attainment. It may be that this was a result of the breakdown of her marriage, which seems to have occurred because of del Renzio's homosexual infidelity. In an undated essay written after the breakup of her marriage, probably in the mid-1950s, Colquhoun relates the difficulties that intelligent, spiritually advanced women have in finding romantic and sexual partners. She notes that in general there will be fewer suitable male partners for such women. She notes, with sympathy, that women of attainment may reasonably find themselves interested in a lesbian relationship, but that ultimately it will stifle the woman's potential for achievement: 'It is understandable if a woman so placed is tempted to back into some kind of lesbian relationship, but if she does so it will be to an adolescent phase and will tend to vitiate what she has achieved.'[73]

By 1943 it appears that Colquhoun's fixation on sexual images had cooled somewhat, but we see the repeated uses of this colour symbolism in her corpus over decades. Even when she was no longer exploring an explicit visual dimension, she was still signalling the centrality of the union of opposites, and the resulting divinity, to her esoteric philosophy. Although she retained a strong sexual element in her work throughout her life, and was committed to subverting and challenging traditional gender roles for women, the references to the hermaphrodite becomes less apparent in her paintings. Colquhoun had other relationships and love interests after her marriage, but somehow the *Hieros Gamos* seems diminished for her. Perhaps this was a result of her marriage to del Renzio, but it is evident that she was still refining her ideas about the impact of alchemical *conjunctio* at a larger scale than the individual. At this stage Colquhoun and del Renzio were in the middle of their André Breton orthodoxy period, and she was striving to promote what she believed to be an authentic Surrealism in Britain that reflected the roots of the movement. To that end, in 1943 she published 'The Water-Stone of the Wise', in the Surrealist journal *New Road*, which Shillitoe identifies as perhaps her most important theoretical piece, hinging on alchemical metaphor and the creation of the hermaphrodite.[74]

Shillitoe notes that 'Water Stone of the Wise' was composed in part as a response to Breton's 1942 'Prolegomena to A Third Surrealist Manifesto (Or Not)', but although Colquhoun is Breton's champion during this period, 'Water Stone' pokes at the Prolegomena, and offers a 'new myth' that Breton would have very likely not had any interest in adopting. In 'Prolegomena', a war-weary and seemingly jaded Breton is commenting on what he sees as conformity in Surrealism twenty years into the movement, and artistic trajectories that have moved disappointingly far from his original radical inspiration. Breton complains that this conformity and lack of originality threatens the core ethos of resistance that he believes to be at the core of the movement, and through which freedom can be attained. But how to shift direction? He asks: 'What should one think of the postulate that "there is no society without a social myth"? In what measure can we choose or adopt, and impose, a myth fostering the society that we judge to be desirable?'[75]

In 'Water Stone of the Wise' Colquhoun presents her response. Colquhoun was always a champion of myth, seeing it as a force that both guided and reflected the spiritual position of humanity, and she suggests here that a new guiding myth needed to be both radical and explosive. The title of her essay comes from the alchemical treatise *The Sophic Hydrolith*, written in 1619 by printmaker Johann Ambrosius Siebmacher, which is one of many texts in *The Hermetic*

Museum, compiled by A.E. Waite. *The Sophic Hydrolith* reveals that the Philosopher's Stone is the earthly substance of Christ, or the perfect Light of God, that which was known to the patriarchs and to a few adepts throughout history who were pure enough to receive the knowledge. The Stone itself embodies the perfected Adam from before the Fall, when humanity was united with Christ, and thus completely united with the divine, symbolising the fully realised Divine Human. It was this state that Colquhoun sought. She wanted humanity to aspire to and reach its divine potential, but to do this a new mythic foundation needed to emerge. As Breton suggested the need, Colquhoun prepared her response, which as ever was complex and uncompromising.

While *The Sophic Hydrolith* is thickly Christian in its sentiment, Colquhoun continues her fixation on the necessity for overcoming the bonds of gender, yet since this is in the realm of the mythic she does not exactly suggest a practical programme for doing so:

> No more tyrants and victims, no more the fevered alternations of that demon star which sponsored the births of de Sade and von Sacher-Masoch – but the hermaphrodite whole, opposites bound together in mitigating embrace by a silkworm's thread. The new myth, the myth of the Siamese Twins, will make of him a forgotten bogey.
>
> In one of the planets' airy houses live the Twins, a boy and a girl, perpetually joined by an ectoplasmic substance which is warmed by the solar and lunar currents of their bodies. They cannot part, nor do anything apart. They eat and breathe each other day and night.
>
> They are united face to face, having passed forward to the condition of the androgynous egg. Their faculty is dream, their body-of-fate the stream of images – sensual transpositions – induced by the incandescence of their own body and mind. They have no privacy from each other, and desire none, since

> theirs is a unity conscious of its own elements. They weigh down equally each scale of the Balance, and as the two Fishes, are held together in watery dance by a single cord.[76]

Although this sounds somewhat like its own condition of eternal bondage, for Colquhoun, this was a myth of liberation, two souls eternally conjoined as a 'hermaphrodite whole', and in their perfection having the ability to live in the superconscious world of dreams, the realm of myth. The imagery suggests the visions of alchemical conjunction, where the King and Queen lie together in a vessel, but it also mirrors Mathers' *Kabballah Unveiled*, where the King and Queen are also joined together, quietly and blissfully throughout eternity, 'together they are at rest; the one ceaseth not from the other, and the one is never taken away from the other'.[77]

Colquhoun envisioned this cocoon as the place of gestation for a liberated and evolved society, since this is the vision of the perfected state which existed in the garden of Eden prior to the separation of man and woman. *The Kabballah Unveiled* specifically dictates that liberty of sinners and the fallen is to be found through the Mother, and this was the liberty that Colquhoun wanted available to us all. This essay may also echo the redemptive qualities and social application of alchemy found in Yeats's *A Vision*, which probably found its roots in the same sources. As a small yet mighty manifesto, 'Water Stone of the Wise' serves as the outward-facing and more explicitly political expression of this part of Colquhoun's alchemical journey. After this point her focus turns more inward, and her interest in the androgyne shifts.

Later, Colquhoun's fixation on the androgyne transmutes into an interest in parthenogenesis, and the degree to which women can transmit currents of esoteric mystery without the aid of men. By 1959, when she is writing her dream-based novel *I Saw Water*, she writes of the possibilities of female parthenogenesis supporting the enlightened state: 'wherein the lunar soul that perceives and feels is fertilised by (a long eclipse over) rays from its own hidden brightness (brilliance) to bring forth at last the radiant child.'[78] A small undated watercolour titled *The Virgin on the Knees of Saint Anne* features two women in a Tantric pose, and references the idea that St. Anne was a pure vessel transmitting that purity to her daughter, Mary, so she could carry Jesus. In the sketch Mary is cloaked in blue and scarlet, Colquhoun's colours of the transcended and perfected being.

In Pursuit of the Golden Thread

Colquhoun did not abandon her magical studies while she was married to del Renzio, but her focus was different. At the end of war, and the end of her marriage, she needed time to regroup and embrace new directions and new locations. At the end of the 1940s, Colquhoun started to split her time between Cornwall and London, embracing the quiet community of Lamorna, countered with a bustling life in London. From the beginning of the 1950s, Colquhoun's visual work seems to take on more of a private and contemplative nature and her painting output decreased for nearly a decade, while the public focus of her art switched more to poetry and writing. She tried her hand at journalism and essay writing during this period, and also experimented with publishing short stories. Some of her earliest work in occult journalism was completed for a local London paper called *The London Broadsheet*, edited by her Fortean friend Antony Borrow, whom she knew as editor of *The Glass*. Borrow was interested in the occult goings-on in Britain and got Colquhoun to write profiles of Gerald Gardner (1954) and Austin Osman Spare (1955), as well as more theoretical material on Thelema and divination. She contributed ten pieces to *The London Broadsheet* in 1954 and 1955, ranging from poems and short stories of a Surrealist bent to proto-Fortean topics such as research into the paranormal and UFOs. Although much of the focus of her writing in the 1950s was on longer works, she also started writing for *Prediction* magazine, completing a four-part series on the Kabballah in 1958. As with many of Colquhoun's pieces, her 'introductory' Kabbalistic essays were sure to plunge the novice reader into deep water.

Colquhoun's social networks were also converging in such a way that various magical orders were becoming more accessible to her, after her initial disappointment with the Golden Dawn. The players on the 1940s and 1950s occult stage overlapped considerably; they knew each other, were frequently members of each other's orders, and were sometimes at each other's throats. It was a time of innovation, cross-pollination, collaboration and rivalry. Aleister Crowley, Cecil Williamson, Dion Fortune, Gerald Yorke, Doreen Valiente, Gerald Gardner, Ross Nichols, Kenneth and Steffi Grant, Austin Osman Spare, and W.B. Crow were all part of the British occult scene and very likely all of them were known to Colquhoun, even if they were not in her immediate sphere

Colquhoun was actively responding to the call of the Golden Dawn Secret Chiefs that she believed had touched her etherically after her first contact with the Order in the 1930s, and she was compelled to follow their call through seeking legitimate initiations that would connect her to 'the current'. World War Two had caused the fragmented Golden Dawn lodges to disband, and so she had to wait since there was no Golden Dawn lodge readily available.

But because she also believed that there were many avenues to the Secret Wisdom, authenticity and proficiency were her primary criteria in evaluating a magical group. She started to approach magical orders that had some sort of connection with the original Golden Dawn lodges. In 1952 she started her studies with the Society of the Inner Light, the esoteric organisation that was founded by Dion Fortune. Fortune had been a member of the Alpha and Omega Golden Dawn lodge where Garstin was Cancellarius. Colquhoun and Fortune might have had some contact, but no correspondence between them has yet come to light, although in *The Sword of Wisdom* Colquhoun does note having attended a 1934 lecture given by Fortune in Glastonbury, which potentially inspired her approach to sacred sites. Nevertheless, Fortune was a formidable occult mind and Kabbalist, and in Colquhoun's mind the Society had legitimate links to the Golden Dawn, so it was no surprise that through them Colquhoun would have heard the call of the Secret Chiefs. Further, given the centrality of Glastonbury to Fortune's work, the added layer of native British mysticism focused on myth and landscape would have appealed to Colquhoun's interests in pursuing localised aspects of the 'ancient mysteries'. Like Fortune, Colquhoun believed that much of the ancient Celtic wisdom tradition was derived from the sunken continent of Atlantis, and she would probably have liked the idea that she was tapping into a magical tradition that combined many of the elements she was already attracted to. She probably also appreciated that the organisation had a high barrier for initiates who would then be allowed to access the real Inner Plane beings.

Despite Colquhoun's commitment to their curriculum, full membership in the Society of the Inner Light was not to be. In a letter to Colquhoun dated April 16, 1956, she was told that her work was 'adequate on the mental level' but that she was not deemed to be suited for initiation.[79] This seems quite remarkable in that she had already been working in their correspondence course for four years. Colquhoun noted in a draft of *Sword of Wisdom* that she believed that she was rejected because she kept asking questions and pointing out contradictory teachings in their material. In her scathing reply to their letter she called them 'disingenuous'. She believed that she was a gifted student, and that it was the fault of their curriculum that it could not withstand her scrutiny. It may well be that Colquhoun was being assessed on other qualities aside from her coursework. Today's Society of the Inner Light admits that the road to initiation is not easy, and they expect members to demonstrate a certain commitment to citizenship, including solvency, family life and procreation, and service to 'the race'.[80] Whether those were being assessed at the time, and how they were evaluated, are not at all clear, but it is likely that some aspect of Colquhoun's character fell under indictment.

Further seeking the true current of initiation, in 1952 Colquhoun also joined the O.T.O. She had a long-term, love-hate relationship with the writings and theories of Aleister Crowley, being both inspired by him and highly resistant to many of his magical conclusions. In several autobiographical accounts, including the one reproduced in *Sword of Wisdom*, Colquhoun recounts her first encounter with the Crowley mythos, reading Betty May's newspaper accounts of Crowley's Abbey of Thelema while she was on the loo as a girl in around 1923. This seems to provide a fitting metaphor for the ambivalence she had towards Crowley's work and legend throughout her life. Crowley's legacy remains a force to be reckoned with, and he cannot be ignored. His work and life kept intersecting with Colquhoun's, even down to knowing the family of the mother of his son in Cornwall. But with her love of Yeats, and his own hatred of Crowley, one can predict which side she would come down on given the animosity between the two magicians.

In *The Living Stones* Colquhoun claimed to have been in the same room with Crowley only once, while he was giving a lecture at the Atlantis bookshop in London, but she also knew many of his acquaintances and was well read in his works. Fast moving adept and rebel in the Golden Dawn, Crowley quickly took over the leadership of the German Ordo Templi Orientis and fashioned it into a religious order focused on ideas of religious and personal liberty and breaking social and cultural barriers based on his Rabelais-inspired notion of Thelema – Do What Thou Wilt. His channelled 1904 *Book of the Law*, known within Thelemic circles as *Liber Al*, was intended to be the holy book of the New Aeon. Perhaps unsurprisingly, Colquhoun believed that the source of *Liber Al* was actually his wife at the time, Rose, whom she believed acted as the channel for the text, so that it was her work, not his.[81]

Colquhoun seems to have had little time for Crowley's deities or his *Liber Al*, but she certainly made use of *Liber 777* and drew on the correspondences within, explicitly naming it as a source for a number of visual experiments in the 1950s. However, she does not seem to have been a fan of the Libertarian sensibilities suggested by 'Do What Thou Wilt'. She once made a random and well observed note about its potential pitfalls regarding the social order:

> One typical result would be drastic change in the environment. Since all organisation is precluded from Crowley's programme – each man is to work as he will – the community would seize up rapidly and catastrophically. While a Yin motivation is just compatible with Crowley's ideas, a Yang motivation is totally at variance with them, and its only possible outcome would be (and that briefly) an exaggeration or caricature of the system that at present prevails over most of the world resulting from centuries of Yang directed brain wash.[82]

Colquhoun's relationship with Crowley's magical order, the Ordo Templi Orientis and Kenneth Grant's Nu Isis Lodge which followed, is not entirely clear. In a draft of *The Sword of Wisdom*, she writes of a young couple with whom she was acquainted that was trying to revitalise Crowley's work but they courted social discord with their efforts, and she did not wish to delve into the matter more closely as she was not involved long. That couple was Kenneth and Steffi Grant, who built upon Crowley's work to form the Nu Isis Lodge and what would ultimately become known as the Typhonian O.T.O. Although there are a number of stories about the break of Kenneth Grant's O.T.O. from the order that Crowley headed, he apparently officially splintered off in 1954 and started the Nu Isis Lodge in 1955. At that point, the Grants went in a different direction from Crowley, developing an emphasis on extra-terrestrial contacts and working with demonic or darker entities.

What is known from Colquhoun's own archives is that she became involved with the O.T.O. under Kenneth Grant in 1952, prior to his own split with the order, and this split seemed to cause her some difficulties in her desire to continue with them. Some grade work and examinations from 1952 and 1953 remain in her papers at the Tate, but it is unclear how far she progressed, even though she did have notes for the IX degree. In one draft version of *The Sword of Wisdom* she writes that while she learned a great deal of theoretical knowledge from her time with the Grants, and followed their reading list, she did no ritual with them. Although she would have been in their social network, there were certainly some gaps. For instance, she reportedly only met Austin Osman Spare once.

Perhaps the most enduring legacy from her time with the O.T.O. and also the Society of the Inner Light, was her magical motto, *Soror Splendidor Vitro*, which translates to 'More Sparkling than Crystal' and which she selected in 1952. Shillitoe notes that the motto refers to Horace Ode 3.13 'To the Spring of Bandusia', in which Horace writes to the deity of a spring to which a sacrifice will be made. This piece would have resonated with many of Colquhoun's preoccupations, including animism, her interest in fountains, springs and wells, the hidden energies living underneath the earth, light and colour. Also, a vessel which is brighter than crystal can be penetrated by the divine light while also reflecting it. Ten years later, in 1962 during another flurry of magical order joining, she begins using a monogram of the motto as the signature on her paintings, suggesting that she believed she was integrating her artistic self and her magical self even more fully.

As both Colquhoun and Steffi Grant were esoterically minded artists they would have had a lot in common, and they clearly were engaged in similar visual mapping projects through the 1950s. From the illustrations to *The Carfax Monographs*, a collection of essays written by the Grants from 1959 and 1963, we can see that both Steffi Grant and Colquhoun had an interest in the visual culture of the Golden Dawn. In fact, we see Colquhoun producing similar images of the various crosses that Golden Dawn initiates used during their grade work, but there is no indication that these explorations formed a part of their work together, especially since Steffi Grant was less interested in the Golden Dawn as a magical system. Very likely, however, the magical exchange between Colquhoun and the Grants would have gone both ways, because even though Colquhoun sought O.T.O. initiation with them, she was certainly well advanced by that time. Colquhoun and the Grants would have had a number of shared interests, including the importance of the Divine Feminine and Tantra, but it seems likely that the Grants wanted to take their magical order in a different direction.

Correspondence in 1953 between Colquhoun and Karl Germer, the head of the O.T.O. following Crowley’s death in 1947, suggests that Colquhoun was very much aware of Grant’s shift in direction even at an early stage, and was seeking clarification about his position within the order.[83] Colquhoun was seeking the genuine current, and perhaps she believed that it was being compromised. The Grants claimed Colquhoun as a member of Nu Isis Lodge, but the degree to which she was still magically involved with them by the mid-1950s is unclear. Nevertheless, Colquhoun and the Grants stayed friends and exchanged holiday cards for many years.

There were many aspects of Thelema that were probably not compatible with Colquhoun’s own quest, but she was clearly compelled by Crowley and could not shake his influence. In 1955 she wrote a short piece called ‘The Dying Kick of The Dying God’ for *The London Broadsheet*, where she claimed to be assessing his contributions to esoteric theory.[84] She addressed the writing of *Liber Al* and what he attempted to do with it, but although she judges that his work is worthy of study, her essay is hardly a ringing endorsement.

It was also in the mid to late 1950s that she wrote a chapter for *The Living Stones* called ‘Crowley in Cornwall’, noting that although most stories about Crowley in Cornwall were untrue, they still had an impact on perceptions of Cornwall as a place of occult activity, and that even twenty years after his seemingly benign holiday visit, tales of his ‘black magical’ activity still persisted. She established that Crowley had not performed ritual in Cornwall, based on his diaries that Gerald Yorke had provided for her to examine.[85] Most of the chapter, however, was an opportunity for Colquhoun to question common assumptions and moral assertions about the occult and ritual magic. She used the chapter to comment on what she believed were generally hypocritical positions about issues such as blood sacrifice and drug usage, stating that most people don’t have enough understanding of ritual magic to condemn it. This ends up being yet another interesting personal expression in a far from standard ‘travelogue’.

But Crowley did have a relationship with Cornwall through the conception and birth of his son, and Colquhoun took the opportunity to write about it in the late 1970s when she wrote an odd mish-mash biography called *Crowley Lasting Out*. To be honest, it is a mess as manuscripts go. She tried on several occasions to get it published, yet despite some juicy tales it was deemed unpublishable. It's possible that this was an opportunistic play on her part to release the interesting local history that she knew, but it is also likely that it was part of her wider interest in, and struggle with, Crowley as a personality and occult figure. Two sections from the original manuscript made their way into private hands and were eventually published in 2012 in *Starfire: A Journal of the New Aeon* as 'Two Fragments on Ataturk'. These contain a fascinating account of the magical conception and early life of Crowley's son, Randall Gair, aka Aleister Ataturk. Ataturk's mother, Deidre Patricia Maureen Doherty, was an acquaintance of Colquhoun's and lived down the road from her in the Cornish village of Newlyn at Wheal Betsy, the house built by one of the founders of the Newlyn School, Thomas Gotch. In fact, Gotch was Doherty's grandfather and it is likely that his estate may in some way have supported some of her eccentricities. Deidre was born into wealth and was even presented to the Queen as a debutante at age 18, but Colqhuoun's account of her suggests she did not exactly conform to conventional expectations.

Colquhoun gives a compelling account of Doherty's pursuit of Crowley and the conception of their son, while also providing some interesting insights into the occult history of Cornwall in the early part of the 20th century. Although this manuscript never became public, it may be one of the more detailed accounts we have of this relationship, provided to Colquhoun directly from Doherty. Deidre, also known as Pat, had been sexually involved at a very young age with a shady character known as Major Robin Thynne, born Robert Tinn, who had been in the Royal Air Force at the end of WWI. He was an associate of Crowley's who ran a small Kabballah study group in Cornwall, and an investor in the original Mandrake Press. Pat was part of Robin's esoteric study group and ended up moving in with him, despite their age difference and his declining marriage. Probably because of his reputation and her interest in magic, the young woman took an interest in Crowley – so much so that she travelled to London to try to meet him during what was known as the 'Laughing Torso' libel trial in 1934, when Crowley was defending his character against accusations of 'black magic'. Before long Pat and Crowley were in a sexual relationship, and she would visit him in London. She was determined to conceive a magical child, and believed Crowley to be the only real choice to father it. The pair did ritual sex magic to produce a 'Sun Child' in a makeshift solar temple, and when she became pregnant, Robin Thynne accepted paternity. Much of this essay is an interesting account of Pat's relationship with Crowley and his kindness, although not material support, toward their child. Colquhoun also gives some indication that even if the occult scene in Cornwall was not particularly coherent in the 1920s and 1930s, there was still a number of practitioners. She suggested novelist Mary Butts and writer William Arnold-Forster as potential Cornish based occultists of a Hermetic bent, and said that even if she was incorrect about the latter, she could think of 'a dozen or half dozen' people in West Cornwall who might have been magically inclined.

In another chapter, Colquhoun recalls visiting a much older Aleister Ataturk at his flat called 'Tally Ho', which was situated in the old workhouse in the village of Madron, and from which he was about to be evicted.[86] During this period in the mid-1970s, he was referring to himself as Charles Edward D'Arquires, and had started his own political organisation The Supreme Council of Great Britain, for which he received some local publicity in *The Cornishman*, the local newspaper of West Cornwall. Colquhoun's account shows Crowley's son to have been a chip off the old block, madly eccentric and with clear delusions of grandeur. Colquhoun claimed Ataturk was functionally illiterate, although talented in other ways. She paints a picture of his mother's home at Wheal Betsy in a constant state of chaos and drunkenness, with many children and dogs running around. It is not a flattering portrayal. Colquhoun reports that Pat was selling all of the old family paintings and furniture just to keep their heads above water. It is a sad story, but one of the most compelling and detailed pictures we have of Crowley's son, who died in a car accident in 2002.

In these two chapters it is clear that while Colquhoun respected aspects of Crowley's work and legacy, she didn't think much of him as a person. She also didn't seem particularly impressed by the antics of Pat Doherty and Crowley's son. She gives a vivid picture of chaotic and messy lives, and the squandering of resources and goodwill.

A Traditional turn

After parting company with the Society of the Inner Light and the O.T.O., from the late 1950s onward Colquhoun's magical interests took a decidedly Traditionalist and more conservative turn as she became involved with Druidry, Freemasonry and Martinism. It is evident that the circle of friends with whom she had surrounded herself through Druidry had inspired an exploration of mystical orders which had more of a focus on mystical Christianity. Although it would be simple to suggest that she was brought into these orders primarily through her social circles, it is evident that they were satisfying her interest in orders with a strong sense of lineage and internal mythology about connection to an ancient wisdom tradition. It is also during the early 1960s that she writes *I Saw Water*, exploring Catholicism, Brittany, Druids and dreams.

During the early 1960s, coinciding with her visits to the Breton *Goursez*, Colquhoun started to visit France more, and seems to have begun a relationship with the French occult writer Serge Hutin. Hutin was a prolific popular French writer on the occult, specialising in 'secret societies' and later in life more 'Fortean' topics such as extraterrestrials. His work is little known among English readers even though he wrote over 40 books. In 1959 he collaborated with Belgian artist Aubin Pasque on the international movement known as Fantasmagie, but more formally as Centre International de l'Actualité Fantastique et Magique (CIAFMA). The aim was to promote a movement of fantastic and esoterically motivated art, and Colquhoun became involved for over a decade. This may represent the first shift into categorising her work as esoteric or fantastic art. She exhibited with the group four times from 1962 to 1969. They also produced a publication, *Fantasmagie*, to which Colquhoun contributed three pieces. It may well be that it is through CIAFMA that Colquhoun and Hutin first met.

Over the next several years Hutin's letters to her were both intimate and restrained. He called her pet names, and sent her packages of ribbons and adorable postcards with kittens on them. It is hard to know how far their relationship was emotionally mutual. Colquhoun had a habit of getting frosty when gentlemen got too intimate, and although it is clear that she and Hutin were close for a number of years, it is likely that she kept him at a distance. Nevertheless, in 1966 he presented her with a pair of white Masonic gloves, which he told her symbolised that he admired her most of any woman in the world. It is likely that she did not return the sentiment in equal measure. However, he, too was a Freemason and a Martinist, and it is possible that she had at least found some sort of partner to share The Work with.

1961 was a good year for Colquhoun. She successfully published the manuscript she had worked on for decades, *The Goose of Hermogenes*, became a Co-Mason, and was ordained as a member of the Ordre Martiniste et Synarchique. Given her interests, it is easy to see why she would gravitate to Martinism. The primary objective of Martinism is to assist with reintegration of the human with the divine to the period before the Fall, which had long been Colquhoun's driving preoccupation. One of the key Martinist texts, Martinès de Pasqually's *Treatise on the Reintegration of Beings* from 1775, presented the legend of humanity before the Fall as being contained in an androgynous being. Although Martinism is heavily reliant on the idea of Christ being the vehicle for divine reintegration, it also has a Perennialist streak with a belief in the unified ancient wisdom tradition. It is lineage-based, initiatory, concerned with secret ruling elites, and also heavily centred on the Kabballah. Martinism dovetailed with, and was even a logical extension of, Colquhoun's other magical preoccupations. She would have encountered Martinists through her wider occult networks, and as was the case with her other heterodox Christian affiliations, she may have come to this particular order through her friend Ross Nichols, who was a member. She seems to have become involved with it around the same time that she became a Co-Mason, and given the historical relationship between the two traditions that makes perfect sense, although unlike other orders the Ordre Martiniste et Synarchique did not require Masonic initiation.

This particular branch of Martinism only became active in Britain in 1958, so Colquhoun was a fairly early British member. It was founded by Victor Blanchard, one-time secretary to 'Papus' (born Gérard Encausse), the founder of modern Martinism, as a way to circumvent previous stipulations that some Martinist orders maintained that members must also be Freemasons. That requirement would have been a barrier to the participation of women, whom Blanchard allowed in his order. It adopted the principles of synarchy at its outset, complete with right-wing resonances of shadowy elites, and had a particularly monarchic orientation. Martinism was perhaps the most Traditionalist of all the orders Colquhoun could have joined. In fact, René Guénon, now considered the father of modern Traditionalism and an influence on Colquhoun's thought and work, was also a Martinist for a time, earlier in his life. Although her archives suggest that she undertook a fairly extensive curriculum with this group, it is difficult to assess the degree to which Martinism ultimately resonated with her. Her relationship with Co-Masonry was more longstanding.

Colquhoun seems to have started her involvement with the Theosophically influenced Co-Masonry in 1961, and was a member of several lodges until 1978. She was also Holy Royal Arch and received notices from the Chapter of The Trois Lois lodge, located in London, until quite late in life, which suggests that she was more than just a casual member. Given the relationship between Freemasonry and almost every esoteric society Colquhoun was interested in, her membership makes perfect sense. Becoming a Co-Mason was a requirement for entry into the Order of the Pyramid and Sphinx, but it is likely that Colquhoun was a member earlier than that. In terms of the impact of Masonry on Colquhoun's body of work, it may be most visible in her experimentations with sacred geometry, although some of her work with the tarot also reflects Masonic symbolism.

The Goose of Hermogenes

Colquhoun's inner journeys at the start of the 1960s were matched by the publication of her alchemical Surrealist novel *The Goose of Hermogenes*. In many ways, *Goose* represents an earlier phase of her spiritual interests, but it was still consonant with the spiritual focus of her life at the time, and we can see her subsequent attempts at fiction expanding on some of the themes and images in this work. Colquhoun had been working with Peter Owen for some time, and he had already published *Crying of the Wind* and *The Living Stones*. Despite Owen's reputation for taking a chance on unconventional projects, *The Goose of Hermogenes* was a risky publication. He did a test run of some segments in a 1958 literary anthology which also included her strange memorial poem 'Elegy on the Hermetic Order of the Golden Dawn'. Even with its billing as a Surrealist gothic novel, which may have set some expectations for its audience, it is arcane, tricky and challenging. Nevertheless, this was an important creation for Colquhoun, and she was determined to have it published. This odd little work has become important in the historical rediscovery of Colquhoun, showing both her Surrealist and occultist capacity.

Colquhoun had been crafting *The Goose of Hermogenes* for several decades, pulling together dreams, magical allegory and the many themes which were central to her Surrealist fiction, including islands, women, sex and arcane rituals. The beautiful description of two moths described by the Anchorite in Chapter One was initially published in the Surrealist journal *The London Bulletin* 10 in 1939 as 'The Moths'. 'The Echoing Bruise' and 'The Volcano', from *The London Bulletin* 17 were other short pieces that ended up in *Goose*. The rest of the book, with its focus on alchemical conjunction, is consonant with the other work that was consuming her at the end of that decade. We see the roots of the project in Colquhoun's earliest alchemical writings in the 1920s, sharing themes with her play *The Bird of Hermes*, about unlocking a young woman's potential for integration and enlightenment. In fact, the title *Goose of Hermogenes* was taken from the same text as *Bird of Hermes, Metamorphosis of Metals* by Eirenaeus Philalethes (believed now to have been George Starkey):

> It is our door keeper, our balm, our honey, oil, urine, maydew, mother, egg, secret furnace, true fire, venomous dragon, theriac, ardent wine, Green Lion, Bird of Hermes, Goose of Hermogenes, two-edged sword in the hand of the cherub that guards the Tree of Life.[87]

The Bird of Hermes / Goose of Hermogenes, representing alchemical mercury, was a central magical theme in Colquhoun's early life. Vaughan characterises the Bird of Hermes and the Goose of Hermogenes as the womb-like environment in which the seed of the alchemical operation must be deposited, and conceives of alchemical mercury as essentially feminine in character:

> Hence it is clear that our Mercury is not common mercury; for all common mercury is a male that is corporal, specific, and dead, while our Mercury is spiritual, female, living, and life-giving. Attend closely to what I say about our Mercury, which is the salt of the wise men. The Alchemist who works without it is like a man who draws a bow without a string. Yet it is found nowhere in a pure state above ground, but has to be extracted by a cunning process out of the substance in which it exists.[88]

For Colquhoun this was the female principle that is necessary for the alchemical transaction to occur and for the ultimate creation of the Philosopher's Stone.

As with most of Colquhoun's fiction, the structure of the work, in this instance based on the *12 Keys of Basil Valentine*, provides the wider narrative that shapes the story. Each chapter is assigned to a stage of the alchemical process, although it is hard to see the correlation when reading the narrative. Our protagonist is a young woman narrating a bizarre, colourful world and strange characters with the remarkable detachment that is another stylistic hallmark of Colquhoun's writing. She frequently narrates unsettling images and events in a cold and emotionless way, but with exceptional visual detail. The story begins with our narrator traveling to stay at her Uncle's creepy, sprawling island home. We are not told why she is making this journey. Her Uncle is said to be involved in alchemical pursuits, and in order to achieve his goal he believes he needs the jewels of the narrator. We know little of them or their properties, except that they are precious and beautiful, and perhaps more than a little euphemistic.

> I somehow guessed that my Uncle wanted me in his house because of my jewels, which were beautiful as children's sweets and which he probably fancied to be possessed of alchemistic powers. But he had to obtain them from me by some no too-openly disreputable means, and this was not easy since I always wore them.[89]

As with most of Colquhoun's fiction, *Goose of Hermogenes* has no characters, only archetypes, seemingly motivated by large eternal forces. When our narrator stumbles upon a magical text featuring the tale of the alchemical lover twins, she is engrossed and sees herself in the story. The tale itself, 'Corolla's Pinions' in the chapter titled 'Conjunction', is the tale of two cousins who are destined to marry and become one, to become the hermaphroditic whole. They are drawn together, but not in a way that is at all passionate. Their union has quenched all desire, which is symbolic of the unified state of the hermaphrodite in paradise, existing prior to the need for desire, prior to separation. The narrator is overcome with pathos upon reading the tale and realises her situation is perilous, and that her Uncle may have dangerous intentions toward her. We wander with our protagonist through dreams, visions, fantastic landscapes and narrative vignettes. It is frequently less like a journey and more like snippets of visions that have been loosely woven together.

One stunning episode finds our protagonist in a cave of sea Goddess statues and entities. This may be one of Colquhoun's more explicit portrayals of the Divine Feminine. This shrine is a space of forgotten Goddesses, once powerful, but still alive. These Goddesses are saints, mermaids, mothers and warriors, as old as Atlantis, but now debased. It seems likely that in this description, Colquhoun is creating an emblematic tutelary deity she calls Vellanserga, Celtic and warrior-like, who still lives in the fertile landscape. Vellanserga was an estate near Lamorna upon which, at one time, sat a chapel near the sea.

> She overthrew the Norsemen. She melted the Romans down. It was she who led the people. She fought on the hill of stones, she wore the tunic of battle, she wielded the sword. She rode. A breastplate of stone and glass covers her egg-ribs; and it is said that small living creatures dwell within but she can scarcely comprehend their gnat-like life.[90]

In the tale, Vellanserga was once worshipped locally as a saint, but is really the Goddess embodied in the land itself. Vellanserga is still worshipped by the locals in their revels, and stone monuments to her power come to life during the full moon. Although Colquhoun laments the waning power of the Goddess, she recognises that she still lives in the land and is easily awakened.

> Still bemused by the gaze of the statue woman, I cannot but search for her everywhere; and I find her in the land's own long memory.[91]

Goose of Hermogenes is saturated with Colquhoun's signature style and themes that define both her written and visual work. The descriptions are lush, filled with colour and texture, and almost overwhelming for the reader to grasp, because in the mind's eye they become incongruous and dreamlike. The story is set on a chain of islands, which is also the setting for her other novel-length tales. In fact, the book is dedicated to the Azores. Although the descriptions of the landscape and flora call to mind the Mediterranean, Colquhoun's descriptions quickly give the landscape a fanciful turn. These islands are unreal, invoking other mythic submerged landscapes such as Ys, Lyonesse and Atlantis. Colquhoun's fictional islands are mirrored by several paintings she completed of submerged islands, including the *Linked Islands I* and *Linked Islands II* from 1947, and *La Cathédrale Engloutie* (1952) and its companion piece *Rocky Island* (1969). Architecture in this world also has a strange quality. Buildings are odd and sprawling, with many rooms in seemingly strange relationship to each other. We see the centrality of volcanos, alternative religious orders and ecstatic ritual. While *Goose* shares these themes with her other novels (and with her visual art), they are not exactly linked texts. These are images and ideas that Colquhoun worked with and worked through for decades, and we might envision them as being viewed from a number of angles rather than trying to enforce any linear narrative on them.

This world is also filled with strange taboo, frequently of an incestuous nature. In one passage she escapes her uncle's home, and finds herself in a house with her four sisters and her brother. As it turns out, her mother is a sort of spiritual madame who has been prostituting her children out to spirits. In the climax, our protagonist finds herself transported to a ritual circle, naked except for her jewels, where she is flogged into an ecstatic state by her uncle. In the final colourful chapter the narrator seems to escape her Uncle's house only to end up at the home of her father, who is now only a ghost. She ends up in a conservatory chamber, which sounds quite like an alembic, and ends the tale facing the mountains of the east just as the dawn is breaking.

In the 2018 edition, Richard Shillitoe adds a chapter found only in draft manuscripts, called '*Hexentanz*'. As Shillitoe notes, it was ultimately rejected as it does not fix thematically or stylistically with the rest of the piece, yet it does contain some remarkably raw and taboo sections, one of which becomes the very disturbing 'Happy Families', filled with incest, disfigurement and effluvia, which remains unpublished.

Goose of Hermogenes is not easy. It is overflowing with occult imagery and emblems of Colquhoun's personal mythology. Yet here we see a key to many of the themes which preoccupied her for decades, and which emerge in her artistic and symbolic language throughout her life. That the text took over two decades to complete and be finally realised with publication shows the degree to which Colquhoun believed these ideas were important.

Witchcraft

Colquhoun's relationship with witchcraft is still somewhat of a mystery. She was clearly interested in witchcraft of all kinds, whether it was as a part of existing folk tradition and belief, or the growth of religious witchcraft which emerged with Gerald Gardner in the 1950s. In the 1950s and 1960s, after the repeal of the Witchcraft Act in 1951, British culture was undergoing a rapid shift in its views on folk healing and beliefs such as 'ill wishing' or the evil eye, and there were, in fact different categories of folk practitioner still operating in Cornwall. There still are today. While during this period belief in 'ill wishing' people and livestock was on the decline, folk healers were still commonly used to treat skin conditions, aches and pains, and respiratory ailments. Many areas of Cornwall were, and still are, remote, with healthcare difficult to obtain, and people would turn to traditional and community-based solutions for minor ailments. Colquhoun herself was a believer in traditional healers, and her archives show correspondence with a variety of traditional healers in Cornwall and Ireland whom she contracted to do remote healing on her, for a variety of health concerns, until very late in life. One of her Irish healers even proclaimed on his letterhead that he was the '7th Son of a 7th Son'.

When Colquhoun first met Gerald Gardner is unclear. He would have been a member of her wider occult network as it emerged in the 1950s, as he was close to Ross Nichols, and also knew Kenneth Grant and Gerald Yorke, all of whom were in her network. Probably because of her social circle, Colquhoun was asked to write a piece on Gardner for Antony Borrow's *London Broadsheet*, and her archives suggest that she met with Gardner in 1954 to learn about Wicca, but it is likely they were already acquainted. In 1958 Doreen Valiente wrote to Colquhoun recalling that they had once met at Gardner's home, but at this point Valiente herself was expressing frustration with Gardner's focus on publicity. Ultimately, Colquhoun did not choose either Wicca or Traditional Witchcraft as a path, despite all of the groups and orders she would ultimately join. It is likely that the ecstatic element of the religion would not have suited her, as she generally liked her magical orders to contain a more intellectual and Hermetic component. While she writes in *Sword of Wisdom* that Gardner had clearly been influenced by Mathers' work, especially regarding the importance of women in magic, Wicca was evidently not part of the initiatic current that she was seeking. However, she did believe that witchcraft was real and that Gardner's Wicca did represent an authentic tradition.

It is also possible that her view of Gardner may have been affected by her relationship with Cecil Williamson, Gardner's great rival, who eventually established the Museum of Witchcraft in Cornwall. Cecil Williamson befriended Gardner in the late 1940s as a result of their mutual interest in witchcraft traditions, and their shared experience as civil servants who had spent time overseas learning about the religious traditions of 'exotic' peoples. Williamson claims to have first learned about witchcraft in Devon during the Second World War, and during his youth encountered various wise women who taught him about divination, healing and curses. In 1948, Williamson opened his Museum of Witchcraft in Castletown in the Isle of Man, and by 1951 had hired Gardner to work there as his 'Resident Witch'. But the two had very divergent ideas on what the nature of witchcraft was and how it should be promoted, and both wanted the public notoriety of being the expert on the subject, so unsurprisingly they soon fell out. Gardner took over the collection on the Isle of Man in 1952, and Williamson moved his personal collection to several different locations, finally settling on the present one in Boscastle, Cornwall, in 1960. He tried to launch a number of other attractions as well, including The Museum of Smuggling, The House of Cats, The House of Shells, The Hangman's House, and The Witch's House.

The animosity between Williamson and Gardner has continued to affect the trajectory of witchcraft in Britain, including Cornwall, and there is no doubt that Colquhoun's own researches would have been swayed by the debate. Williamson objected to Gardner's Wicca on a number of grounds, one being that he did not believe that it authentically represented the folk practices of actual British witches. He believed it was too moral, and too sanitary. In his view, real witches were mostly solitary, worked alone, and were not afraid to get their hands dirty with the nasty business of cursing. He also recognised that many of the folk traditions that have become associated with witchcraft, including healing and cursing, were carried out within a Christian framework. In Colquhoun's early correspondence with Williamson from 1954, around the time of her visit to him, he was clear that he felt Gardner was going down the wrong path. She corresponded with Williamson on matters related to witchcraft on and off for many years, and in one of his later letters to her he noted that she was the one to have suggested that he move the Museum of Witchcraft to Cornwall! Eventually, though, he seems to have become frustrated that she sometimes called on other sources for information, and it seems as though their friendship tapered off in the mid-1960s, when he evidently felt that he was not achieving the recognition as a witchcraft expert that he felt he deserved.

Yet Colquhoun was clearly compelled by ideas of a 'Witchcraft revival' with ritual and religious continuity to a Pagan British past. Even though she seems to have not been involved with Wicca, she was still very interested with the portrayal of witches in the 1960s, and kept a file of all the media sensationalism around Gerald Gardner and Alex Sanders. She was very serious about her own researches into witchcraft in Cornwall and had a reputation as a local expert, sometimes receiving requests to find covens. Of course, she was interested in ritual and folk magic in many forms, and would have wanted to draw parallels between emerging witchcraft traditions and the Hermetic and Freemasonic traditions with which she was already deeply involved. In 1967 she received a letter from Ron 'Chalky' White, who was publicising a new Traditional (non-Gardnerian) Witchcraft group called 'The Regency' which he hoped would promote Traditional Witchcraft within emerging Neo-Pagan culture in Britain. He told Colquhoun it would be based on the worship of two tutelary Gods in the person of King Arthur and Robin Hood, and a Goddess, and their ritual year would mirror their story.[92] It is currently unknown if Colquhoun participated, but one could see how this might have been interesting to her.

In 1965 and 1966 Colquhoun worked on another manuscript, *Destination Limbo*, which was again woven together from her dreams and which she had characterised as being about a witch cult. It shares some features with her other Surrealist novels, *Goose of Hermogenes* and *I Saw Water*, in that it is set on imaginary yet loosely Greek or Mediterranean islands, and features interactions with a group of ritualists; in this case, she calls them witches. It's clear that Colquhoun was continually refining ideas about the imaginal operations of a highly developed ritual magic group. In the case of *Destination Limbo*, the participants are much more sexually motivated, and it was expected that they would engage in sexual activity with each other, which is consistent with some of the more sensationalist press accounts of religious witchcraft as it was emerging in the mid-1960s. However, the manuscript was never completed, and a contract for publication, based on her sample chapters, was never secured.

Colquhoun was so inherently witchy, in so many ways, that one wonders why she did not become involved with some form of initiatory or participatory witchcraft. There must have been so much that might have appealed to her, especially the focus on the inherent sacredness of the British landscape, particularly given her belief that witches used the ancient sacred sites of Cornwall as meeting places. However, one can also see aspects that might not have appealed. Again, many witchcraft traditions include an ecstatic element that may not have suited her ritual sensibilities, more rooted in the allegorical performance one sees in Freemasonry or the Golden Dawn. Additionally, Colquhoun was attracted to systems that fitted the Perennialist narrative of an ancient wisdom tradition, and while much of witchcraft at this time was proclaiming that it was, indeed, an ancient religious tradition, it was of a different flavour than those related to Hermeticism. It lacks the heavy reliance on correspondences, for example. And it may also be that Colquhoun frankly was more invested in an idea of enlightenment based on a theurgic ideal, and that religious witchcraft was too earthy. Yet she doubtless engaged in some folk magic and other practices that would have been in the repertoire of many witches, and she resonated with the Divine Feminine, although it is unclear how the idea of a Goddess fitted into her spirituality. Today Colquhoun sits among the pantheon of Cornwall's witchy ancestors, and would probably have been proud to wear that label.

I Seek the Light of Hidden Knowledge

In *The Sword of Wisdom*, Colquhoun recounts a very personal and intimate tale. In 1967 she received a remarkable gift, from a relative of a member of the Alpha Omega lodge. It was the now-famous portrait of MacGregor Mathers in his Egyptian-style Golden Dawn nemyss, painted by his wife Moina, that had been rescued from a fiery fate. When the painting arrived, Colquhoun fell to her knees, and kissed the image on its lips. She recalls that she had fallen in love with the image in the portrait, believing that his spirit was reaching out through the ethers, and that in it she could see his true nature; mystic, martyr, angel, priest. On the Winter Solstice of that year, she performed a ritual in front of the portrait where she dedicated a sword to his memory, and she could feel him reaching out to her from beyond. Perhaps Colquhoun had found her match, a spirit soulmate who could finally understand her.

Although she was never able to join a Golden Dawn lodge with direct lineage from Mathers, which would have been her ultimate dream, the Golden Dawn system of magic was one of Colquhoun's great, lifelong loves. It captivated her from the 1930s onward, and informed her work and magical art experiments to the end of her life. There would have been many aspects of Golden Dawn theory and practice that would have dovetailed with her interests, and she shared an artistic and educational legacy with two of the most important members of the order, Florence Farr, who also attended Cheltenham Ladies College, and Moina Mathers, who was trained at the Slade. But Colquhoun's interest in Golden Dawn ritual magic would have set her apart from other Surrealists, who tended to be more attracted to the symbolism of alchemy, tarot and folk magic idioms, but for the most part did not see their artistic production within a framework of Western occult practice.

As a magical system, the Golden Dawn is rich and multi-layered, and its curriculum is essentially a primer for the Western occult tradition, incorporating astrology, tarot, geomancy, Egyptian deities, and the Kabbalah. The Kabbalah forms much of the basis of study for the initial degrees of the Golden Dawn system, and members are expected to have a command of Hebrew letters in addition to their magical correspondences. Notably, the Golden Dawn was the first complete and coherent magical curriculum in the Hermetic tradition that admitted men and women on an equal basis, and the idea that men and women could participate in ritual on an equal basis would have certainly attracted Colquhoun. In many ways, given the structure of its rituals, the Golden Dawn can properly be considered a para-masonic organisation, and its ritual and symbolic influence touched most of the occult and esoteric movements that followed in the course of the 20th century, including Wicca and esoteric Druidry.

The Hermetic Order of the Golden Dawn is considered to be a Rosicrucian Order which situates its philosophical and symbolic origins in Ancient Egypt, and in the Renaissance 'Rosicrucian' allegorical texts *Fama Fraternitatis* (1614), *Confessio Fraternitatis* (1615), and *The Chymical Wedding of Christian Rosenkreutz* (1617). These 'manifestos' tell the story of Christian Rosenkreutz, the father of the Rosicrucian tradition, who travelled to the East and gained occult wisdom, and shared it with a secret group of initiates. The texts, now considered allegorical, inspired Renaissance Hermeticism and created the backstory for a variety of initiatic orders. The Golden Dawn uses the story of Christian Rosenkreutz, with his death and discovery of his body in a seven-sided tomb, as the basis for some of the order's pivotal ritual moments.

Another feature of Golden Dawn practice which is reflected in Colquhoun's interests is the use of Egyptian symbolism and deities. Most of the early innovators within the Golden Dawn system, and within the early 20th century occult milieu in general, including Samuel 'MacGregor' Mathers and Aleister Crowley, used Egyptian lore as a foundation for their rituals and esoteric curricula. In fact, many of the occult groups of the early and mid-20th century would have traced their spiritual lineage to Egypt, including some Druidic orders. While the Golden Dawn system synthesises a number of influences from the western esoteric tradition, including Egyptian deities, kabbalah, alchemy, geomancy, astrology, and planetary magic, it can be argued that early Golden Dawn practice was focused on imaginatively reproducing the ritual conditions of a mythical Egypt steeped in Hermetic practices.

There are six grades of advancement in the First or Outer order of the system, and most initiates would spend the bulk of their time learning the material in this section. Each grade involves meditations, ritual work, memorisations and learning correspondences. Within each of the rituals, which have structural similarities to Masonic ritual, the ritual officers and stations represent Egyptian Godforms.

The Neophyte Hall and the initiation process is based on principles of judgment in *The Book of Coming Forth by Day*, known as the *Egyptian Book of the Dead*. When the initiate is ready to prepare for the Second Order, she or he undergoes the death and rebirth of Christian Rosenkreutz.

Scholars of art and literature are mainly familiar with the Golden Dawn as a result of its illustrious membership, including W.B. Yeats, Allan Bennett, Aleister Crowley, theatre pioneer Annie Horniman, and writer Arthur Machen, among others. Scholars of religion and the occult are focused on the fact that the Golden Dawn system was the first systematic curriculum of Western occultism designed for practical use, and that it was equally offered to men and women. There seems to be a perception among scholars that Golden Dawn participation was primarily for socialising, and as a result the curriculum and activities of Golden Dawn lodges are rarely discussed in depth when looking at its membership and their creative output. In fact, actual spiritual engagement with Golden Dawn material has frequently been overlooked by scholars who are uncomfortable with the idea of occult practice.[93] However, to progress in the Golden Dawn curriculum required dedication and study, as well as complex ritual advancements from grade to grade, so it is quite likely that this material would have had a significant emotional and spiritual impact on the creative work of active members of the order. It is hard to imagine that initiates who took the material seriously would not be changed by it, and it's pretty clear that for many Golden Dawn members, including Yeats, Florence Farr and others, their magic was very real and not just an interesting intellectual or symbolic construct.

Colquhoun probably first heard of the Golden Dawn through her fascination with Yeats, whom she had been reading since the mid-1920s. She recalled that she first learned of the Golden Dawn in one of his early essays, some of which were published in the collection *Ideas of Good and Evil*. His passionate writing about his belief in magic must have been compelling to the young Colquhoun:

> I have now described that belief in magic which has set me all but unwilling among those lean and fierce minds who are at war with their time, who cannot accept the days as they pass, simply and gladly; and I look at what I have written with some alarm, for I have told more of the ancient secret than many among my fellow-students think it right to tell. I have come to believe so many strange things because of experience, that I see little reason to doubt the truth of many things that are beyond my experience; and it may be that there are beings who watch over that ancient secret, as all tradition affirms, and resent, and perhaps avenge, too fluent speech.[94]

Although Colquhoun was not a member of an actual Golden Dawn lodge, through the orders that she did join, and her own resources, she was still able to explore many of the esoteric aspects of the order that appealed to her. Even prior to Israel Regardie publishing the Order's rituals and papers in 1937, Crowley had published a number of Golden Dawn documents in *The Equinox*, and Colquhoun was familiar with many of the documents on the Golden Dawn reading list from the books that her cousin Edward lent to her. Crowley's publication of *Liber 777* may have been the most helpful document to her, providing a list of correspondences that she could use to guide her colourful compositions, so in reality she had been working with the Golden Dawn current for years.

In the early 1960s, Colquhoun encountered Tamara Bourkhoun, who remains an enigmatic figure in the mid-century British occult scene. Records show that Colquhoun knew of Bourkhoun by 1960.[95] In the late 1950s Colquhoun was engaged in correspondence study, conducting remote Tantric and Hermetic practice in a system titled in her notes as 'The Magian Philosophy'. Her correspondent was someone called Terence, who also appears to be an associate of Bourkhoun. Probably the best account we have of Bourkhoun to date is from Timothy d'Arch Smith in his memoir *The Times Deceas'd*.[96] He tells us that she was born in Manchuria in 1915, and lived in the US from 1940 until she relocated to London in 1963. Although she was previously a Theosophist, in 1949 she purchased Regardie's Golden Dawn and started down a new spiritual path, believing it was her destiny to form a new Golden Dawn order. She started corresponding with Regardie around 1952. Although she was clearly well read in the Golden Dawn system, much of her own spiritual authority came from her own visionary work and her contacts with inner plane adepts. D'Arch Smith describes how she had been working to make contacts with members of the British esoteric community, including Druids and Co-Masons, and then in 1963 moved to London to found a new order based on a message from an Enochian contact. It was this order, the Order of the Pyramid and Sphinx, that Colquhoun joined in the early 1960s.

Bourkhoun was heavily interested in Enochian magic and focused much of the ritual and teaching around it. It may be that part of the interest in Enochian for Colquhoun would have been a reinforcement of her ideal state of humanity before the Fall, since this was supposed to have been the angelic language spoken before that unfortunate occurrence. Bourkhoun took purity very seriously. Her lifestyle rules and expectations were very strict and she demanded that all of her members be Co-Masons, vegetarian and celibate, according to Michael Howard.[97] Colquhoun did become a Co-Mason, although this was likely before she became involved with Bourkhoun, and appears to have abided by Bourkhoun's other restrictions for some time. She was clearly very active in the order, occasionally traveling to London to attend rituals. Apparently, there is ample correspondence between Bourkhoun and Regardie around the establishment of the Order, but it remains in private hands, as does most of her correspondence with Colquhoun.

However, what is available indicates that Colquhoun was very involved in helping to create temple materials for the Order, and was very likely working on a tarot deck for them. Although Colquhoun had been using various Golden Dawn colour schemes in her work for decades, her archives also show many sketches of items that would have been used in a Golden Dawn ritual context. There are talismans in flashing colours, different studies of the crosses that Golden Dawn initiates use in their grade studies, and esoteric renderings of some of the tools of the Order and how they are positioned on the Tree of Life. There is also evidence of some Enochian work, with paintings of coloured pyramids surrounded by gold leaf paint.

In February of 1966 when Colquhoun was deep in her work with the Order of the Pyramid and Sphynx, she undertook what must have been a pilgrimage-style trip to Egypt to visit the pyramids and other sacred sites of the Egyptian deities. The centrality of the Egyptian pantheon to Golden Dawn practice would have made this quite a journey for her. She was right in seeing Egypt as the 'fountainhead' of Golden Dawn tradition, and, given her own Perennialist sensibilities, she may well have believed that Egypt was, in fact, the cradle of the whole Western esoteric tradition. She visited a variety of sites – Luxor, Nag Hammadi, Abydos, Amarna – and when she could she performed rituals in the temples, frequently salutations to Thoth. In an interesting interpretation of Golden Dawn theology, she even wondered if the Goddess Sekhmet was, in fact, her Holy Guardian Angel.

She chronicled her pilgrimage in an unpublished manuscript, *The Blue Anoubis*, which was her attempt to do for Egypt what she had done for Ireland and Cornwall in her previous two travelogues. As with the first two, the manuscript is intensely personal and unconventional. She included her private rituals, and esoteric interpretations of the sites she visited, as well as her everyday observations of the Egyptian people and her hope that they would not yield to the pressures of 'progress'. As usual, she includes commentary on noise and modernisation, complaining about the use of a loudspeaker to announce the calls to prayer, claiming it 'ruined the praxis of holy ascent to the mountain.' There were also intended illustrations, beautiful and delicate blue-lined renderings of Egyptian deities and motifs. She submitted the manuscript for publication several times, but as usual she had little sense of market or audience. It is a challenging read even for someone with an occult background, and too filled with personal commentary to be widely accessible. At one point, she even describes hiking her skirts to pee behind a pyramid.

Given the centrality of the Golden Dawn system to Colquhoun's work, it is unclear why she left the Order of the Pyramid and Sphinx after such close association for over a decade. It is very possible that Colquhoun and Bourkhoun clashed somewhat, and that Bourkhoun's lifestyle prescriptions were too constricting for Colquhoun, or that Bourkhoun's ego became more than Colquhoun wanted to manage. It is notable that neither Bourkhoun nor the Order of the Pyramid and Sphinx receive mention in *The Sword of Wisdom*, which would have been published after their association ended. Nevertheless, there is no doubt that Colquhoun's time with this group affected her view of Mathers' influence on the history of Western magic. However, the greatest flowering of Colquhoun's Golden Dawn interests was to come after she split from Bourkhoun, and in the later part of her life.

The Sword of Wisdom, published in 1975, is widely considered to be a curious and somewhat strange book, but historically of interest. It may have been Colquhoun's most successful and widely read publication, having been picked up by G.P. Putnam. Very likely the occult gossip content was what sold it, given its unconventional nature. The title was taken from a Georges Bataille poem 'Du Haut de Montserrat', where he invokes Paracelsus:

Colquhoun's translation reads:

> . . . his two hands resting
> On the sword of wisdom
> The intimate of stars and gems.[98]

She compares Bataille's vision of Paracelsus to the painting of Mathers holding a gem-encrusted sword, which forms the emotional core of the book.

The Sword of Wisdom made Colquhoun's name known within the occult community and gave her a visible profile even after her death. In no way is *The Sword of Wisdom* a conventional Golden Dawn history, or even a definitive biography of Mathers. As with most of Colquhoun's books, it is highly personal, punctuated with anecdotes, observations and not so subtle commentary. It is primarily Colquhoun's proclamation of love to the Golden Dawn; it is her goal to establish the place of the Golden Dawn as the order which gives birth to practically every significant occult movement in the 20th century, and she makes a compelling case. Golden Dawn scholars tend to feel that Colquhoun's account is too anecdotal and an unreliable work of bad history. However, the gossip and snarky observations are part of the enjoyment of the work, and come from a writer who has been completely immersed in the British occult milieu for much of her life, so nothing should be dismissed outright. In fact, the amount of lore documenting the British occult milieu of the first half of the twentieth century is quite astounding. The manuscript exists in several versions, some with interesting handwritten notes in the margin which never made it to the final version. Although many of the anecdotes are not verifiable, it is likely that they resulted from her years of personal knowledge of the occult community.

The Sword of Wisdom starts, unusually for a biography of someone else, with the author's own magical autobiography, much of which had been written earlier in an unfinished manuscript. The first section chronicles her own interest in the occult, her encounters with the Golden Dawn lodge of her cousin, and other occultists and orders she engaged with on the road to connecting with the true current. Here, she details her genuine beliefs in the workings of the Secret Chiefs which guard and maintain the initiatory wisdom current. She wonders about the nature of the Secret Chiefs, and whether or not they are corporeal or existing on another plane, but she fully believed that they had a strong hand in directing her spiritual advancement. Much of the book does detail Mathers' life, stories of his wife Moina, biographies of various Golden Dawn members, offshoot temples, splits and schisms.

There are also odd graphs and pronouncements about the typical psychological profile of a Golden Dawn initiate, including a propensity for childlessness, or as she puts it, 'Golden Dawners Don't Breed'. One might speculate that this was also an attempt to convince herself that she was well suited, despite Mrs. Weir's assessment.

Some of the most interesting chapters of the book are at the end, where Colquhoun shows her own esoteric expertise. After she finishes the Golden Dawn history section, she includes essays on Enochiana, alchemy and sex magic instruction in Western magical orders. These pieces show not only her command of the material, but the ways that various occult actors in this milieu engaged with these topics. Unfortunately, these pieces fail to be truly informative, as the topics are too broad, and she seems to be unable to condense all she wants to say about them, other than how other occultists viewed them. What is clear, however, is that she could have written her own volume on any of these subjects, and we are poorer for her never having done so.

The Visual Impact

One cannot truly understand Colquhoun's corpus without understanding the Golden Dawn, especially the Kabbalistic colour attributions and the Golden Dawn theories of colour usage which inspired her to the end of her life. She truly believed that the Golden Dawn presaged significant moments in art history, developing both collage and 'op art', long before they became adopted by the art world. Overall, Colquhoun displayed a symbolic and emotional attachment to the Golden Dawn system that might not always be apparent in her paintings, due to their non-representational nature, but once you understand the principles she was embracing you see them everywhere, particularly when there is a link to the Kabballah.

Given the tendency to want to link artistic production to biographical moments, it would be satisfying to pin Colquhoun's paintings to her time in various orders to see what leaked through to the canvas, but it is not that simple. Just as esoteric curricula tend to be built upon layers of folk and received wisdom injected with the occasional innovation, so the Golden Dawn system of magic reflected a variety of ideas, beliefs and techniques, many of which were available to Colquhoun. As she shows in *Sword of Wisdom*, it is hard to disentangle much of what is considered to be 20th century Hermetic practice from the Golden Dawn curriculum, which was so effective at compiling, rebranding, and building on a Hermetic magical tradition. Colquhoun had access to a variety of publications whose authors had in some way experienced the touch of the Golden Dawn, just as she had. But while much of the Golden Dawn material was drawn from earlier sources, it was probably their genuinely unique contributions to modern magic that most affected Colquhoun, with the equal inclusion of women, development of the visual Kabbalah, and magical colour theory.

Colour

Although Theosophy, with its colourful thought forms, made more impact on the art world of the early 20th century through the influential writings of Kandinsky, the work of the Golden Dawn, using modern colour theory for magical ends, was right in line with Colquhoun's interests. Understanding the Golden Dawn use of colour helps us to understand a key part of Colquhoun's own art and magic.

The Golden Dawn curriculum developed the use of colour in magical contexts in sophisticated and complex ways that had not been previously possible, and colour theory is central to the Order's magical teachings. This not only sets the Order apart from other magical schools of thought, it demonstrates that through the science of colour theory, which was motivated in the late nineteenth century by the development of artificial pigments, the Golden Dawn cultivated an interesting engagement with elements of modernity. When the Golden Dawn was founded in 1888, a new era of colour experimentation was emerging, with the development of a wider range of artificial pigments with bold hues that didn't require blending to produce. Moina Mathers and Florence Farr, both trained artists, provided the theoretical foundation for the experiments with colour that the Golden Dawn formulated in their ritual practice. What developed as a result is an exciting set of ritual practices and meditations which combine traditional esoteric colour correspondences, and the idea that colours were themselves entities which could be invoked, with newly emerging ideas about the effect of colour on physiology and the psyche. Many Golden Dawn magical practices are designed to produce spiritual experiences triggered by the physiological response to colour. In this way, we see the Golden Dawn taking the role of magical engineers, employing scientific discourses of the day to produce experiences with colour that they believed were not only mythic in scope and narrative, but also repeatable.

Many components of the Golden Dawn system focus on the colours associated with the various sephira and paths of the Tree of Life. Although there were colour themes for the sephira prior to the Golden Dawn, Golden Dawn magicians expanded and refined them, and essentially built the colour schemes that people use today. Understanding how these colours are generated, and having a thorough knowledge of them and their correspondences, remains an essential part of the curriculum and is a key to progressing into the Second Order. One of the key symbols of adepthood is the Rose Cross, which contains a colour wheel at the very centre, with each colour representing one of the twenty-two paths of the Tree of Life. This central portion of the device was developed along with the colours released by the Winsor & Newton paint company in the 1890s, thus providing magicians a richer way of playing with and experiencing an expanded range of sacred colour. The precision of colour mixing was highly important to Golden Dawn magicians. If the colour is not precise, the correct result may not be obtained. It's hard for us to imagine today, with our lives being filled with oversaturated colours, how radical this was when it was first developed as a magical technology. Colour mixing was a specialised skill. Not everyone knew how to mix colours accurately with any degree of sophistication, and many pigments weren't readily available. Yet these colours were connected to entities and very real powers, 'The Signature of Forces', and if you wanted to contact them you needed the right signature, which required precision.

One of the most interesting and innovative uses of colour in the Golden Dawn system is in the use of the Vault, one of the system's primary initiatory devices, which is used to incubate a new adept and also for lodge members to undertake visionary and divinatory work. The Golden Dawn vault may have grown out of the Masonic Chamber of Reflection, which is a small room containing allegorical symbols for the initiatory candidate to consider prior to initiation. However, this practice itself is said to share a legendary Rosicrucian origin with the Golden Dawn vault. The Golden Dawn vault is a seven-sided chamber supposedly designed after the tomb of Christian Rosenkreutz. The walls of the vault are covered with squares containing symbols in an opposing colour to the background. This phenomenon is known as simultaneous contrast. The desired effect is that the symbol-covered squares appear to vibrate, and thus cause an intensely immersive experience for the candidate. Additionally, simultaneous contrast of colours can also cause retinal burn, so potentially the symbols might remain visible to the candidate for some time after the ritual. This would have the effect of reinforcing the intensely embodied experience of colour while making the symbols inscribed in the chamber seem to take on a rather spectral life of their own. This is again a reason why the precision of colour mixing in the Golden Dawn was such an important concern. Not only were these colours themselves entities to be invoked, but a lasting magical impact on the candidate needed to be ensured. This technique was employed in a variety of Golden Dawn magical practices, including the building of talismans and astrological or elemental tablets for meditation, and also in creating tarot cards, which members were encouraged to do.

Colquhoun worked with Golden Dawn colour schemes not only in her automatic works, but also in a variety of more recognisable magical experiments starting from her alchemical pieces in the late 1930s.

She had her own version of the Golden Dawn colour wheel, which forms the centre of the Rose Cross, and which aligns colours with the 22 Hebrew letters and paths of the Tree of Life. Her archives show drafts of astrological templates and ethereal paintings of archangels in flashing colours. In a 1979 essay she explained that flashing colours worked by sending a signal from the material world to the world of formation, producing a hypnotic effect in the viewer, and ultimately a change in consciousness.[99] Her archives also contain scores of colour experiments of blocky humanoid forms employing different Kabbalistic colour schemes, and there are even sketches of a vault that she may have been designing for use with the Order of the Pyramid and Sphinx. It seems that after she left the Pyramid and Sphinx she created some of her most sophisticated works inspired by Golden Dawn principles. In the mid-1970s she started to focus more intently on working in enamel, another recommendation found in Golden Dawn documents, and in 1977–78 she completed a number of small enamel pieces. Most of these pieces do not appear to have thematic links with Order material, her 1977 Taro and the *Decad of Intelligence* being exceptions. The key to understanding Colquhoun's relationship to colour and its impact is that from her earliest days of art school training she was aware that colours were not only signposts or symbols of larger principles, but functioned as gateways and were themselves forces.

Tesseracts, Crosses and the Fourth Dimension

Colquhoun's Golden Dawn interests and Surrealism came together in her quests to traverse other dimensions. For Colquhoun the true form of spirits was not humanoid; they lived in the realm of colour and shape, unlocked by principles of sacred geometry. Her interest in the relationship between visual art and other dimensions is one of the key concepts of her artistic production. She touches on this in her own characterisation of her automatic processes in 'The Mantic Stain', but we start to see evidence of it in her work as early as 1940–41 with sketches of tesseracts and human figures in cubes of space. She applied dimensional theory to a wide variety of pieces throughout her life, including landscapes and murals, and we also see it in a number of occult visual experiments linked more explicitly to the Kabballah and later to her Golden Dawn work. Colquhoun's interest in the tesseract and extra dimensional portals spanned several decades of her life, and cuts across her engagement with esotericism, science and art theory. In fact, as with many areas of interest for Colquhoun, the resonances of extradimensional theory that she was encountering both in the art world and in occult writings would have continually enriched and reinforced her own experiences, which is one reason we see this theme emerge in so many contexts over the decades of her life.

Although she had studied and worked with Platonic solids in her various art school curricula, the initial defining moment for Colquhoun would have been, as previously noted, her encounter with the ideas of Roberto Matta when she was in the Surrealist enclave at Chemilieu in 1939. Matta's ideas were part of a much broader interest in the art world about the visual construction of extra dimensions, but for Colquhoun, this artistic and scientific conversation would have perfectly coalesced with complementary theories emerging in esoteric circles. Her goal can be characterised as artistically cultivating the ability to transfer energy and forces between different planes of existence. Over the course of her life we see the influence of a variety of thinkers including Ouspensky and Gurdjieff, Charles Hinton, Paul Foster Case, and Claude Bragdon, many of whom were building on each other's work and were part of a wider dialogue about the nature of space and human limitation. Linda Henderson, in fact, argues that discussions about the fourth dimension are a defining motif in developing ideas of modernity, continually reasserting itself during periods where human consciousness becomes a wider cultural area of focus.[100]

We saw earlier how Colquhoun's conceptions of automatic processes became the vehicle by which she would contact other dimensions, and much of the theoretical basis for her work was established by a succession of metaphysical and esoteric theorists who were trying to reconcile evolutionary theory with physics and spirituality.

'A stream of power, set in motion': Occultism

Colquhoun's interest in extra dimensions was part of a wider interest in the fourth dimension that ran through science, art and spirituality in the early twentieth century, impacting the development of Cubism and Surrealism as well as the occult. Although people weren't sure what the fourth dimension was, they were sure it existed. 'The fourth dimension of these texts was not time but an extra supersensible dimension of space, of which our three-dimensional world might be merely a section or boundary.'[101] As with many philosophical notions of the late nineteenth and early twentieth century, the developing language of science played with esoteric thought (and vice versa), since many of these ideas connect with theories of expanded consciousness and the permeability of material planes. As these theories about other dimensions intersect with the western esotericism of the time, they become refracted through a Neoplatonic framework, where moving through various dimensions becomes transferred to the metaphor of emanations, and becomes mapped on to the world of the Kabbalistic tree of life. Because Colquhoun's work was so deeply informed by these theorists, it is worth taking a detour into fourth-dimensional theory.

Thinkers have always been curious about the nature of space, but in the late nineteenth century the debate renewed with some vigour: is it time? Nothingness? Another dimension? Can 'space' contain any matter at all? The ideas which emerged from those debates were a collision of several theoretical perspectives, embracing esoteric theory, philosophy, and mathematical debates about N-dimensional geometries. Although the public understanding of the theory of relativity ended scientific debate on these matters, they remained fodder for esotericists still keen to explore supersensual spaces and phenomena. When extradimensional theories intersected with the human potential movement of the late nineteenth century, the 'space' of theoretical extra dimensions morphed into a moral imperative for the developing superhuman. As a result, the impact on art, speculative fiction and occult subcultures continued as people embraced alternative ways to interact with 'consciousness'.

There were several key writers on extra-dimensional theory during this period who impacted the worlds of art and magic as they tumbled into modernity. At the leading edge of this movement was the eccentric British mathematician Charles Hinton. In 1888 Hinton published his esoteric mathematical treatise *A New Era of Thought*, establishing much of the thinking and visualisation of the fourth dimension by successive thinkers and esotericists. Synthesising sources such as Plato and Kant, Hinton examines the possibility of accessing dimensions not readily intelligible by normal sensory means. In some ways his theories echo the influential 1884 novella *Flatland*, by Edwin Abbott, which was one of the first works to address the moral realities of dimensionally stifled consciousness, yet Hinton takes a much more mathematical and less allegorical approach. Hinton coined the word tesseract to refer to his model of the fourth dimension as represented in the second, using three-dimensional perspective. Hinton's tesseract is depicted as coloured cubes jutting out at right angles to all the planes on a central cube. If you were to dissect this figure, you would produce a hypercube, a cruciform shape with a cube jutting out of the central portion.

Hinton proposed a series of exercises and visualisations using coloured cubes to help people access their own extra-dimensional consciousness. His work became exceptionally influential for occultists and artists in the early twentieth century and inspired a number of texts by other thinkers who were essentially extrapolating from his original theories. He followed his 1888 publications with several other influential works, such as *The Fourth Dimension* (1905), which is only slightly more readable than *A New Era of Thought*. Hinton's works were essential reading for turn-of-the-century occultists. Crowley placed Hinton's works on his A*A* reading list, and he even gets a small cameo appearance in Crowley's novel *Moonchild*. It is also worth noting that in *Liber 777* Crowley makes the tesseract one of his geomantic figures.

Hinton, like those who followed, described the characteristics of the fourth dimension with recourse to the other three dimensions, theorising that the fourth dimension certainly exists in an unseen world just beyond ours. Hinton took Plato's analogy of the cave quite literally, in that the two-dimensional shadows teasing the prisoners in the cave are akin to the realities of higher dimensions which lie beyond our senses, of which we can only comprehend mere 'shadows'. Hinton believed that exposure to these forms, and understanding their interactions with our sense of reality, could help humans wake up to their higher capacities to access other planes.

> In our world these various relations are found by the most simple observations; but a plane-being could only acquire them by considerable labour. And if he determined to obtain a knowledge of the physical existence of a higher world than his own, he must pass through such discipline.[102]

So, to help cultivate fourth dimensional vision, Hinton proposed that one construct a series of cubes coloured with each of the faces of a tesseract, so that one could concentrate on them and build visionary discipline that would free people from the limitations of three-dimensional space and direction. In this way, humanity could progress further in sciences and technology by using these new capacities. Yet, his programme was not exactly easy to achieve. Hinton's description of his tesseract and how it can be constructed is complicated to say the least. Each plane, face and intersecting point is assigned a different colour, and he describes how they can be arranged and how each section can be conceptualised to move in space. One can see why Hinton's work appealed to Colquhoun, even though much of the description is nearly unreadable. His tesseracts are designed with a variety of rich colours and demand precise thought and exceptional visualisation.

While Hinton introduced a metaphysical aspect to the fourth dimension that humans could access with higher faculties, Claude Bragdon's expansion of Hinton's work injected a moral and symbolic element. It is likely that Colquhoun was familiar with Claude Bragdon's rather charming 1913 *Primer of Higher Space*. Based in New York, Bragdon was, like several of Colquhoun's inspirations, an accomplished architect, and also a Theosophist who was influential in merging Western Esotericism with contemporary ideas of 'natural' architecture. He believed that universal forms found in nature, when applied to architecture and ornament, would inspire the better impulses of humanity to help overcome societal discord. Bragdon was so taken with the potential of promoting higher dimensional thought that in 1923 he translated and published P.D. Ouspensky's *Tertium Organum*.

Bragdon believed, like Hinton, that with the right sort of moral and physical discipline one could access higher dimensions, but he went further than Hinton in his characterisation of what benefits might be accrued by these practices. Bragdon believed that developing fourth dimensional capacities could produce superhuman abilities. In fact, he believed that the fourth dimension was the spatial location where both clairvoyance and reincarnation took place, and that with the right sort of training this unseen area could be fully unlocked. Bragdon's 1913 publication presented many of Hinton's ideas in a simplified form, illustrated with diagrams to prove some of his key points. The similarity of some of these diagrams to some of Colquhoun's drawings of energetic bodies from the 1940s is striking, and it is likely that she was using Bragdon's text as a source. Bragdon integrated existing esoteric theory about cubes into his treatise, making subtle allusion to masonic teachings, the Bible and of course Theosophy. Cubes represent the spiritual in the perfected material, alluding to Biblical descriptions of the New Jerusalem, which in the Book of Revelation was given the dimensions of a cube. Bragdon also explicitly incorporated Christ imagery, refracted through a Theosophical lens, into fourth dimensional theory. He demonstrated that when one dissects a cube, the result is a crucifix made of squares, representing the state of the perfected human in this plane. 'If the cubes be taken to represent the higher selves of individuals in a higher space world, "the plane" our phenomenal world, the cross sections would then represent the lower space aspects of our higher selves.'[103] For Bragdon, the tesseract represented a higher spiritual aspiration.

Ouspensky rehearsed many of the arguments of Hinton and greatly expanded them, practically and philosophically. Colquhoun very evidently knew his work as well, since Ouspensky provides guideposts to many of her 1940s preoccupations ranging from alchemy to the spirit of stones. It's possible that she first became aware of Ouspensky during her time at the Quest Society in the 1930s. Ouspensky's work became popular with many artists in the 1920s, in part supporting the daring visual perspectives of Cubism, but there were other and perhaps more tactical reasons that his writings became popular with artists. Ouspensky spoke directly to the role of the artist and the artist's ability to help uplift humanity to fourth dimensional consciousness and the beginning of a new era of human evolution:

> In art it is necessary to study 'occultism' – the hidden side of life. The artist must be a clairvoyant: he must see that which others do not see; he must be a magician: must possess the power to make others see that which they do not themselves see, but which he does see.[104]

Through the work of artists who have achieved fourth dimensional vision, humans can be liberated from this three-dimensional world, just as those who suffered in Plato's cave could ultimately be brought to light by the philosopher kings. For Ouspensky, 'Christ' is not a saviour, but a metaphor for cosmic consciousness that can be achieved by the right people. This mission is not for everyone, and Ouspensky's conclusions are somewhat elitist. Spiritual evolution can only be achieved by the 'higher man', one fitting to act as a conduit for these unseen forces, the initiate, the artist, the one who is uplifted by the sort of culture that will support this evolution. He believed in the freedom of the individual, but not in human equality. Deeply anti-materialist, he longed for the day when a universal religion will dominate our waking hours, and when the spiritual caste will rule lower men.

In this model Colquhoun, like many of her Surrealist peers, ultimately fashioned herself as a seer and would have envisioned herself as part of this revolution, helping to communicate the psychic life through artistic production. She would have also been attracted to Ouspensky's latent animism; he characterises the nature of stones as being qualitatively different according to their place and function. Stones can speak to us, if we know their language and listen to them:

> The poet understands that the mast of a ship, the gallows, and the cross are made of different wood. He understands the difference between the stone from a church wall and the stone from a prison wall. He hears 'the voices of stones,' understands the whisperings of ancient walls, of tumuli, of mountains, rivers, woods and plains. He hears 'the voice of the silence,' understands the psychological difference between silences, knows that one silence can differ from another. And this poetical understanding of the world should be developed, strengthened and fortified, because only by its aid do we come in contact with the true world of reality. In the real world, behind phenomena which appear to us similar, often stand noumena so different that only by our blindness is it possible to account for our idea of the similarity of those phenomena.[105]

By the time that Colquhoun visited Chemilieu in 1939 she herself had become heir to these influences, which she integrated into her own dimensional theories. These took a variety of expressions over the decades, ranging from work with cubes and Platonic solids, to theories about dreams and remote visions, theories of automatism and the cultivation of place and body as astral portal. It is likely that the works inspiring Matta and Onslow Ford were in some measure already known to Colquhoun, and their preoccupations just helped to support her direction philosophically. Ultimately, Colquhoun came to believe that clairvoyance is essentially fourth dimensional vision that would allow people to access space, time and materiality in a fluid manner. Yet despite Colquhoun's spiritual preoccupation, time and again she saw science as playing a supporting role in proving metaphysical claims. For instance, Henderson notes the way in which the development of X-ray technology changed how people viewed the nature of reality and the permeability of physical boundaries. If X-rays were 'energy waves' that allowed for the penetration of bodies, perhaps people could cultivate a similar type of vision that would also allow them to see differently by manipulating their own energy. As Bragdon implicitly drew on these ideas in his own theories about clairvoyance, Colquhoun made them explicit in her own visual studies of the energy rays and internal organs within human bodies, which show the capacity of the clairvoyant to see beyond flesh into the various internal planes of the body. The artistic expression of an extra-dimensional portal represented an important spiritual concept for Colquhoun, namely that we are surrounded by other worlds and Otherworlds, and that with the right spiritual technology we can contact them. She believed that people in other times had the ability to move between the worlds, and she was not only interested in apprehending those dimensions herself, but longed to represent their mysteries to others.

Colquhoun was evidently taken with the idea of the tesseract early on, and she incorporated its features into a number of works and magical experiments ranging from human bodies to landscapes. We see her first sketches of tesseracts in the early 1940s, and she returns to them with her exploration of Platonic solids in the 1950s, and then with simple, clean renderings of tesseracts in the 1970s, the last decade of her life. The sides of Colquhoun's tesseracts when painted are complex, as a tesseract has many sides and planes, yet in simplified formats they are read as green, orange, blue and vermillion. However, she did experiment with tesseracts of different colours, incorporating Kabbalistic correspondences in her colour schemes. When Colquhoun adapted tesseracts to a different context they can be identified by a square, or pyramid figure bounded by one of these colours, which she projected on to landscapes and human figures. For instance, around 1941 we see a preliminary sketch of *Sunset Birth*, an image of the *Mên-an-Tol* with a figure passing through the centre of the monument, encased in a pyramid shape in these colours. It is likely she was suggesting

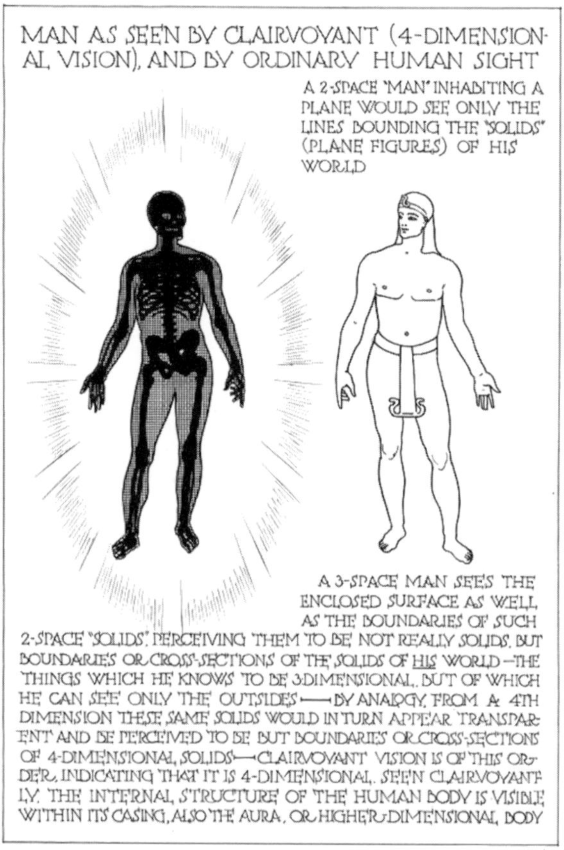

ABOVE Bragdon shows how cultivating higher dimensional vision allows clairvoyants to see both internal organs and auras.

that megalithic monuments are extra dimensional portals. Also, again around 1941, in a piece that appears to have been done around the same time as the *Diagrams of Love* series, we see a loose rendering of a figure, with a red and blue hexagram at the heart, and the torso encapsulated in what appears to be a rough sketch of a cube in tesseract colours. Is this another conceptualisation of the cube of space, or does it suggest something else about the spatial placement of a human with fourth dimensional capacities?

RIGHT Hinton cubes figures to aid in extradimensional perception.

Views of the Tessaract.

No. 1.

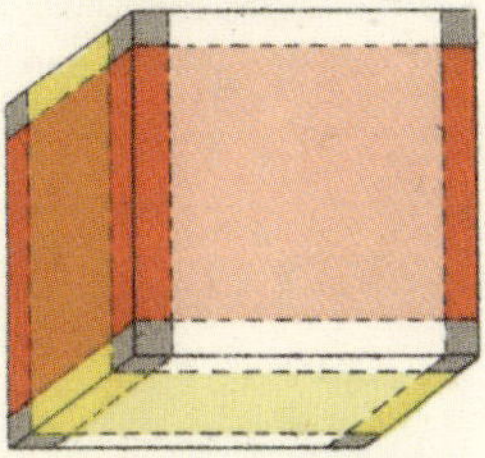

No. 2.

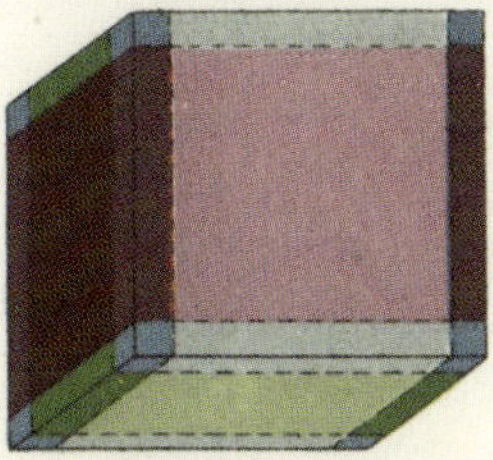

No. 3.

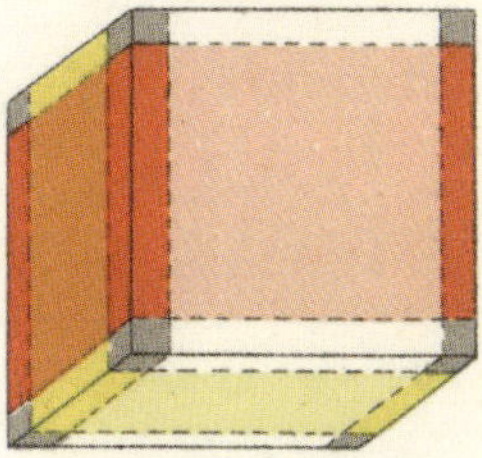

No. 4.

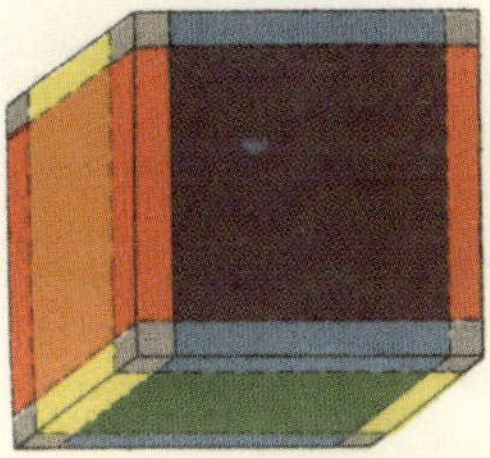

No. 5.

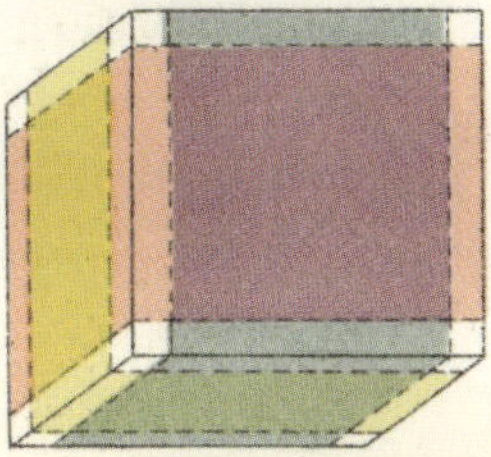

No. 6.

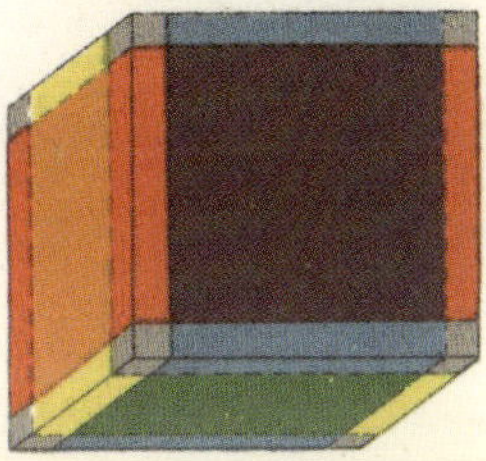

No. 7.

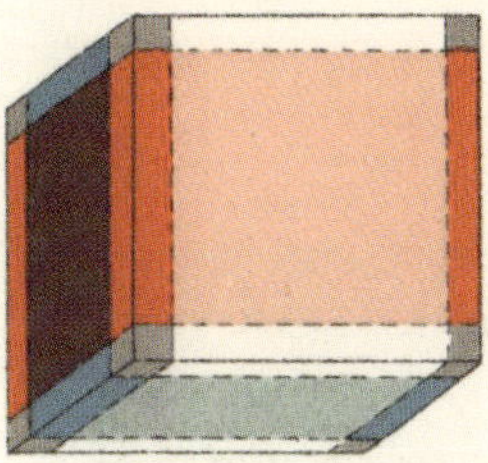

No. 8.

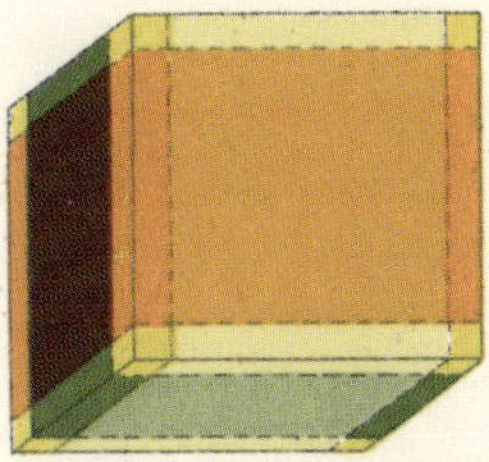

No. 9.

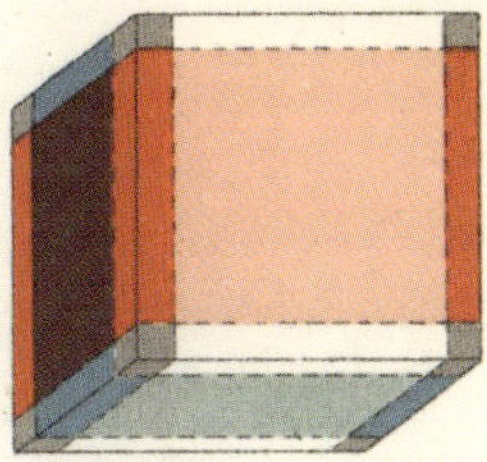

No. 10.

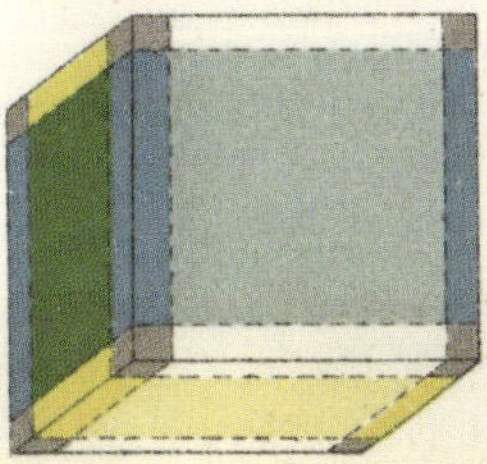

No. 11.

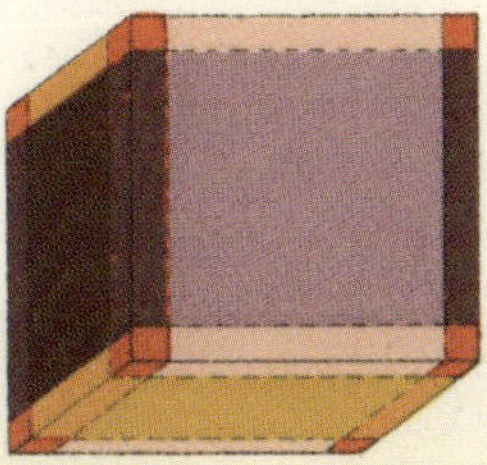

No. 12.

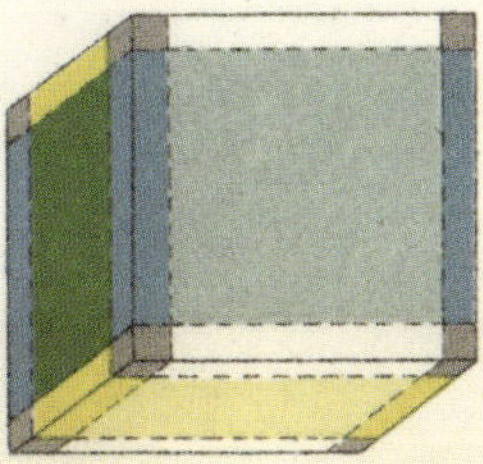

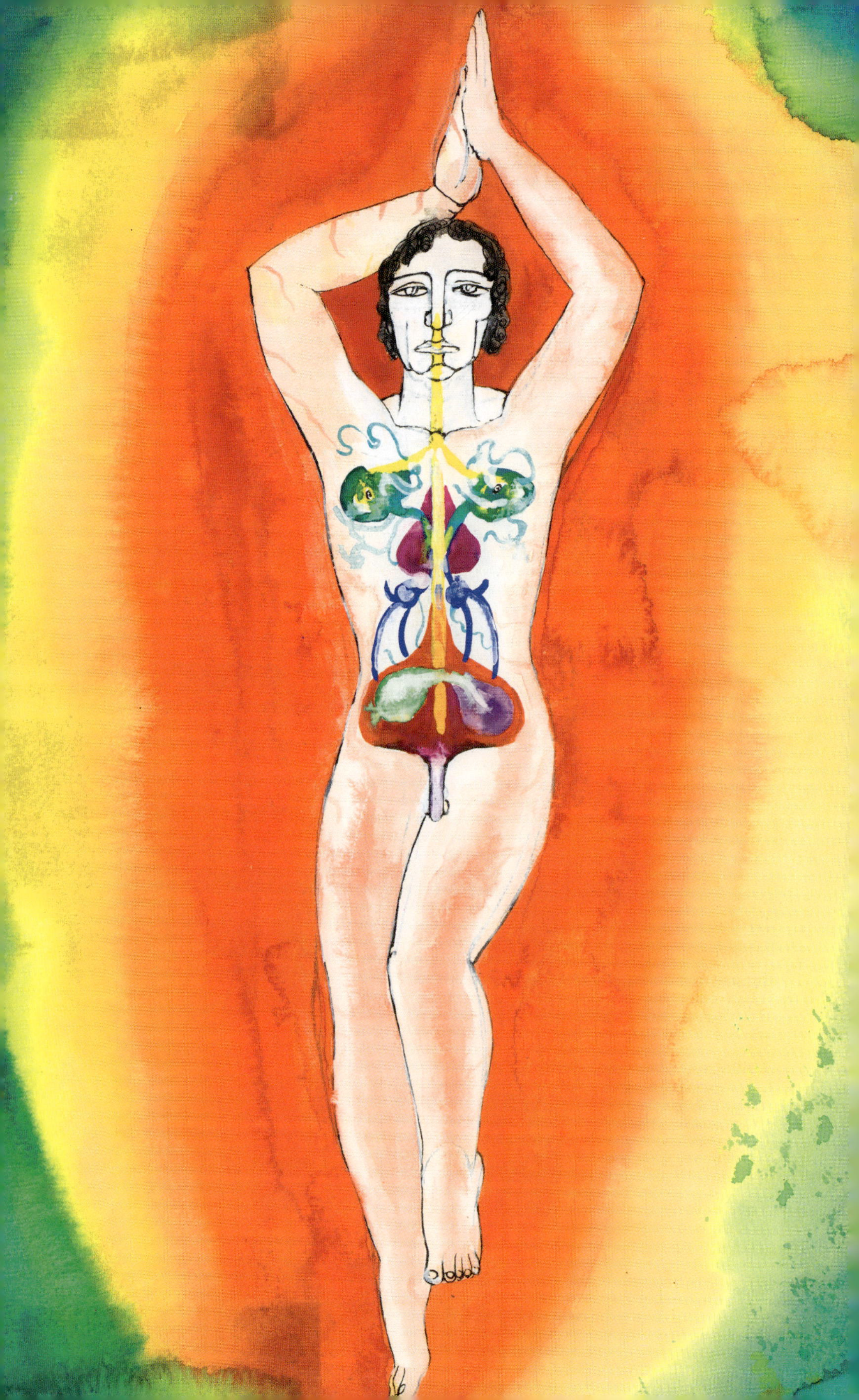

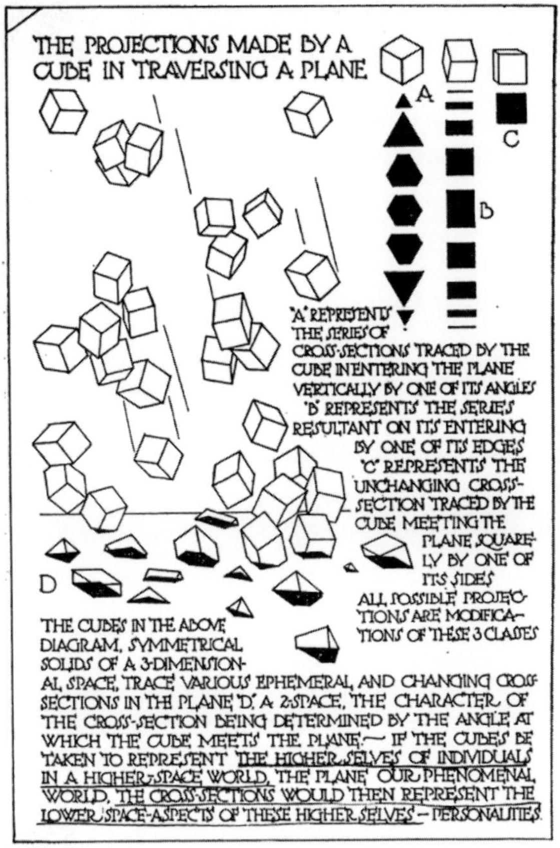

PLATE 30

ABOVE Bragdon's diagram indicating the two dimensional plane view of three dimensional objects.

Starting in the early 1950s, Colquhoun started an esoteric project of reducing figures graphically to cubes and squares. Some of Colquhoun's work is meant to represent a level of human evolution which can be attained by meditating on mapping esoteric colours and diagrams onto the human body, envisioned as cubes or crosses. Paul Foster Case's 'Cube of Space' would have also provided a model for Colquhoun in her dissections of cubes. Interestingly, Case was clearly inspired by Bragdon, and Case and

LEFT One of several studies of humans with bright auras and internal organs on view, c. 1942. Note the similarities to Bragdon's sketch.

Bragdon met in 1900 when Case was only 16 years old. Case related that Bragdon had asked him about the nature of the tarot, which helped inspire his future researches. Case's Cube of Space was inspired by a passage in the *Sepher Yetzirah* which associates Hebrew letters with various directions. Case believed that this was a diagram for a cube, so he aligned each edge and axis of the cube with Hebrew letters, which also correspond to tarot cards. For Case, as with Bragdon, the cube represents the manifested universe as we currently experience it. Of course, Colquhoun was not the only one in the 1950s to have been working with notions of the cube and the perfected human. We see it in Dalí's 1955 *Corpus Hypercubus*, meant to give the viewer an experience of Christ in, or potentially as, a higher dimension.

By comparison, Colquhoun's cross figures were blocky, almost robotic, and they were the culmination of long-term meditations on the etheric results of placing squares atop one another. Given the dates of some of the larger paintings which reflect these themes, she may have completed a large number of these in the early 1950s, during the time she was working with Kenneth and Steffi Grant in the O.T.O. Some of these works were clearly magical experiments, studies in form and colour, where the human form was mapped not only onto a simple cross but also coloured in with various colours corresponding to the Kabballah. In one series she used Francis Barrett's *The Magus*, as well as *Liber 777*, to generate the colour schemes. We also see sketches of boxy angelic figures using a cruciform base and Kabbalistic colours. While many of these experiments would not have been meant for display, she did create a number of pieces which were intended as murals. *Heads of Angels* (1953) and *Crucifixion* (1953) were mural designs for Maze Hill Congregational Church in Greenwich. Her *Game of the Year* (1953), a large piece painted for the Football Association 90th anniversary exhibition titled 'Football and the Fine Arts', used some of the same features. Sadly, it was not selected for exhibition. It seems likely, given her preoccupation with building up figures in this way, that she intended to interject an esoteric dimension into a seemingly secular work. Woven into these pieces were

RIGHT
Horus (c. 1957)

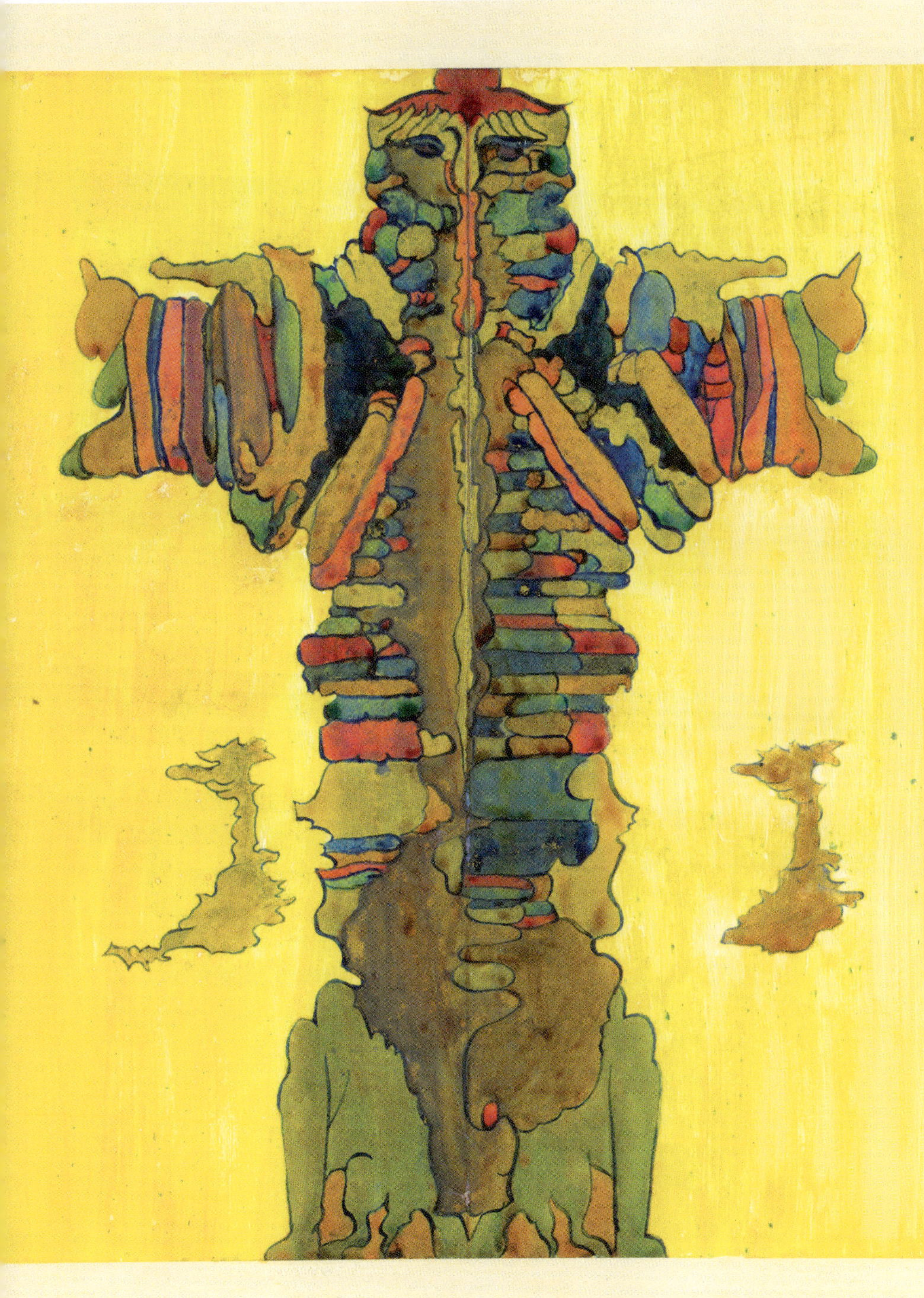

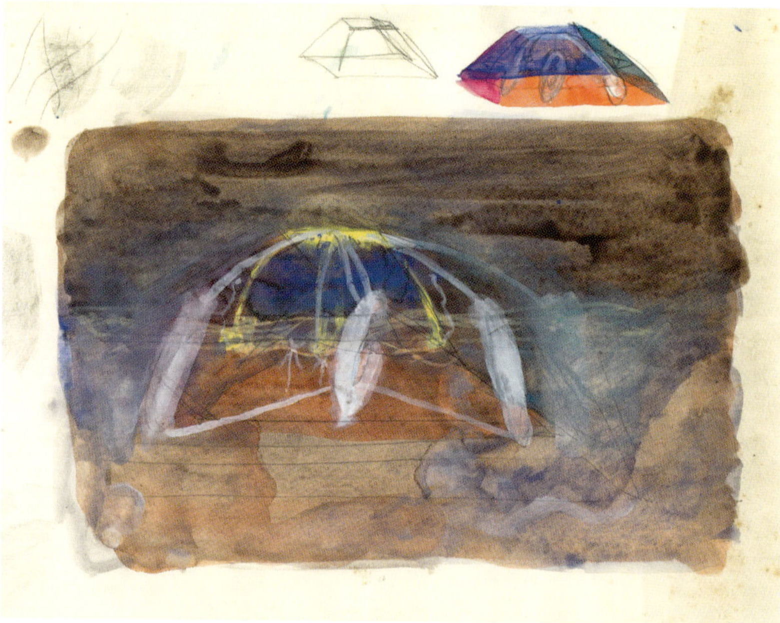

ABOVE

Mên-an-Tol sketch with Tesseract (c. 1942)

esoteric principles about the perfected human, that the everyday viewer would have been oblivious to.

Although Colquhoun's creations of these human/cross images appear to have peaked in the 1950s, we see her revisiting these visual motifs as late as 1981 with the Sufi-inspired *Torso*, a delicate work employing the *Lataif-e-sitta*, or areas of extrasensory perception cultivated in the body by Sufi mystics. Each area is represented by a particular colour, and Colquhoun's image is broadly a cruciform/human shape, with colour blocks representing these metaphysical centres. Colquhoun was mapping these principles on to the wider ideas of the cruciform representing the contact that can be made with higher dimensions through spiritual discipline.

RIGHT

Figure with Tesseract (c. 1940s)

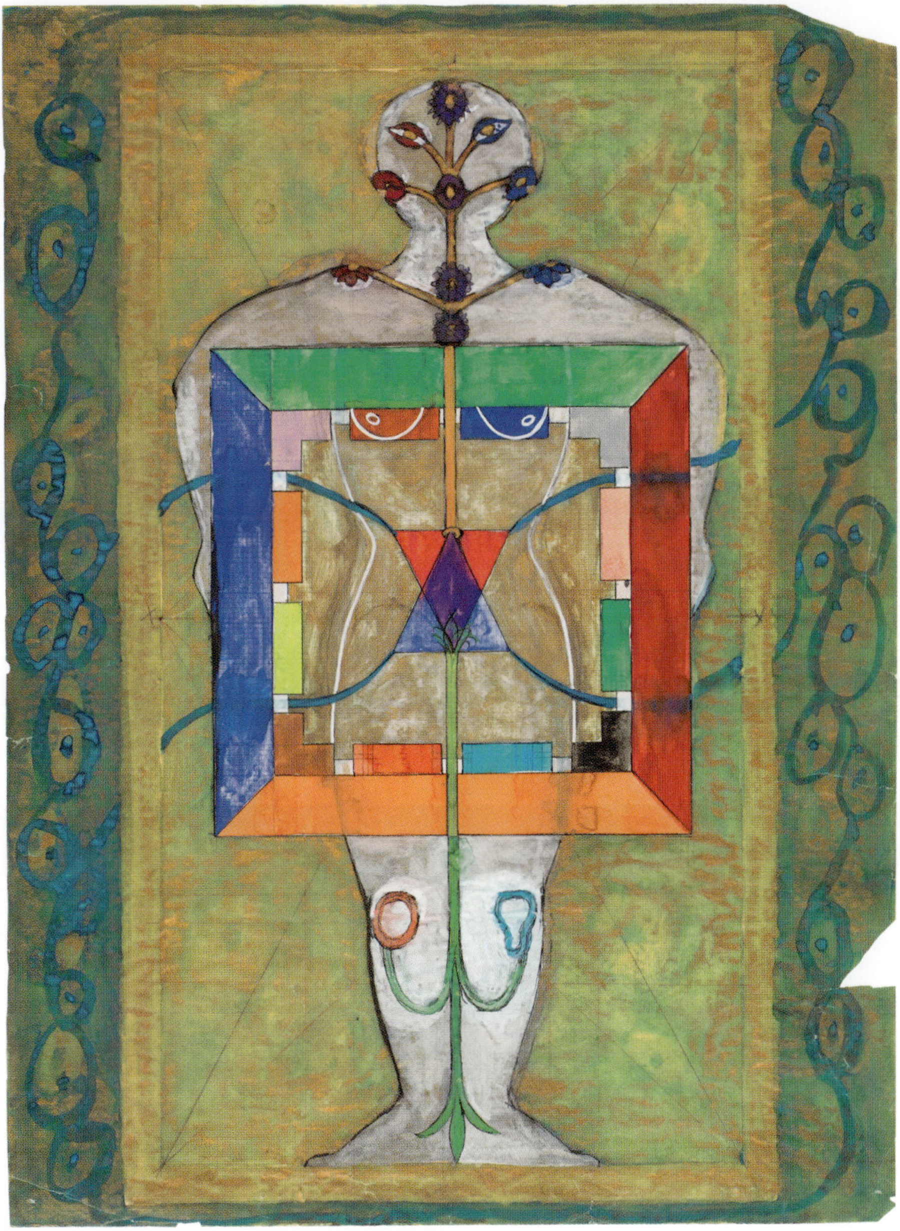

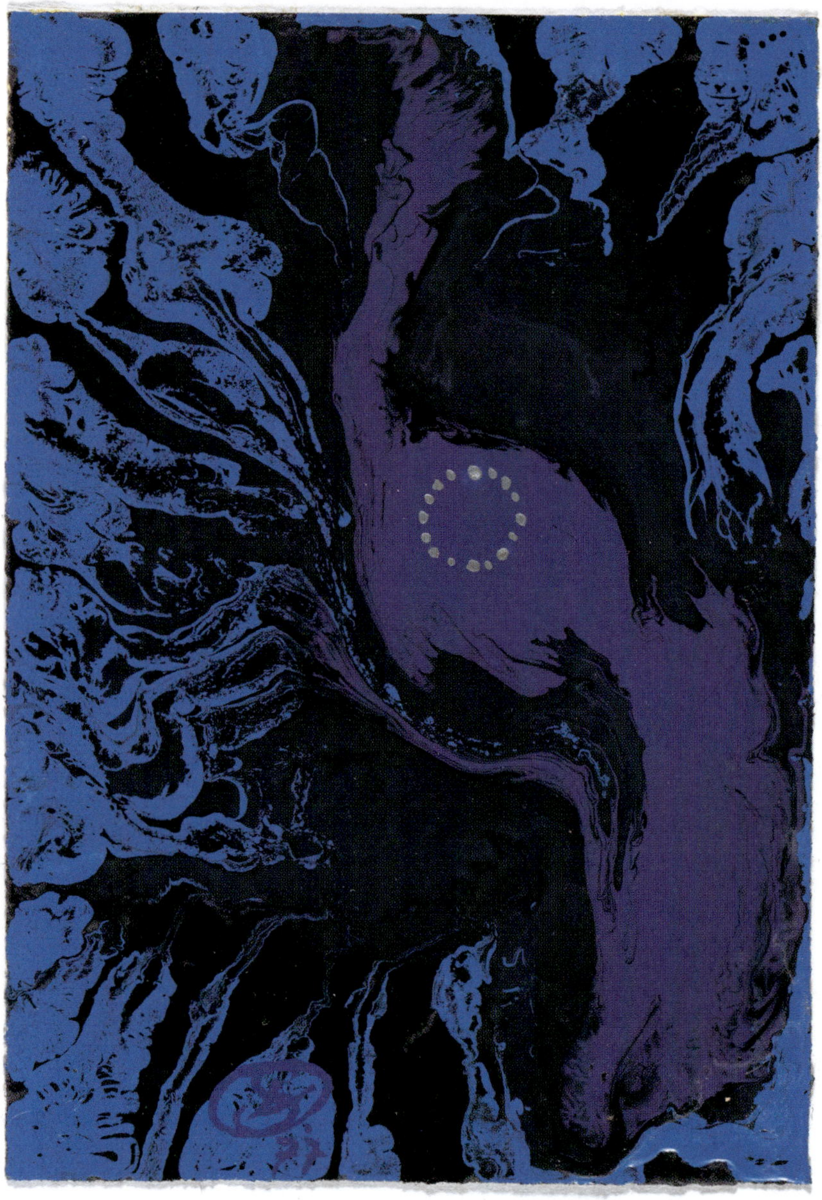

The Princess of the Echoing Hills. The Rose of the Palace of Earth

It was possibly in the late 1960s, in conjunction with her work with Tamara Bourkhoun, that Colquhoun started a project of dissecting cubes and hypercubes, and then working the dissected cubes into various forms. This was probably a project designed to help her cultivate fourth-dimensional vision. She wrote an unpublished essay on this theme entitled 'Dimensional Interrelations: A Meditation on the Platonic Solids', which addresses her experiments with creating, building up and breaking down Platonic solids and geometric forms. Although her ultimate intention is not clear, she may have been attempting to cultivate a particular way of seeing, as one might do with a set of Hinton cubes. As she described the process in the essay, she would start with a two-dimensional form, and then build it up into three dimensions, only to open it flat, and build it up again. She called this process 'Dimensional exchange', and she would continue this project until the form began to lose spatial integrity. She noted that the cube was the form which maintained integrity the longest, that one could build up and break down the most times. She completed this process with a square and expanded it to a form of 106 squares and 26 cubes. Her reporting on this project sounds somewhat obsessive, but is worth getting a taste of it to understand her thought process:

LEFT
Princess of the Echoing Hills
from *Taro of Colour* (1977)

> Though the rhythm of dimensional exchange has been carried two stages further than in the case of the tetrahedron, it would seem that this second cross is the final product of the square, unless it can be extended into a fourth dimension. But there is the possibility of a 'third dimension plus' in constructing the cross of the six directions...[106]

She never defined what the 'third dimension plus' means, or how it would be experienced. She continues instructing the reader on adding cubical arms to the 26 cube structure, opening them into the second dimension, building them up and breaking them down again. Her records show that she was undertaking these experiments herself with a number of figures, including swastikas, pyramids, dodecahedrons and octahedrons, and this was clearly an important magical experiment for her. Sacred geometry formed the basis of many of the magical traditions Colquhoun was involved in, from the Golden Dawn to Freemasonry.

The Golden Dawn intersected, in a rather literal way, with Colquhoun's interests in Platonic solids and crosses as ways to represent and contact etheric beings and dimensions. Colquhoun's archives show that she also completed a number of detailed studies and renderings of crosses which were used in the degree work of the Golden Dawn, meant to instruct the candidate about aspects of sacred geometry, their relationship to the Kabballah and the spiritual position of the candidate herself. The Golden Dawn uses a variety of crosses in its grade work, marked in different colours and symbols, including the *fylfot* cross or swastika, cubed crosses, ten-square and thirteen-square crosses. Each cross suggests a different focus of contemplation for the candidate, and before candidates enter the Second Order they are reintroduced to each of the crosses and must write a paper on their contemplations upon them. We find many of these sketches among Colquhoun's archives, possibly completed independently or as a part of her later work with the Temple of the Pyramid and Sphinx. It is important to remember, however, that these crosses are not necessarily evidence of the centrality of Christianity to Golden Dawn practice; they represent a wide variety of configurations, so one should be careful when attributing this symbolism to Colquhoun's work. In fact, the Calvary Cross is only one cross of many in the Golden Dawn system, placing the Christian death and resurrection into a wider cosmic and mythic framework. And it is in this wider realm of forms and myth that we find Colquhoun's own interests flourishing as part of a wider interest in sacred geometry, the fourth dimension and intersecting planes that she was able to apply to other magical projects, such as her Taro cards.

The 1977 Taro Deck and *The Decad of Intelligence*

In the 1970s Colquhoun's magical projects take on a new vibrance and polish. In addition to publishing *The Sword of Wisdom* in 1975, she finds a whole new set of homes for short essays and poems. There are a number of reasons why this time may have been more fruitful for Colquhoun than before. First, an increase in occult publications and 'zines in the 1970s provided more opportunities for her. We also see a return and refinement of her Hermetic roots for audiences that could handle her depth. In 1979 she published four pieces in Adam McLean's *Hermetic Journal*, a publication featuring a variety of sophisticated takes on esoteric topics. Colquhoun contributed three short but innovative pieces on occult colour theory, one of which provided commentary on a colouring scheme for Dee's *Sigillum Dei Aemeth*. A fourth was a memoir of her cousin Edward Garstin.

In the late 1970s Colquhoun also undertook a series of projects making small enamel paintings on thick watercolour paper or board. Her focus on enamels was a nod to Golden Dawn teachings; William Wynn Westcott advocated the use of enamel or lacquer when creating Golden Dawn implements and tablets to get the best and purest colour. This choice may also reflect the influence of similar enamel experiments of Gordon Onslow Ford in the late 1930s which, like Colquhoun's Taro, referenced metaphysical ideas of extra dimensions. Again, Colquhoun was not bound by fashion or times in how she expressed her influences. Many of the enamel pieces from this period would on the surface appear to be quite similar to one another. They were small, and the paint was applied to the paper in thick drips, with the result being multi-layered coloured ovoid shapes. Many of these paintings reflect natural themes, flowers, sunrises, clouds and underwater flora and fauna.

From these enamel studies two specific magical projects emerged, both designed primarily for contemplation; *Decad of Intelligence*, a colour study of the four scales of the ten sephiroth of the Tree of Life, and her Taro deck. Colquhoun describes her artistic approach to these projects in the terms of Matta's 'psychological morphology', again signalling that these were culminations and a synthesis reflecting a lifelong commitment to automatic techniques. In these paintings Colquhoun was working with colours that she believed to also be independent entities, and as such the technique would have provided access to dimensions and spaces which were not simply a reflection of her own emotional or psychological landscape, but which were representative of other planes of reality. The abstracted Taro and *The Decad of Intelligence* show an astonishing depth of esoteric theory and practice combined with an artistic sensibility that stretches the boundaries of what is conventionally considered to be esoteric art. These are striking in their abstractions. We see no tantalising representations of deity or spirit, no secret sigils to be decoded. Instead, Colquhoun provides , for the viewer, direct access to other places. These pieces communicate on an etheric level, not through the logical mind.

The first of these projects was her Taro, exhibited at the Newlyn Art Gallery in Cornwall in 1977. Over her lifetime she wrote a number of essays on the tarot and made sketches of individual cards prior to the creation of her own deck which occurred, interestingly, only toward the end of her life. Perhaps most intriguing of these tantalisingly unfinished projects is the undated remnant of a decalcomania of what would have been an Ace of Wands. In *The Magical Writings of Ithell Colquhoun*, editor Steve Nichols includes a series of undated essays on the conventional trump cards, mainly concerned with representational aspects and narrative symbolism.[107] These essays are highly syncretic in nature and draw on a variety of esoteric traditions, as one might expect in a system so reliant on correspondences. In addition to commenting on how they might function in divination, Colquhoun links the cards to Freemasonic ideals and Golden Dawn ritual practice.

In 1967 and 1968 Colquhoun completed a series of personal meditations and visions on the conventional tarot in conjunction with the Temple of the Pyramid and Sphinx. Some of these meditations and notes were the subject of correspondence between Colquhoun and Bourkhoun regarding Colquhoun's command of tarot material. The notes show that she was bringing together a variety of approaches, including Crowley and Harris's Thoth Deck, Case's Builders of the Temple of the Adytum deck, the Golden Dawn and the Rider/Waite/Smith deck. Although no figurative attempts at creating a deck for this order have been discovered, correspondence between Bourkhoun and Colquhoun does indicate that the two of them were working towards creating such a deck. Yet it is only in 1977 that Colquhoun completes her own set of cards, and very much on her own stylistic terms.

Colquhoun's Taro deck (Taro was her preferred spelling) looks simple in its abstraction, but it was a remarkably complex enterprise. It is likely that this project was considered to be a refinement of her ideas about art and magic, and less about the production of a functional deck. Colquhoun's Taro deck was created in prototype from enamel on paper and exhibited only once in her lifetime. Running from July 26 – August 13 1977, the exhibition was accompanied by a short essay, 'The Taro as Colour' which outlines the guiding principles of the deck's design and organisation.[108]

Colquhoun's deck represents her thoughts about tarot cards in a very stripped down and concentrated form. Yet the structure and form of the deck is complex, and the accompanying essay is almost unreadable for anyone not deeply immersed in the theories which underlie it. One wonders how this small exhibition was received. While the pieces themselves are beautifully executed, the theoretical framework is, still, somewhat impenetrable, especially for a viewer with little occult background. Despite the theoretical complexity of the deck, the viewer is relieved of the burdens of imagery, storytelling and interpretation. Rather, with this project (as with her life's work) there is a focus on revelation for the viewer. As with the images of the *Decad of Intelligence*, this deck was designed for use in meditation and contemplation, not divination.

Ever since the Freemasons and other esotericists adopted tarot during the 18th and 19th centuries, the cards have been at odds with themselves. While the court and suit cards have historical connections to gaming and cartomancy, the cards of the Major Arcana are often framed as an allegory of the road to spiritual enlightenment. Thus, the purpose of the cards often feels fractured in supporting documents: divination is base and material, and tarot should be primarily supporting the spiritual journey; but if you do need to use them for some material insight, direction is provided. However, the Major and Minor Arcana are distinct in their visual qualities and often lack obvious integration in a single system. Colquhoun's deck goes some way toward integrating the Major and Minor Arcanas by removing the visual symbolism, backgrounding the narrative aspects and foregrounding the Kabbalistic and elemental connections between the cards. Although the Major Arcana remain visually distinct from the rest of the deck, the journey takes on a different quality.

Colquhoun came to believe, as did many early occultists, that divination was a debasement of the cards. While the Golden Dawn teachings did provide methods and descriptions that are suited to divination, there was a separate set of practices reserved for contemplation, and she was promoting that function with this deck. This non-divinatory approach also reflects the view of Paul Foster Case's esoteric school, the Builders of the Adytum, on how the tarot should best be used. Colquhoun had arrived at a rather low opinion of anything that might suggest material rather than spiritual pursuits. As such, the design of each of the cards was to work as a source of illumination and visioning, which also made them well-suited to the environment of an exhibition, since museums and galleries invite reflection.

Colquhoun's vision for this deck is wholly unique. It is one of the first abstract tarot decks, and an early deck relying wholly on Kabbalistic colour schemes. Much of the structure of Colquhoun's deck is outlined in her essay 'The Taro as Colour', where she helps the viewer understand the underlying principles and connections of the cards. Each card can be taken on its own terms, as each has its own distinct title, derived from the Golden Dawn source text on the tarot 'Book T', and reflects the Order's inner teachings about the nature of each card.[109] In Colquhoun's accompanying essay, she notes that the titles of the cards 'act as a mantra to the design's yantra'. For people familiar with tarot decks derived from the Rider/Waite/Smith deck these card titles may seem unfamiliar, yet their unfamiliarity allows the viewer to approach each image on its own terms; an important aspect of this project.

A defining feature of the structure is that Colquhoun does not separate out the major arcana from the minor arcana, or 'decanate cards', named for the 36 astrological decans, and the court cards. As with Golden Dawn decks in general, the Aces and court cards in her system take a more preeminent role than in other decks, which often emphasise the Major Arcana and their narrative of the seeker's esoteric journey. Colquhoun's Major Arcana colour scheme follows directly from her *Decad of Intelligence* project, where she constructs each of the sephiroth out of the colours of each of the four worlds. The colours of the Major Arcana in this deck are derived from the colours of each path in each of the four worlds, with the King at the centre, radiating outwards to the Queen, Emperor and Empress scales. Throughout the deck she uses 'flecking' and 'raying' which are techniques for expressing various colour scales, particularly the Princess scale, as outlined by Florence Farr in Golden Dawn documents.[110] Colquhoun groups her Major Arcana cards according to element and then incorporates them more broadly into each suit.

While the Kabbalistic affinities drive the colour schemes for each card, the structure of the whole deck emphasises the elemental affinities of the cards. The colour patterns of the deck are regularised so as to reinforce the structure of the deck. The elemental colour scheme of each suit is revealed through the Aces, emanating from the centre of the card to eventually become the background of each suit card: indigo for earth, lighter blue for water, red for fire and yellow for air.

Although the Golden Dawn normally used black to represent earth, Colquhoun here uses a deep purple or indigo, which appears to be an elemental colour scheme also found in some of her experimental colour studies of gnostic crosses and cubes, and which reflects another influence from Case.

Each card in a suit emanates down from the Ace. The Court cards form the link cards between the Aces and the decanate cards, somewhat like a web. The colours of the court cards link the Aces of each deck to the decanate cards. The yellow of air, indigo of earth, red of fire and light blue of water are repeated at the centre and focal point of each court card, and these ultimately become the background of each of the decanate cards, as though they are bursting forth from the centre of the court cards. It is a remarkably complex scheme, and only when they are all laid together, in the order that Colquhoun gives in her essay, can one see how they are visually connected. This is not how they were displayed in the exhibition, so one can only wonder how it was received. Did the viewers at the Newlyn Gallery see them there, all 78 cards packed tightly together in five frames, as merely a wild art project?

Although the *Decad of Intelligence*, created in 1978 and 1979, is in some ways a distinct project from Colquhoun's Taro, it is still conceptually and visually linked and can be considered a companion piece. *The Decad of Intelligence* is based on the list of sephirotic intelligences set out in the *Sepher Yetzirah*. Although the text and images were at some point separated, possibly after Colquhoun's death, it was designed to be a small book of ten enamel pieces, each depicting a different sephira, accompanied by a description of the properties of each one. Colquhoun likely intended *The Decad of Intelligence* to be a complete work, although it is not clear whether she envisioned this as a singular artifact for private or group-based meditation, or if she had wider interest in distribution or just exhibition. Colquhoun had partially completed several different illustrated magical projects in her life, including *Diagrams of Love* in the 1940s, and a project structured around the Celtic tree alphabet in 1972, and none of these was fully realised.

Colquhoun's text for the *Decad* is regular, sparse and poetic, and provides a list of the correspondences of each sephira, including its location, corresponding section of the body, elemental and planetary associations, fragrances and flowers, alchemical associations, and the vision that the sephira is intended to inspire. Most of these correspondences are drawn directly from Aleister Crowley's *Liber 777* and the *Sepher Yetzirah*, but despite her accompanying text, the bold enamels were designed to bypass intellectual processing.

As with the Taro, it is clear that Colquhoun intended this work to be used as a guide to contemplation for understanding the deep nature of each of the sephira. The paintings are masterful, with the paint thickly laid on the paper. Each is a colour study, encompassing the colours of each of the four different colour scales of the Tree of Life. The colours for each sephira generally move from the King Scale forming the centre, surrounded by the Queen Scale, the Emperor Scale and the Empress Scale, the latter generally finished by hand. The sephira are not portrayed as round, but more generally oblong and irregular, with the colours running together in ways that may defy the visual expectations of some practitioners. The layout of the enamel on the paper shares some features with the Taro deck, yet the shapes are much more vulvic and entirely contained, probably representing the Golden Dawn teaching that the sephira are essentially feminine. However, each sephira also represents the hermaphroditic formula that is at the heart of Colquhoun's belief about the fourfold nature of the Kabbalah.

Colquhoun's Taro and the *Decad of Intelligence* represent an accomplished culmination and beautiful synthesis of her magical work and her Surrealism. She executed bold and bright automatic enamels, which is a challenge in itself, supported by subtle and complex esoteric theory. She continued to make esoterically informed art after these pieces, but these are a high point.

Ithell Colquhoun's life and work was informed by and in service to the occult. Although in her essays we can get a glimpse of the breadth and depth of her knowledge, one feels cheated by not having had access to a wider and more coherent slice of her esoteric expertise. She routinely sent novels and short stories to publishers, but no full-length didactic manuscript on any occult topic by Colquhoun exists. It is not as though she didn't have the capacity to produce such a work. But, like many women, she was more comfortable in the realm of the memoir and of subjectivity than she was in the position of authority. But what Colquhoun did leave behind, showing us how deep her waters were, are so many pieces of art and esoteric experiments that give us a glimpse of how she saw the world, and imagined the world beyond.

'More Brilliant Than Crystal':

VI – The Legacy

NEXT PAGE The Hand of Ithell altar from Steve Patterson's Ancient Scent project in 2016.

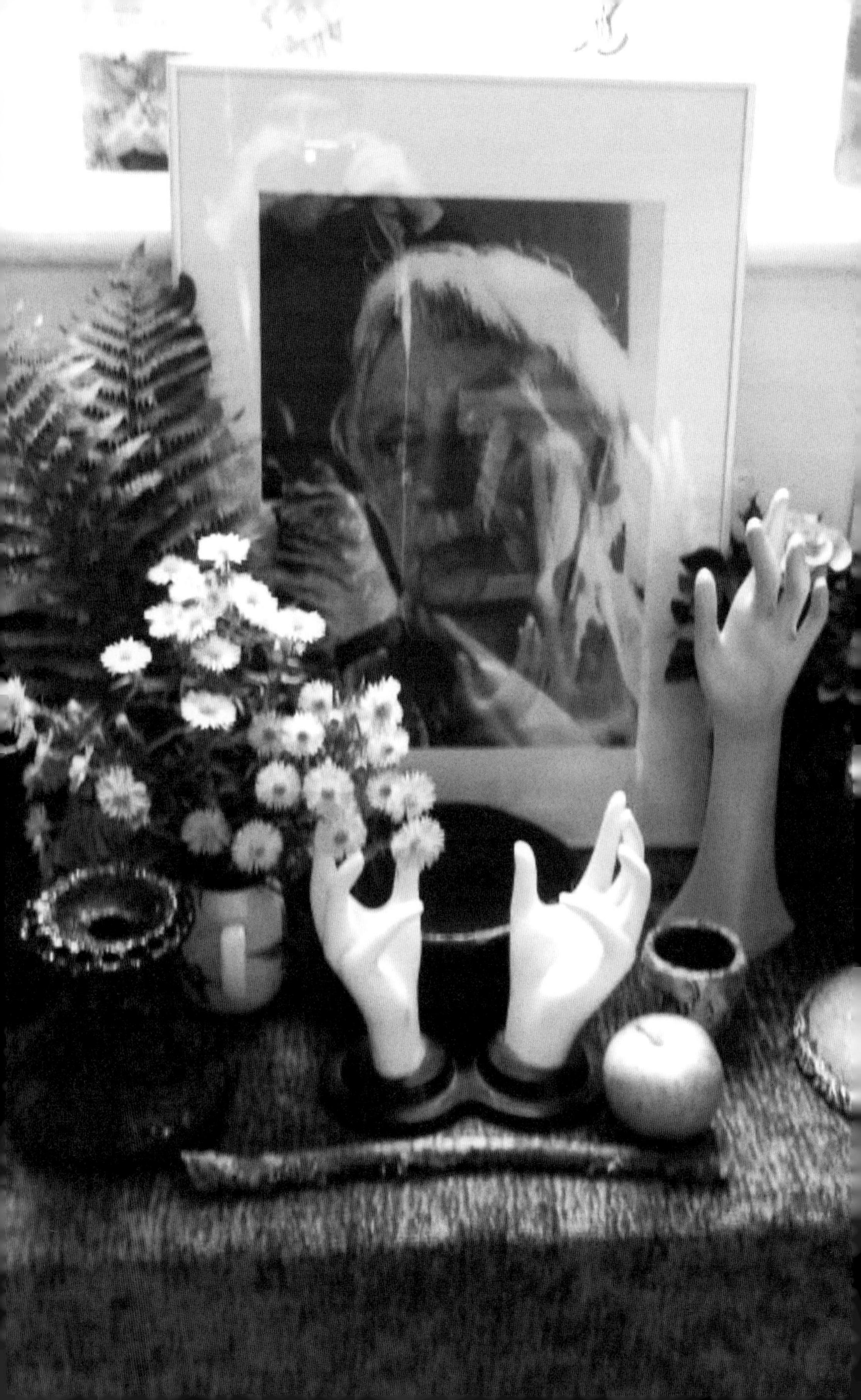

VI

> I prefer individual achievement, or even individual obscurity to reflected glory. If my intimates prove disappointing, my universe does not collapse. If I win success, I want it rewarded openly and in my own name; and if I go to pieces, I have only myself to thank. If I have talent, I want to develop it myself, rather than delegate to descendants, who may not be trustworthy. But then, I am an altruist.
>
> – Ithell Colquhoun, from 'Clever Women'[III]

The last decade of Colquhoun's life was not easy. Her letters show that she struggled with isolation, phobias and depression. Her health had always been fragile, and her solitude in the tiny village of Paul, at a distance from so many health and support services, was taking a toll on her. However, as was her way, Colquhoun was not complacent. She sought help, sometimes in unconventional places, and was generally frustrated by an inability to get the support she needed. Letters show that she wrote to both the BBC and Westward, the local commercial television station at the time, to complain about a lack of services in Cornwall for depression. She also sought out alternative treatments, as she had done throughout her life, availing herself of psychic and remote healers who worked with energy telepathically. Cornwall has been chronically underserved for mental health, and it was both brave and futile for Colquhoun to have reached out as she did for help. It seems as though the balance that she had struck earlier in her life between beloved and quiet privacy and some form of community had fallen into loneliness and anxiety. Yet from photos it is clear that she found solace in her garden tending to her plants, and her ginger cat, and enjoying beautiful views out to the Atlantic that she could see from the front of Stone Cross Cottage.

She kept creating visual art until around 1983, although her production in the early 1980s was very diminished. In her final years, Colquhoun returned to her beloved Lamorna where she was a resident of Menwinnion House, now called Menwinnion Care Home. She died of heart failure on April 11, 1988, and her ashes were scattered on the beach near Lamorna Cove. When she died in 1988, she left an odd sense of defeat behind her. Her will is confusing, even though it bespeaks an attempt to be generous in remembering the agencies and institutions that had given her comfort during her life. Her home and the contents of her studio were willed to the National Trust, who were directed to sell it all to help keep undeveloped spaces of land in West Cornwall. Although this was clearly intended to be a noble gesture, it shows the degree to which she had stopped thinking about her legacy. This was a woman who had saved nearly every scrap of paper, every piece of art she had ever created. One wonders what her studio must have looked like! Instead of thinking about where she might house her works for future generations, she told the National Trust to sell it all. This put the National Trust in a difficult position, since they became unwitting conservators of a collection that is hardly in their area. This collection was a gift to the nation and to the world. To separate it might dilute the power of this woman's artistic voice. Yet keeping it poses its own problems in terms of conservation, access and space. Colquhoun was no stranger to the world of art and archives. Did she feel so defeated that she accepted that her work was to be scattered to the four winds? Luckily, her work has been well preserved and in 2019 the Tate acquired the National Trust collection which will undoubtedly help promote and secure her legacy.

There is always a sense in looking at Colquhoun's body of work that she was ahead of her time, even though she identified as a Traditionalist. Ironically Colquhoun's vision of returning to a 'Golden Age' is, in some ways, deeply conservative, but her idea of what it would take to get humanity back to that place would require radical shifts, and her vision of enlightened and genderless beings seems oddly progressive, especially today. We know she was forward-thinking from some of the theories she was exploring in her art and writing, and more importantly in the degree to which she was not interested in compromising her vision because of social expectations about women's roles and societal position. Yet even twenty years after her death, people were only starting to awaken to the real scope of her vision. No longer the 'lost Surrealist', she is now being rediscovered as a mystic and an esoteric artist. At her home in Cornwall, she began to take on the status of a magical ancestor, her spirit tied to the essence of the land. In the Autumn of 2015, Cornwall-based artist and magician Steve Patterson, inspired by Colquhoun's work and magic, started an immersive community art project called Ancient Scents, that wove art, ritual and automatism together. Patterson writes:

> The tale begins back in 2015 when a group of artists, performers, writers, and sorcerers gathered together in Lamorna Village Hall in West Cornwall and hatched a fiendish plan to invoke the genius loci of Lamorna Valley, with the Surrealist artist and occultist Ithell Colquhoun (1906–1988) as our guiding force and tutelary spirit.[112]

Patterson had a special relationship with Colquhoun's work and writing about the sacred places of Cornwall. He used her essay 'The Mantic Stain' as a template for his project, and each month for a year, artists would meet up for workshops where they conducted rituals, completed divinations and created art based on Colquhoun's automatic techniques. The year concluded with an exhibition in Lamorna Village hall, complete with an altar to Colquhoun herself. In 2017, several of the artists completed a second Ancient Scents project based in Ireland, inspired by *Crying of the Wind.*

Colquhoun is having a continuing impact on the art world. A new crop of contemporary artists are discovering her unique blend of art and magic, and have taken her unconventional ways and committed feminism as inspiration for their own works. Feminism will continue to increase the visibility of Colquhoun's legacy. Colquhoun was a woman artist who unapologetically focused on women's sexuality and societal roles; she was interested in empowerment for women on a mythic level, and to share her vision and her magical reality she had no compunction about shattering taboos. Colquhoun's feminism initially seems to reify stereotypical associations about the nature of woman, especially if it is read as an equation of woman with nature or receptivity, but her feminism was complex, and intersected with her queerness.

Colquhoun's fearless qualities have inspired British punk artist Linder Sterling, known as Linder. Initially known for producing album covers for bands such as the Buzzcocks, much of her work has explored the condition and objectification of women, using collage, cut-ups and photomontage, frequently using fashion and household magazines to create bizarre and sensual visual juxtapositions. In many ways Linder's corpus intersects with Colquhoun's earlier works in their approach to taboo and the challenge of the male gaze. In recent years Linder has also expanded into installations, ballet and musical performances. In 2014 Linder completed a residency at the Tate St. Ives which piqued her interest in the work of Colquhoun, especially her status as outsider to the art scene in West Cornwall.

I spoke with Linder about the continuing influence that Colquhoun has had on her work since her 2014 residency. I had mentioned to her Steve Patterson's experience of what he calls 'The Hand of Ithell' effect, where when you come into contact with the spirit of Colquhoun, she starts to shape your life. The notion resonated with Linder the way it did with me. Her encounter with Colquhoun entirely reshaped her own approaches to her art:

> The Hand of Ithell is a curious phenomenon. The hand has a light touch which can easily be mistaken for coincidence

> or serendipity. I sometimes wilfully call out to the Hand of Ithell Colquhoun though, especially during my ongoing act of homage to her mantic stain technique.
>
> In 2014, the Hand of Ithell held my hand as I laid down the surgeon's scalpel that I'd used for over four decades to create photomontage. In exchange for sacrificing the blade, the Hand of Ithell then offered me enamel paints to let spill over the surfaces of found photographs. I'd found a large stash of *Health & Efficiency* magazines in a bookshop in Penzance, the shop was a stone's throw away from the Newlyn Gallery. The naturist magazines all date from the last years of Colquhoun's life, another coincidence or the Hand of Ithell at work?
>
> The leap in faith from the precise cut of a scalpel to suddenly having only the slenderest amount of control over enamel paints took some time to adjust to. The Hand of Ithell has taught me to be far more fluid in my image making and to not only contemplate the surface image but to see through it and beyond it. 'Mind pictures' emerge from the enamels as they slowly congeal and my fascination for the mantic stain technique became such that I wanted to know what a mantic chord would sound like and which ingredients a mantic perfume would contain and what sort of mind pictures would it conjure up in the wearer?[113]

Her residency also resulted in two interconnected pieces inspired by Colquhoun's work for the British Art Show.

> In 2015 I was very fortunate to work with Northern Ballet and the choreographer Kenneth Tindall to explore how the mantic stain principle could influence choreography. My son Maxwell Sterling was encouraged to create a mantic hallucinogenic soundtrack and I worked with Dovecot Studio in Edinburgh to create a rug that could shape shift amidst the dancers. Nothing

> was ever quite what it seemed in the Children of the Mantic Stain ballet, we were all touched by the Hand of Ithell.

Linder named her brightly coloured rug: *Diagrams of Love: Marriage of Eyes*, inspired by Colquhoun's art and poetry series of the 1940s. The piece is a riot of colour, incorporating eye motifs that give it the feel of a giant floating, undulating moth. The second piece was a commissioned ballet called *Children of the Mantic Stain*, based on Colquhoun's essay of the same title. Linder has said that the ballet was an imaginative reconstruction of a meeting between Colquhoun and Barbara Hepworth at the Penwith Arts Ball in 1956.[114]

The rediscovery of Colquhoun has come with what might be considered a wider 'Shamanic turn' in art, with an increase in installations and performance pieces intended to inspire contemplation and spiritual experience in the audience. However, many of these inspired artists are not performing within a religious context as adherents of particular practices. The artists may be providing a commentary on religious behaviour or iconography, although they frequently employ elements of ritual or religiosity to cause a change of consciousness or awareness in the audience. The 2009 *Dark Monarch* exhibition at Tate St. Ives was a forerunner here, with a focus on magic and the esoteric in Modernist art and particularly on the ways these are expressed in British landscape art. This raised Colquhoun's profile as there were some pieces of hers in the exhibition, and her occult book collection was on display. But, again, many of the selections were more about what they might invoke in the viewer, rather than explicitly about art as esoteric practice.

RIGHT Linder, *Sisters of the Mantic Stain VIII* (2019)

Esoteric art is emerging as a distinct category, but what it means is still not well defined. It is too easy to say that it is 'occult art' rebranded, yet it is not the same as simply religious art or even visionary art, although it shares features with both. Although Colquhoun would definitely have identified with specific labels as an artist during her

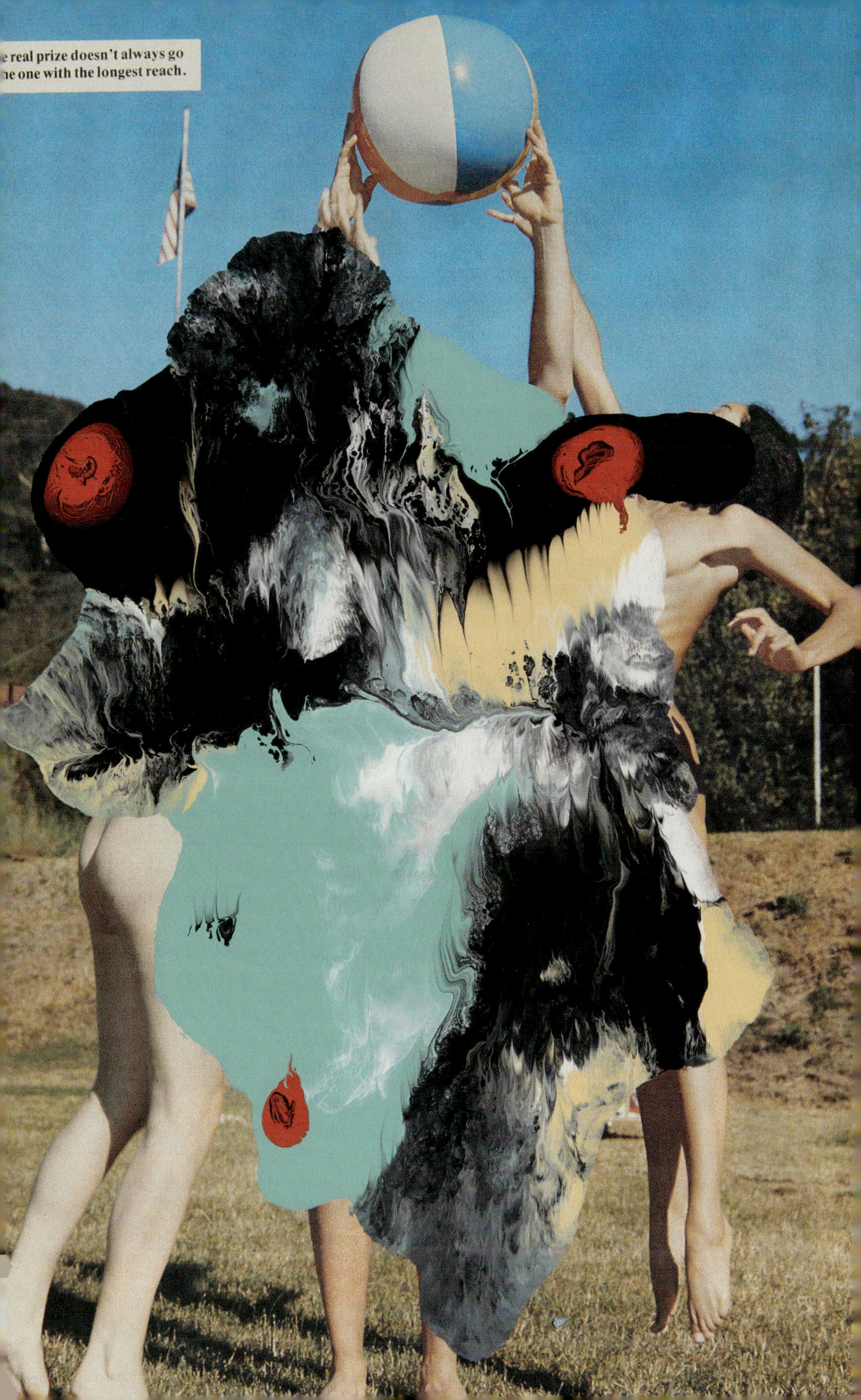
e real prize doesn't always go
he one with the longest reach.

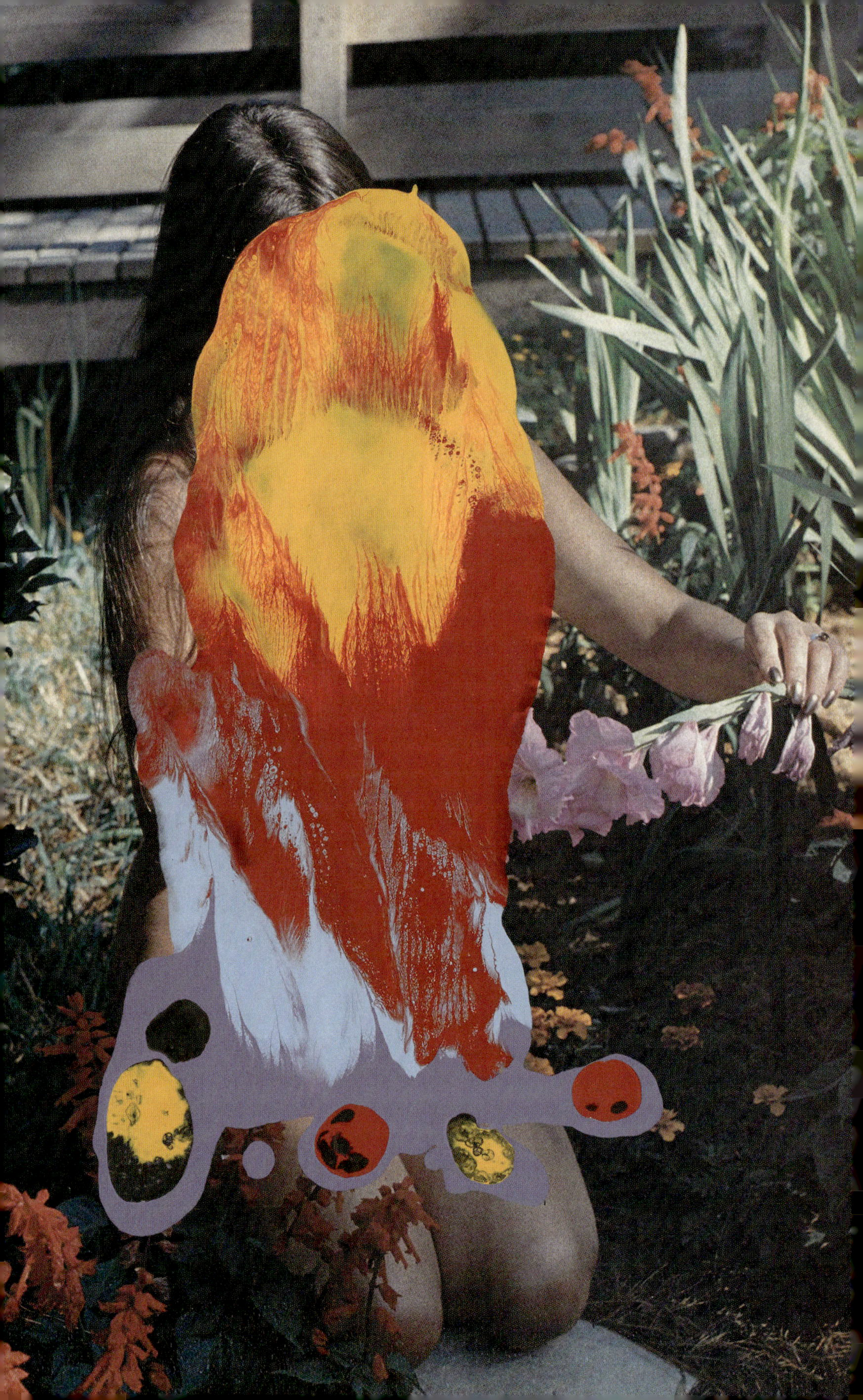

life – Surrealist, and she might even have accepted Fantastic – new understandings of the occult as a motivator for artistic practice are being examined as never before, and it is the flowering of the idea of esoteric art as its own category that is supporting the rediscovery of Colquhoun and her work. The rise of interest in esoteric art, as shown by the recent wealth of academic books, conferences and exhibitions, helps create a new cultural space that had previously been poorly defined and without much institutional support. The success of the *Hilma af Klint: Paintings for the Future* exhibition at the Guggenheim museum in 2018–2019 demonstrates the growing wider interest in esoteric art as practice, and highlights the historic contributions of women artists to pioneering this trend. It may well be that Colquhoun may be just as fruitfully examined in the company of artists such as the early twentieth century Dutch Theosophist Olga Fröbe-Kapteyn and the Swiss Emma Kunz whose abstractions were explicitly designed to bridge the viewer with spiritual realms. However, despite growing interest, the role of practice and belief on the part of artists, audiences and associated communities may still have an isolating effect on this category because of persistent associations with the irrational, the marginal and the taboo. And that is not necessarily a bad thing, because by its very nature the esoteric is not for everyone.

LEFT
Linder, *Superautomatism XVIII* (2015)

Esoteric art engages with spiritual practices and systems that are unorthodox, which run alongside or even counter to mainstream religiosity. For decades the idea that artists may have a sustained occult practice, or in other words that they 'actually believed that stuff', was a difficult pill for art historians to swallow. And not just art historians, but academics and literary scholars. It was more comfortable to look at the role of the occult either as a cultural motif, or perhaps as a sign that the artist belonged to a certain order or had specialist occult knowledge. But art and literature as practice, ritual, divination and invocation moves into a realm of religiosity that is still uncomfortable for some scholars. Suddenly art moves beyond artifact and becomes the playground for the anthropologist, ethnographer or religious

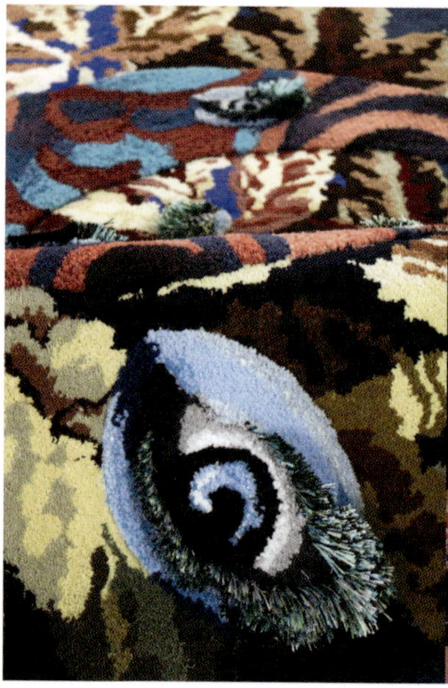

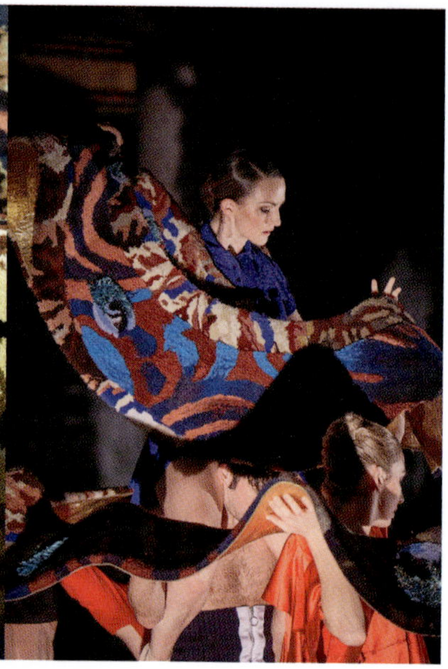

ABOVE LEFT
Linder, *Diagrams of Love: Marriage of Eyes* (2015)

ABOVE RIGHT
Linder's ballet, *Children of the Mantic Stain* performed in Leeds in 2015, featuring *Diagrams of Love, Marriage of Eyes* (2015)

studies scholar, looking at meanings, world views and experiences in addition to the ever-attractive hidden symbol. In this way Ithell Colquhoun's body of work is ripe for a new generation of scholars and artists to mine for inspiration, because we can now see the whole of the artist, her doodles, sketches, writings and magical experiments as part of a complex and coherent worldview, the result of a lifetime of study and practice, and the cultivation of a very particular way of seeing the world.

Future generations may see her as decoupled from the history of Surrealism, and view her work through the lenses of the esoteric and, importantly, feminism, as we continue to hear the echoes of a rare and uncompromising woman. Colquhoun left us so much, yet in knowing her genius, I mourn for the kinds of work we never saw from her, the books and essays that would tell the world exactly what she was trying to do, that would teach us her secrets, and establish

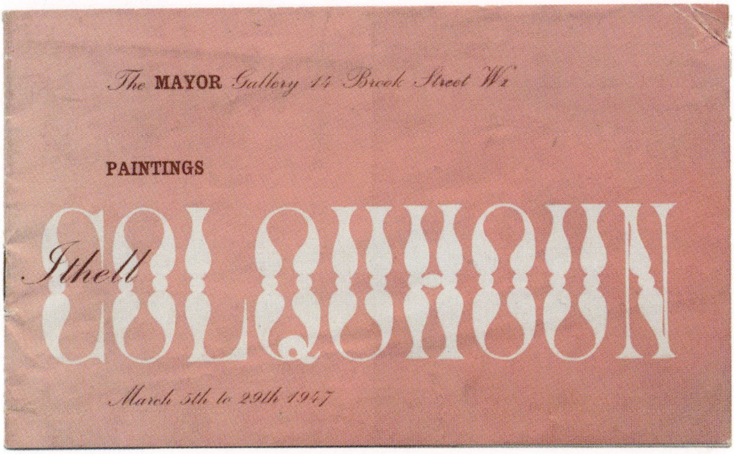

ABOVE
Catalogue image from 'Ithell Colquhoun: Paintings', Mayor Gallery, 1947.

her as the expert she was, because so many of us are desperately hungry for the rare exemplar of women's authority to jump out of the past and fill that historical void. But Colquhoun did not live in a time that supported who she was. She didn't have a network that would nurture her capacities, and there were no platforms for a voice so strong and resistant. It is only now that we are starting to reshape history through the inclusion of silenced and unacknowledged women. There is no doubt that Colquhoun would have utterly hated many things about the world as it has progressed since her death, yet ironically it would have been a much more accommodating world for her. I think she would love the fact that so many are reaching through the dimensions of space and time to find her now, and bring her back.

NEXT PAGE
Dryad: Vine (1971)

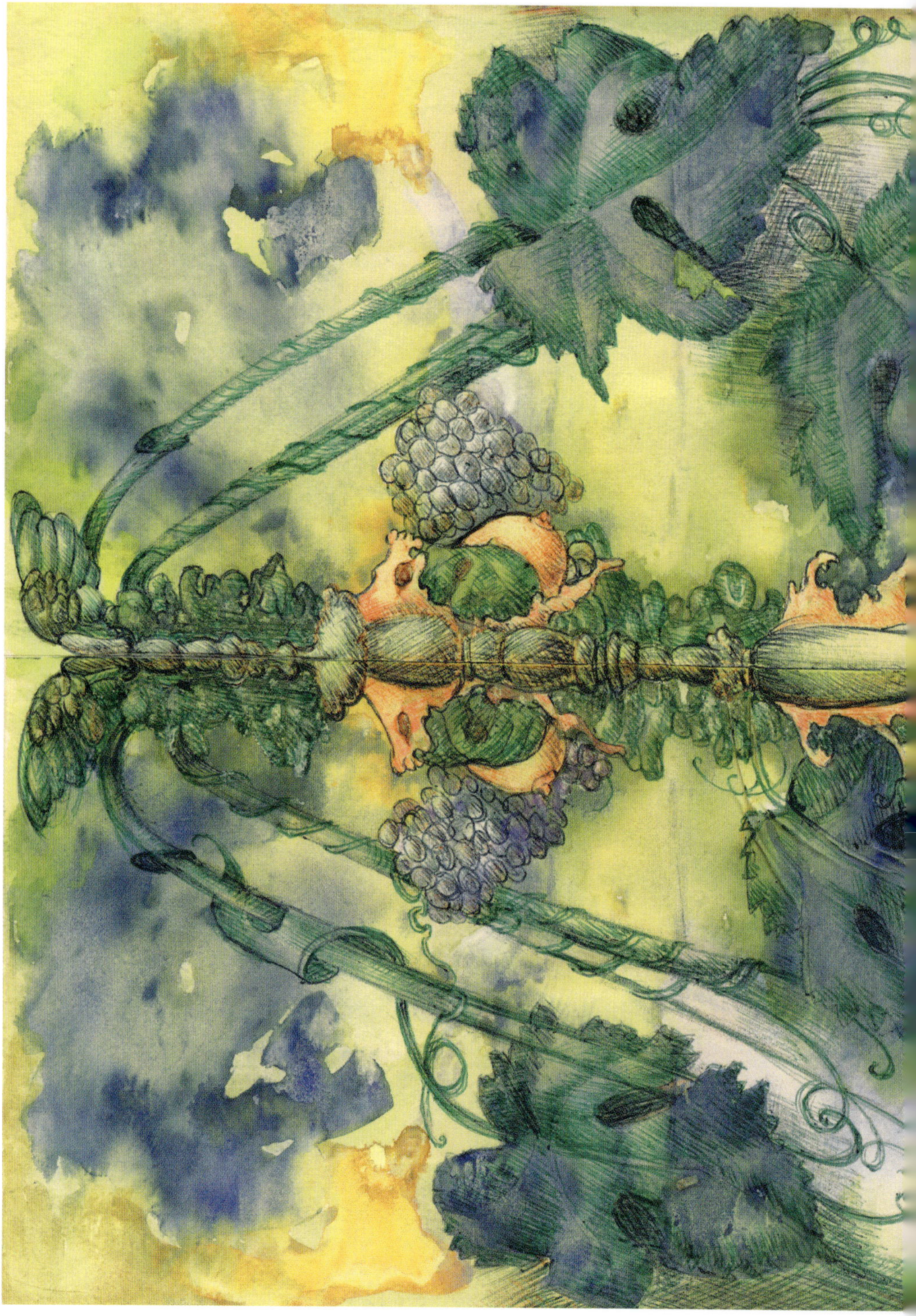

Image Credits

Permission for all images kindly granted by Spire Healthcare, The Noise Abatement Society and The Samaritans. Medium and dimensions derived from Shillitoe (2010), The Ithell Colquhoun Catalogue of the Tate Gallery Archives, and personal estimation.

p. 10 Colquhoun in her Garden at Stone Cross Cottage. © Philip Stokes 1984

p. 24 Photograph of Colquhoun as a young girl. © Tate Gallery

p. 31 Colquhoun dancing at Cheltenham School of Art. Photograph by Hugo van Wadenoyen

p. 42 The chateau at Chemilieu, France, 1939. Photograph by Elisabeth Onslow Ford Rouslin. Image from the Gordon Onslow Ford collection and archive, courtesy of the Lucid Art Foundation

p. 48 Ithell Colquhoun at the Mayor Gallery, 1939. *The Sketch*, 14 June 1939. © Illustrated London News Group

p. 49 Ithell Colquhoun, *Scylla* (1938) Oil on board. 36 x 24in. (91.4 x 61cm.) © Samaritans, Noise Abatement Society and Spire Healthcare

p. 50–52 Ithell Colquhoun, *Gouffres Amers* (1939), Oil on canvas. 28½ x 36in (71.2 x 91.3cm). Image supplied courtesy of The Hunterian Gallery. © Samaritans, Noise Abatement Society and Spire Healthcare

p. 54 Colquhoun with Gordon Onslow Ford at the Ideal Palace of Facteur Cheval, 1939. Image from the Gordon Onslow Ford collection and archive, courtesy of the Lucid Art Foundation

p. 54 The chateau at Chemilieu, 1939. Image from the Gordon Onslow Ford collection and archive, courtesy of the Lucid Art Foundation

p. 55 At the Ideal Palace of Facteur Cheval, 1939. Image from the Gordon Onslow Ford collection and archive, courtesy of the Lucid Art Foundation

p. 56 Ithell Colquhoun, *Ages of Man* (1944) Oil on panel. 11½ x 7in. (29.4 x 18.2cm.) © Samaritans, Noise Abatement Society and Spire Healthcare

p. 65 Ithell Colquhoun, *Sardine and Eggs* (c. 1941) Watercolour. 8¾ x 6¾in. (22.3 x 17.3cm.) ©Tate

p. 66–68 Ithell Colquhoun, *The Pine Family* (1940) Oil on canvas. 18 x 20in. (45.7 x 50.8cm.) ©Tate

p. 81 Ithell Colquhoun, *Attributes of the Moon* (1947) Oil on board. 33¾ x 13¼in. (86.5 x 34.2cm.) © Samaritans, Noise Abatement Society and Spire Healthcare

p. 82 & 84 Ithell Colquhoun, *Arbour* (1946) Oil on board. 9 x 13½in. (22.9 x 34.3cm.) Image courtesy of Richard Shillitoe. © Samaritans, Noise Abatement Society and Spire Healthcare

p. 83 & 85 Ithell Colquhoun, *Gorgon* (1946) Oil on board. 22¾ x 22¾in. (57.8 x 57.8cm.) Image courtesy of Richard Shillitoe. © Samaritans, Noise Abatement Society and Spire Healthcare

IMAGE CREDITS

p. 87 Ithell Colquhoun, *Autumnal Equinox* (1949) Oil on canvas. 80 x 32in. (205 x 82cm.) Image courtesy of Sacha Llewellyn. © Samaritans, Noise Abatement Society and Spire Healthcare

p. 90 Luna or Large pea-green phalaena illustration from The Naturalist's Miscellany (1789–1813) by George Shaw (1751–1813). CC0 1.0 Universal (CC0 1.0)

p. 92 Ithell Colquhoun, *Oread* (1970) Gouache. Dimensions unknown. Image courtesy of Richard Shillitoe. © Samaritans, Noise Abatement Society and Spire Healthcare

p. 94–95 Lamorna, Cornwall. Photo courtesy of James J. Conway

p. 102 Colquhoun's studio in Lamorna, Vow Cave. © Tate Gallery

p. 103 Architectural drawings for the improvement of Vow Cave. © Tate Gallery

p. 110 Mên-an-Tol from J.T. Blight's *A Week at the Land's End*, Truro: Lake and Lake, 1893.

p. 131 Ithell Colquhoun, *Dance of the Nine Opals* (1942) Oil on canvas. 22½ x 28in. (51 x 69cm.) Slide reproduction of original. © Tate Gallery

p. 132 Ithell Colquhoun, *Dance of the Nine Maidens* (1940) Watercolour and pencil on onion skin paper. 17½ x 11¼in. (45 x 29cm.) © Tate Gallery

p. 135–136 Ithell Colquhoun, *Stalactite* (1962) Oil on board. 58 x 14in. (147.4 x 35cm.) Image courtesy of Richard Shillitoe. © Samaritans, Noise Abatement Society and Spire Healthcare

p. 153 Ithell Colquhoun, *La Cathédrale Engloutie* (1952) Oil on canvas. 51½ x 77in. (131 x 195cm.) image courtesy of Sacha Llewellyn. © Samaritans, Noise Abatement Society and Spire Healthcare

p. 154 Ithell Colquhoun, *Oil and Water Nymph* (1964) Oil on board. 42 x 28½in. (108 x 73cm.) Image courtesy of Richard Shillitoe. © Samaritans, Noise Abatement Society and Spire Healthcare

p. 157 Autumn Equinox ceremony designed for the Golden Section Order Society © Tate

p. 164 Bird of Hermes from The Ripley Scroll. Public Domain, image courtesy of Beinecke Rare Book and Manuscript Library, Yale University

p. 174 Figure 8, *Book of Lambspring*

p. 185 Ithell Colquhoun, Untitled, two lovers (c. 1940–1941) Pen and watercolour, dimensions unknown. © Tate

p. 186 Ithell Colquhoun, Untitled, two women lovers (c. 1940–1941) Ink and pen on celluloid, dimensions unknown © Tate

p. 191 Ithell Colquhoun, *Diagrams of Love: The Bird or the Egg* (c. 1940) Watercolour. 10.3 x 6.5in. (25.5 x 16.5cm.) © Tate

p. 192 Ithell Colquhoun, *Virgin on the Knees of Saint Anne* (ud) Ink and watercolour, 5 x 7in. (approx.) © Tate

p. 248 Claude Bragdon from *Primer of Higher Space*, Rochester, NY, The Manas Press, 1913

p. 249 Hinton Cubes, Charles Howard Hinton. *The Fourth dimension.* G. Allen & Unwin Ltd, 1912

p. 250 Ithell Colquhoun, *Mystic Figure* (after Shillitoe) (c. 1940) Gouache and ink. 14 x 10in. (35.5 x 25.4cm.) © Tate Gallery

p.251 Claude Bragdon from *Primer of Higher Space*, Rochester, NY, The Manas Press, 1913

IMAGE CREDITS

p. 253 Ithell Colquhoun, *Horus* (c. 1957) Ink and wash. 9¾ x 10in. (25 x 26cm.) © Tate

p. 254 Ithell Colquhoun, *Mên-an-Tol* sketch with Tesseract (c. 1942) Watercolour and pen on paper, dimensions unknown © Tate Gallery

p. 255 Ithell Colquhoun, Figure with Tesseract (c. 1940s) Watercolour and metallic paints on greaseproof paper. 14.9 x 22 in. (38cm x 56cm.) © Tate Gallery

p. 256 Ithell Colquhoun, *Princess of the Echoing Hills* from *Taro of Colour* (1977) Enamel on paper. 29½ x 33½in. (75 x 85cm.) © Tate Gallery

p. 268 The Hand of Ithell Altar, (2016). © Photograph courtesy of Steve Patterson

p. 275 Linder, *Sisters of the Mantic Stain VIII*, 2019 Enamel on magazine page. 29.6 x 21cm 11 5/8 x 8 1/4 in. © the artist. Courtesy of the artist and Modern Art, London

p. 276 Linder, *Superautomatism XVIII*, (2015) Enamel on magazine page. 26.6 x 19.4cm 10 1/2 x 7 5/8in framed: 44 x 36.5cm, 17 3/8 x 14 3/8in. © the artist. Courtesy of the artist and Modern Art, London

p. 278 Linder, *Diagrams of Love: Marriage of Eyes*, (2015) Gun tufted rug. 220 x 220cm 86 5/8 x 86 5/8in. © the artist. Courtesy of Modern Art, London and Dovecot Studios Ltd

p. 278 Linder, *Children of the Mantic Stain*. Performance by Northern Ballet, Leeds, 2015. Choreography, Kenneth Tindall, score, Maxwell Sterling. © the artist. Courtesy of Modern Art, London; Northern Ballet, 2015 and Dovecot Studios Ltd. Images: Justin Slee

p. 279 Catalogue image from 'Ithell Colquhoun: Paintings', Mayor Gallery, 1947. Image courtesy of Ossian Brown.

p. 280 *Dryad: Vine* (1971) Gouache. 8 x 8in. (20.3 x 20.3cm.) Image courtesy of Ossian Brown.

ENDNOTES

'Already I knew my own mind' II

1 Colquhoun 'Paganism' ud. Mss at TGA 929/2/1/46

2 *Ibid.*

3 *Tauranga Memories: Battles of Gate Pa and Te Ranga* (1864) William George Nicholas Manley (1831–1901) PERMA.CC/4DSQ-JXG3

4 Colquhoun, Catalogue notes for Surrealism – *Ithell Colquhoun: Paintings, Drawings, Collages 1936–1976*. Newlyn Art Gallery, 1976.

5 'The Seraphic Doctor' is a reference to St. Bonaventure. Colquhoun's 'Lesbian Shore' ud. mss at TGA 929/2/1/33

6 Mr. Seaton White. *Gloucestershire Echo*. 10 February, 1936

'OBJECTIVE HAZARD': Surrealism III

7 John Russell. 'In 1936, Surrealism Ruled the Creative Roost' *New York Times*. 30, March, 1986. PERMA.CC/2C9Q-K4N5

8 Colquhoun, Notes for Surrealism Catalogue, Newlyn Art Gallery 1976.

9 *Ibid.*

10 Autobiographical notes at TGA 929/2/1/68/3/3

11 'Collage Habit' *The Scotsman* Monday 19th June, 1939.

12 Colquhoun, Notes on Surrealist Exhibition, 1976, Newlyn Art Gallery.

13 Martica Sawain. 'Roberta Matta' Latin American Masters. PERMA.CC/FY4P-3H7T

14 Miranda Lash. 'Boxed In: Imagining the Unseen in Roberto Matta's Cube Constructions.' *RES: Anthropology and Aesthetics*, no. 55/56 (2009): 267–78. PERMA.CC/6FGK-WC22

15 Correspondence to Colquhoun from Harrogate Civic Entertainments league at TGA 929/1/853

16 Dawn Ades. 'Notes on Two Women Surrealist Painters: Eileen Agar and Ithell Colquhoun.' *Oxford Art Journal*, 1980: 36–43.

17 Ithell Colquhoun. 'Letter to the Editor.' *Oxford Art Journal*, 1981: 65.

18 Whitney Chadwick. *Women Artists and the Surrealist Movement*. New York: Thames and Hudson, 1985.

19 It may be notable that the phrase 'circumcised hermaphrodite' that we see in *The Pine Family* was also an anti-Semitic slur levelled in 1936 at the French socialist Prime Minister, André Léon Blum, by conservative monarchist Léon Daudet. While *Pine Family* probably refers to mythic themes, the specific nature of this phrase may well have suggested an additional political reading to Francophone audiences, given that Blum was imprisoned by the Vichy government when the painting was completed.

20 'Toni del Renzio: Enfant terrible of English Surrealism'. *The Independent* Friday 12 January 2007 also Obituary: Toni del Renzio. *The Guardian* 18 January, 2007.

21 Silvano Levy. 'The Del Renzio Affair: A Leadership Struggle in Wartime Surrealism.' Papers of Surrealism Issue 3, 2005: 1–34. p. 4.

*All links available via PERMA.CC initiative.

ENDNOTES

22 Richard Shillitoe. 'New Apocalypse'. PERMA.CC/UC8R-H95S

23 Silvano Levy. *The Scandalous Eye: The Surrealism of Conroy Maddox*. Liverpool: Liverpool University Press, 2003., p. 78.

24 Conroy Maddox to Colquhoun, 14 November 1941 at TGA 929/1/1084-1092

25 See letters at TGA 929/1/1084-1092

26 Derek Stanford. *Inside the Forties: Literary Memoirs 1937–1957*. London: Sidgewick and Jackson, 1977. p. 71.

27 Levy, 'The Del Renzio Affair' 2005, 5.

28 Stanford, *Inside the Forties* 1977 p. 103.

29 Stanford, *Inside the Forties* p. 72.

30 Stanford, *Inside the Forties* p.103.

31 Levy, 'The Del Renzio Affair' 2005.

32 Shillitoe notes that this dating may have been an error and added later.

33 Ithell Colquhoun. 'The Mantic Stain.' *Enquiry* 2 no. 4: pp 15–21.

34 Ithell Colquhoun. 'Children of the Mantic Stain.' *Athene* 5 no. 2: pp 29–34.

35 Edward Langford Garstin. *The Secret Fire: An Alchemical Study*. London: Search Publishing, 1932. Chapter 2, PERMA.CC/X3LA-7RQ4

36 Colquhoun, *The Mantic Stain*, 1949.

37 Colquhoun's Chaim poems exist at TGA 929/2/2/3

38 Ithell Colquhoun. 'The Chain Poem.' *TRANSFORMAcTION* no. 5: pp. 22–23.

39 Colquhoun, 'Notes on Automatism.' *Melmoth* no. 2, 1980. pp 31–32 draft typescript at TGA 929/2/1/40/1

40 Ithell Colquhoun, 'Little Anthology of Inadvertent Surrealism' mss at TGA 929/6/4

41 Mary Ann Caws. 'Linkings and Reflections: André Breton and His Communicating Vessels.' *Dada/ Surrealism* 17 1988. pp. 91–100.

42 Some of Alice Buck's correspondence records can be found at PERMA.CC/Y7PC-Z94F

See also Colquhoun's 1955 Essay 'Divination up to Date' from *The London Broadsheet* where she discusses the state of dream research.

43 Buck to Colquhoun 20 May, 1952 at TGA 929/1/235

44 Buck to Colquhoun 30 September, 1961 at TGA 929/1/235-252

45 Philip Payton provides a more Cornish centred commentary on the Newlyn and St. Ives arts movements. See Philip Payton, *Cornwall : A History*, Fowey : Cornwall Editions Ltd, 2004

46 Joshua Blu Buhs. 'Antony Borrow as a Fortean'. 12, July 2016. PERMA.CC/FNQ7-TN8A

47 Ithell Colquhoun. 'Recollection of Kurt Schwitters' 1969 mss at TGA 929/2/1/55

48 Silvano Levy, *The Scandalous Eye*, 2003 P. 136

49 Shillitoe 'Osmazone', PERMA.CC/T7H6-LB3S

50 Ithell Colquhoun, 'Divination' in *Until Twelve* at TGA 929/2/1/68/1

ENDNOTES

Atlantean currents: Celticism

IV

51 Colquhoun, 1955. p. 45.

52 Colquhoun, *The Living Stones*, 1957 p. 126.

53 Colquhoun, 'Pilgrimage.' *Sangreal 2* no. 1, 1979. pp 29–31.

54 Colquhoun, *The Crying of the Wind*, 46.

55 Colquhoun *The Blue Anoubis* unpublished mss, c. 1967. p. 46. Found at TGA 929/2/1/6/8

'A stream of power, set in motion': Occultism

V

56 Also spelled Bourkoun.

57 For the fuller explication of this idea see Wouter Hanegraaff *Esotericism and the Academy: Rejected Knowledge in Western Culture*. Cambridge: Cambridge University Press, 2012.

58 For more detail on the roots of Perennialist philosophy see John Herlihy (ed) *The Essential Rene Guenon: Metaphysics, Tradition, and the Crisis of Modernity*, Bloomington IN: World Wisdom Press, 2009. Also Aldous Huxley's popular introduction to the subject *The Perennial Philosophy: An Interpretation of the Great Mystics, East and West*, New York: Harper Perennial, 2012.

59 Rudolf Steiner, Christopher Bamford, (ed.) *The Archangel Michael, His Mission and Ours: Selected Lectures and Writings*. Gt. Barrington: Anthroposophic Press, 1994, p. 3.

60 Annie Besant. *Esoteric Christianity or The Lesser Mysteries*. 1902 pp. 159–160.

61 Colquhoun from 'Faith' in Until Twelve, unpublished undated mss. at TGA 929/2/1/68/1

62 Colquhoun, 'Bird of Hermes' c. 1926. Unpublished mss. at TGA 929/2/1/5

63 Ithell Colquhoun. 'Memoir of E.J.L. Garstin.' *The Hermetic Journal* no. 6: 11. p. 6.

64 Ithell Colquhoun, 'The Connection Between Mysticism and Blasphemy' c. 1928/1929 unpublished mss at TGA 929/2/3/2

65 Ithell Colquhoun, 'Images of Joy'. Undated mss at TGA 929/2/1/52/38

66 Colquhoun, *The Sword of Wisdom: MacGregor Mathers and the Golden Dawn*. London: G.P. Putnam's Sons, 1975. p. 21.

67 Letter from David Gasgoyne to Ithell Colquhoun 23 March, 1946 at TGA 929/1/768

68 Samuel MacGregor Mathers. *Kabbala Denudata: The Kabbalah Unveiled*, trans. 1912 [1887], pp. 720, 723, 724. PERMA.CC/R2HG-G33W

69 Aleister Crowley. *Book of Lies*, 1913 Chapter 69. PERMA.CC/KME7-YQBZ

70 Ithell Colquhoun. 'Union Pacific' undated mss at TGA 929/2/2/14

71 Edward Garstin. *The Secret Fire: An Alchemical Study*, 1932 text at PERMA.CC/7W4K-UUAF

72 Colquhoun, 'Openings of the Body' *Quest* no 4, 1970, pp. 9–10.

73 From an undated personal note by Colquhoun at TGA 929/1/245

74 Ithell Colquhoun. 'The Water-stone of the Wise.' In *New Road* 1943, edited by Alex Comfort and John Bayliss, Billericay, Essex: The Grey Walls Press 1943 p. 198–199.

75 André Breton. 'Prolegomena to a Third Surrealist Manifesto (or Not)' in André Breton, *Manifestoes of Surrealism*, Richard Seaver and Helen R. Lane trans. Ann Arbor: University of Michigan Press, pp. 279–294. This quote from pages 287–288.

76 Colquhoun, 'Water Stone of the Wise' 1943.

ENDNOTES

77 *Kabbalah Unveiled* Chapter 8, verse 275.

78 Ithell Colquhoun. draft mss of *I Saw Water* at TGA 929/2/1/31

79 Draft letter Colquhoun to Mallock, April 1956. Private collection.

80 See here for the current requirements for full initiation in the Society of the Inner Light: PERMA.CC/RNU2-UDWS

81 Colquhoun, 'Two Pupils and a Master.' Prediction 37 no.10: 12–14.

82 Undated note at TGA 929/1/4

83 Letters from Karl Germer to Colquhoun, 23 June, 1953, 26 July 1953. Private Collection.

84 Colquhoun, 'The Dying-Kick of the Dying-God.' *The London Broadsheet* no. 4, 1955.

85 Colquhoun, 'The Laughing Torso' undated unpublished mss. Private collection.

86 Colquhoun, 'Tally Ho' undated unpublished mss. Private collection.

87 Frontispiece, *The Goose of Hermogenes.*

88 See Eirenaeus Philalethes, *An Open Entrance to the Closed Palace of the King* 1667 'Chapter 1: Of the need of Sulphur for producing the Elixir' text found at PERMA.CC/Z69F-JGSM

89 Colquhoun, *Goose of Hermogenes,* London: Peter Owen 1961 pp. 25–26.

90 Colquhoun, *Goose of Hermogenes*, 1961 p. 98.

91 *Ibid.*

92 Letter from Ronald White to Colquhoun dated 25 June, 1967 at TGA 929/5/31/4

93 For more commentary on how literary scholars fail to deal with actual occult practice, see comments in William Gorski, *Yeats and Alchemy*. New York: SUNY Press, 1996.

94 William Butler Yeats. *Ideas of Good and Evil*, AH Bullen, 1907, p. 67. Full text also at PERMA.CC/R7PR-WXW3

95 Correspondence from 'Terence' to Colquhoun dated 28 October, 1960. TGA 929/5/17

96 Timothy d'Arch Smith. *The Times Deceas'd: the Rare Book Department of the Times Bookshop in the 1960s*. Settrington, York: Stone Trough Books, 2003.

97 Michael Howard. *Wicca: A History from Gerald Gardner to the Present*. Woodbury, MN: Llewellyn Books, 2009 e book location 920.

98 Colquhoun, *Sword of Wisdom*, pp. 41–42.

99 Colquhoun, 'Flashing Colours and the Zodiac'. *Hermetic Journal* 1979. p. 4

100 Linda Dalrymple Henderson. *The Fourth Dimension and Non-Euclidean Geometry in Modern Art*. Cambridge: MIT Press 2013 [1983] p. 2

101 *Ibid.*

102 Charles Hinton. *A New Era of Thought*. London: Swan Sonnenschein and Son, 1888 p. 147.

103 Claude Bragdon. Primer of Higher Space Rochester, NY: The Manas Press 1913, Fig. 30.

104 P.D. Ouspensky. *Tertium Organum: The Third Canon of Thought and A Key to the Enigmas of the World*. Charles Bragdon trans. New York: Alfred Knopf, 1922 [1912] p.162.

105 *Ibid.* p. 161.

106 Ithell Colquhoun. 'Dimensional Interrelation: A Meditation on the Platonic Solids'. Undated unpublished manuscript at TGA 929/2/1/21

107 Steve Nichols. *The Magical Writings of Ithell Colquhoun*. Lulu publishing, 2007, pp. 163–266.

108 Colquhoun, 'The Taro as Colour.' Unpublished mss. that accompanied show at Newlyn Art Gallery TGA 929/2/1/62.

109 'Book T' is the inner Golden Dawn document providing guidance on Tarot and instructions on creating and using a tarot deck. See Samuel Mathers. c. 1896 'Book T – The Tarot.' Book T found in Regardie, 1989 [1937] *The Golden Dawn*, pp. 540–565.

110 Richard Dudschus and David Sledzinski. *Coloring the Classic Golden Dawn Tarot*. Renton, Washington: D&S Publishing, 2005.

'More Brilliant Than Crystal': The Legacy VI

111 Ithell Colquhoun. 'Clever Women' unpublished undated mss at TGA 929/2/1/9

112 Steve Patterson. 'Robert Lenkiewicz, Ithell Colquhoun, 'Ancient Scent' and an Alchemical Experiment!' PERMA.CC/DQK2-7QMR

113 Linder Sterling private communication to author, 17 November, 2019.

114 Richard Foster. *A Cut Above: Linder Sterling On Art & Ludus*, 17 January, 2017.

BIBLIOGRAPHY

Sources

Much of the research for this book was undertaken in the Hyman Kreitman Reading Rooms at the Tate. Documents used from that collection are detailed in the notes, with their Tate Gallery Archives (TGA) reference number. In some cases manuscripts were kindly provided to me from private collections.

To date, Richard Shillitoe has compiled the most complete catalogue of Colquhoun's work, and has also compiled a list of all Colquhoun's published works which can be found in his invaluable *Ithell Colquhoun: Magician Born of Nature.*

Select Bibliography

Aberth, Susan, *Leonora Carrington: Surrealism, Alchemy and Art* (Surrey, Lund Humphries, 2004).

Ades, Dawn, 'Notes on Two Women Surrealist Painters: Eileen Agar and Ithell Colquhoun' *Oxford Art Journal*, 1980: 36–43.

Besant, Annie, *Esoteric Christianity or The Lesser Mysteries* (London, Theosophical Society, 1901) [1898].

Borlase, William, *Antiquities, historical and monumental, of the county of Cornwall. Consisting of several essays on the first inhabitants, druid-superstition, customs, and remains of the most remote antiquity in Britain, and the British Isles, exemplified and proved by monuments now extant in Cornwall and the Scilly Islands, with a vocabulary of the Cornu-British language* (London, Printed by W. Bowyer and J. Nichols, for S. Baker and G. Leigh, 1769).

Bottrell, William, *Traditions and Hearthside Stories of West Cornwall* (Newcastle upon Tyne, Graham, 1970) [1870].

Bowman, Marion, 'Cardiac Celts: Images of the Celts in Contemporary British Paganism', in Graham Harvey and Charlotte Hardman, (eds.) *Paganism Today* (London, Thorsons, 1995).

Bowman, Marion, 'Contemporary Celtic Spirituality', in Joanne Pearson (ed) *Belief Beyond Boundaries Volume 5: Wicca, Celtic Spirituality and the New Age* (Aldershot, Ashgate, 2002) pp. 55–101.

Bragdon, Claude, *Primer of Higher Space* (Rochester, NY, The Manas Press, 1913).

Breton, André, 'Prolegomena to a Third Surrealist Manifesto (or Not)' in *Andre Breton: Manifestoes of Surrealism*, Richard Seaver and Helen R. Lane trans. (Ann Arbor, University of Michigan Press, 1969) pp. 279–294.

Brown, Terence (ed.) *Celticism* (Amsterdam, Brill/Rodopi, 1996).

Caws, Mary Ann, 'Linkings and Reflections: André Breton and His Communicating Vessels', *Dada/Surrealism* 17 1988. pp. 91–100.

BIBLIOGRAPHY

Chadwick, Whitney, *Women Artists and the Surrealist Movement* (New York, Thames and Hudson, 1985).

Chadwick, Whitney (ed) *Mirror Images: Women, Surrealism and Self-Representation* (Cambridge: The MIT Press, 1998).

Chapman, Malcolm, *The Celts: Construction of a Myth* (London, Palgrave Macmillan, 1992).

Choucha, Nadia, *Surrealism and the Occult* (Oxford, Mandrake, 1991).

Cicero, Chic and Cicero, Tabatha, *The New Golden Dawn Ritual Tarot* (Woodbury MN, Llewellyn Publications, 2010).

Colquhoun, Ithell, 'The Water-stone of the Wise', in *New Road* 1943 (eds.) Alex Comfort and John Bayliss (Billericay, The Grey Walls Press, 1943) pp. 198–199.

Colquhoun, Ithell, 'The Mantic Stain', *Enquiry* 2 no. 4, 1949, pp. 15–21.

Colquhoun, Ithell, 'Children of the Mantic Stain', *Athene* 5 no. 2, 1951, pp. 29–34.

Colquhoun, Ithell, *The Crying of the Wind: Ireland* (London, Peter Owen Publishing, 1955).

Colquhoun, Ithell, *The Living Stones: Cornwall* (London, Peter Owen Publishing, 1957).

Colquhoun, Ithell, *Goose of Hermogenes* (London, Peter Owen, 1961).

Colquhoun, Ithell, 'The Chain Poem', *TRANSFORMAcTION* no. 5, 1973, pp. 22–23.

Colquhoun, Ithell, 'Notes on Automatism', *Melmoth* no. 2, 1980.

Colquhoun, Ithell, 'Two Pupils and a Master', *Prediction* 37 no.10, 1971, pp.12–14.

Colquhoun, Ithell, *The Sword of Wisdom: Mac Gregor Mathers and the Golden Dawn* (London, G.P. Putnam, 1975).

Colquhoun, Ithell, catalogue notes for *Surrealism – Ithell Colquhoun: Paintings, Drawings, Collages 1936–1976* (Newlyn Art Gallery, 1976).

Colquhoun, Ithell, 'Memoir of E.J.L. Garstin', *The Hermetic Journal* no. 6, 1979, p. 11.

Colquhoun, Ithell, 'Letter to the Editor', *Oxford Art Journal*, 1981, p. 65.

Colquhoun, Ithell, (eds.) Richard Shillitoe and Mark Morrison, *I Saw Water: An Occult Novel and Other Selected Writings* (University Park, Penn State University Press, 2014).

Colquhoun, Ithell, *Decad of Intelligence* (London, Fulgur Press, 2017).

Colquhoun, Ithell, 'The Taro as Colour', in A. Hale and R. Ansell (eds) *Taro as Colour*, (Somerset: Fulgur, 2018).

Colquhoun, Ithell, *Until Twelve*. Unpublished mss c. 1940s. TGA 929/2/1/68/1

Comte de Lautréamont, *Maldoror and the Complete Works of the Comte de Lautréamont*. A. Lykiard (trans.) (Cambridge: Exact Change, 1994).

Cross, Tom, *Painting the Warmth of the Sun: St. Ives Artists 1939–1975* (Tiverton, Westcountry Books, 1995).

Crowley, Aleister, *The Book of Thoth* (Stamford, CT, Samuel Weiser, 1974) [1944].

Crowley, Aleister, *The Book of Lies* (Newburyport, MA: Weiser Press, 2010).

Cullingford, Elizabeth, *Yeats, Ireland and Fascism* (London, Palgrave MacMillan, 1984.)

D'Arch Smith, Timothy, *The Books of the Beast: Essays on Aleister Crowley, Montague Summers, Francis Barrett and Others* (London, Crucible Press, 1987).

BIBLIOGRAPHY

D'Arch Smith, Timothy, *The Times Deceas'd: The Rare Book Department of the Times Bookshop in the 1960s* (Settrington, York, Stone Trough Books, 2003).

Deacon, Bernard, Andrew George and Ronald Perry, *Cornwall at the Crossroads: Living Communities or Leisure Zone?* (Cornish Social & Economic Research Group, 1988).

Deacon, Bernard, Dick Cole and Garry Tregidga, *Mebyon Kernow and Cornish Nationalism* (Cardiff, Welsh Academic Press, 2003).

Deacon, Bernard, *Cornwall: A Concise History* (Cardiff, University of Wales Press, 2007).

Dietler, Michael, 'Celticism, Celtitude and Celticity: The Consumption of the Past in the age of Globalization', in Sabine Rieckhoff (ed) *Celtes et Gaulois dans l'histoire, l'historiographie et l'idéologie moderne.* Actes de la table ronde de Leipzig, 16-17 Juin 2005, Glux-en-Glenne: Bibracte, Centre Archéologique Européen (Bibracte 12/1), 2006, pp. 237-248.

Dudschus, Richard and Sledzinski, David, *Coloring the Classic Golden Dawn Tarot* (Renton, Washington: D&S Publishing, 2005).

Engels, David, 'Oswald Spengler and *The Decline of the West*' in Mark Sedgwick (ed.), *Key Thinkers of the Radical Right: Behind the New Threat to Liberal Democracy* (Oxford, Oxford University Press, 2019).

Ferentinou, Victoria, 'Ithell Colquhoun, Surrealism and the Occult', *Papers of Surrealism* 9, 2011, pp. 1-24. PERMA.CC/W8MY-QPGH

Ferentinou, Victoria, 'The Iconography of Coniunctio Oppositorum: Visual and Verbal Dialogues in Ithell Colquhoun's Oeuvre', in Peter Forshaw (ed) *Lux in Tenebris: The Visual and the Symbolic in Western Esotericism*, 2016. pp. 363-96.

Ferentinou, Victoria, 'The Quest for the Goddess: Matriarchy, Surrealism and Gender Politics in the Work of Ithell Colquhoun and Leonora Carrington' in Tessel Bauduin, Victoria Ferentinou and Daniel Zamani (eds.), *Surrealism, Occultism and Politics: In Search of the Marvellous* (London: Routledge, 2017).

Fortune, Dion, *The Esoteric Philosophy of Love and Marriage* (Newburyport, MA, Weiser, 2009).

Frazer, James George, *The Golden Bough* (New York, Macmillan and Co. 1963) [1922].

Gardner, Gerald, *Witchcraft Today* (London, Rider and Co., 1954).

Gardner, Gerald, *The Meaning of Witchcraft* (Newburyport, Samuel Weiser, 1971) [1959].

Garstin, Edward Langford, *Theurgy or the Hermetic Practice: A Treatise on Spiritual Alchemy* (London, Rider and Co, 1930).

Garstin, Edward Langford, *The Secret Fire: An Alchemical Study* (London, Search Publishing, 1932).

Gorski, William, *Yeats and Alchemy* (New York, SUNY Press, 1996).

Graves, Robert, *The White Goddess* (London: Faber and Faber, 1948).

Gribben, Arthur, *Holy Wells and Sacred Water Sources in Britain and Ireland: An Annotated Bibliography* (New York, Garland Press, 1992).

Greer, Mary Kay, *Women of the Golden Dawn: Rebels and Priestesses: Maud Gonne, Moina Bergson Mathers, Annie Horniman, Florence Farr* (Rochester, Park Street Press, 1995).

Hale, Amy, *Gathering the Fragments: Performing Contemporary Celtic Identities in Cornwall* (PhD Thesis, University of California, Los Angeles, 1998).

BIBLIOGRAPHY

Hale, Amy, 'In the Eye of the Sun: The Relationship between the Cornish Gorseth and Esoteric Druidry,' in Philip Payton (ed) *Cornish Studies 8* (Exeter, University of Exeter Press, 2000).

Hale, Amy, 'The Land Near the Dark Cornish Sea: The Development of Tintagel as a Celtic Pilgrimage Site', in *The Journal for the Academic Study of Magic* Volume 2, 2004.

Hale, Amy, 'John Michell, Radical Traditionalism and the Emerging Politics of the Pagan New Right' in *The Pomegranate: Journal of International Pagan Studies*, Vol. 13, no 1, 2012, pp. 77-97.

Hale, Amy, 'Reigning with Swords of Meteoric Iron: Archangel Michael and the Politics of Celtic Spirituality' in Joanne Parker (ed) *The Harp and the Constitution: Myths of Celtic and Gothic Origin 1700–2000* (Leiden, Brill, 2016).

Hale, Amy, 'Colours are Forces, The Signatures of the Forces': An Exploration of Colour as Entity, in *I:MAGE Travelling with Unfamiliar Spirits* eds. Robert Ansell and Livia Filotico (Somerset, Fulgur, 2014).

Hale, Amy, 'Introduction', in Colquhoun, Ithell, *Decad of Intelligence* (Somerset, Fulgur, 2017).

Hanegraaff, Wouter, *Esotericism and the Academy: Rejected Knowledge in Western Culture* (Cambridge: Cambridge University Press, 2012).

Hardie, Melissa (ed.) *100 Years in Newlyn: Diary of a Gallery* (Penzance: Patten Press, 1995).

Henderson, Linda Dalrymple, *The Fourth Dimension and Non-Euclidean Geometry in Modern Art* (Cambridge, MIT Press, 2013) [1983].

Herlihy, John (ed.) *The Essential Rene Guenon: Metaphysics, Tradition, and the Crisis of Modernity* (Bloomington IN: World Wisdom Press, 2009).

Hinton, Charles, *A New Era of Thought* (London, Swan Sonnenschein and Son, 1888).
Howard, Michael, *Wicca: A History from Gerald Gardner to the Present* (Woodbury, MN: Llewellyn Books, 2009).

Howe, Ellic, *Magicians of the Golden Dawn: A Documentary History of a Magical Order, 1887–1923* (London, Routledge and Kegan Paul, 1972).

Hunt, Robert, *Popular Romances of the West of England: Or the Drolls, Traditions, and Superstitions of Old Cornwall* (London, John Camden Hotten, 1865).

Hutton, Ronald, *The Triumph of the Moon: A History of Modern Pagan Witchcraft* (Oxford, Oxford University Press, 1999).

Huxley, Aldous, *The Perennial Philosophy: An Interpretation of the Great Mystics, East and West* (New York, Harper Perennial, 2012).

Jenkins, Geraint H., *Facts, Fantasy and Fiction: The Historical Vision of Iolo Morganwg* (Aberystwyth, University of Wales Centre for Advanced Welsh and Celtic Studies, 1997).

Knowles, Elizabeth, Catalogue of the list of works from Ithell Colquhoun's studio. The National Trust (unpublished), 1990.

Lash, Miranda, 'Boxed In: Imagining the Unseen in Roberto Matta's Cube Constructions', *RES: Anthropology and Aesthetics*, no. 55/56, 2009 pp. 267-78. PERMA.CC/6FGK-WC22

Levy, Silvano, *The Scandalous Eye: The Surrealism of Conroy Maddox* (Liverpool, Liverpool University Press, 2003).

Levy, Silvano, 'The Del Renzio Affair: A Leadership Struggle in Wartime Surrealism', *Papers of Surrealism* Issue 3, 2005, pp. 1-34.

Levy, Silvano and del Renzio, Toni, 'Toni del Renzio in extremis: Alter Ego and Doppelganger', *Papers of Surrealism*, Issue 6, 2007, pp. 1-13.

Lingan, Edmund B., *The Theatre of the Occult Revival Alternative Spiritual Performance from 1875 to the Present* (New York, Palgrave Macmillan, 2014).

Mann, Neil, Gibson, Matthew and Nally, Claire (eds), *W. B. Yeats's A Vision: Explications and Contexts* (Clemson, SC: Clemson University Press, 2012).

Mathers, S. L. MacGregor (Samuel Liddell MacGregor), 1854–1918, and Christian Knorr von Rosenroth, *The Kabbalah Unveiled: Containing the Following Books of the Zohar: The Book of Concealed Mystery; The Greater Holy Assembly; The Lesser Holy Assembly* (London, Routledge Kegan Paul, 1962) [1887].

Melly, George, *Don't Tell Sybil: An Intimate Memoir of E.L.T. Mesens* (London, Random House, 1997).

Michell, John, *The New View Over Atlantis* (London, Thames and Hudson, 1995).

Montua, Gabriel Götz, '1925 – Montevideo in the Orient: Lautréamont's Ascent Among the Paris Surrealists', in *Journal of Surrealism and the Americas* Volume 3, nos. 1-2, 2009, pp. 51–83.

Mundy, Jennifer (ed.) *Surrealism: Desire Unbound* (Princeton, Princeton University Press, 2001).

Murray, Margaret, *The Witch-Cult in Western Europe: A Study in Anthropology* (Oxford, Clarendon Press, 1962) [1921].

Nally, Claire, 'The Political Occult: Revisiting Fascism, Yeats and A Vision', in Neil Mann, Matthew Gibson and Claire Nally (eds) *W. B. Yeats's A Vision: Explications and Contexts* (Clemson University Digital Press, 2012).

Nichols, Steve, *The Magical Writings of Ithell Colquhoun* (Raleigh, North Carolina: Lulu Enterprises, 2007).

Ouspensky, P.D., *Tertium Organum: The Third Canon of Thought and A Key to the Enigmas of the World*, trans. Charles Bragdon (New York, Alfred Knopf, 1922) [1912].

Owen, Alex, *The Place of Enchantment: British Occultism and the Culture of the Modern* (Chicago, University of Chicago Press, 2004).

Payton, Philip, *The Making of Modern Cornwall: Historical Experience and the Persistence of 'Difference'* (Redruth, Dyllansow Truran, 1992).

Payton, Philip, *Cornwall: A History* (Fowey, Cornwall Editions Ltd, 2004).

Pearson, Joanne, *Wicca and the Christian Heritage: Ritual, Sex and Magic* (London, Routledge, 2007).

Philalethes, Eirenaeus (George Starkey), *An Open Entrance to the Closed Palace of the King.* (Seattle, Amazon Digital Services, 2010) [1667].

Philalethes, Eirenaeus, *The Three Treatises Of Philalethes: The Metamorphosis Of Metals; The Celestial Ruby; The Fountain Of Chemical Truth* (Montana, Kessenger Publishing, 2010).

Piper, Raymond Frank, *The Hungry Eye: An Introduction to Cosmic Art* (Los Angeles, DeVorss and Co., 1956).

Polizzotti, Mark, *Revolution of the Mind: The Life of André Breton* (New York, Farrar, Straus & Giroux, 1995).

Ratcliffe, Eric, *Ithell Colquhoun: Pioneer Surrealist Artist, Occultist, Writer and Poet* (Oxford, Mandrake Press, 2007).

Regardie, Israel, *The Golden Dawn: The Original Account of the Teachings, Rites & Ceremonies of the Hermetic Order: An Account of the Teachings, Rites and Ceremonies of The Hermetic Order of the Golden Dawn* (St. Paul MN: Llewellyn Publishing, 1989) [1937].

Remy, Michel, *Surrealism in Britain* (Aldershot, Ashgate, 1999).

Rosemont, Penelope (ed.) *Surrealist Women: An International Anthology* (Austin, University of Texas Press, 1998).

BIBLIOGRAPHY

Sawain, Martica, 'Roberta Matta' *Latin American Masters.*

Sedgwick, Mark, *Against the Modern World: Traditionalism and the Secret Intellectual History of the Twentieth Century* (Oxford, Oxford University Press, 2009).

Semmens, Jason, *The Cornish Witch-Finder: Henry William Paynter and the Witchery, Ghosts, Charms and Folklore of Cornwall* St. Agnes: Federation of Old Cornwall Societies, 2008.

Shillitoe, Richard, *Ithell Colquhoun: Magician Born of Nature* (Raleigh, North Carolina: Lulu Enterprises, 2010).

Shillitoe, Richard (ed.) *Medea's Charms: Selected Shorter Writings of Ithell Colquhoun* (London: Peter Owen Publishers, 2019).

Souhami, Diana, *Gluck: Her Biography* (New York, Open Road Media, 2014).

Stanford, Derek, *Inside the Forties: Literary Memoirs 1937–1957* (London, Sidgwick and Jackson, 1977).

Steiner, Rudolf, *The Archangel Michael, His Mission and Ours: Selected Lectures and Writings*, Christopher Bamford, ed. (Gt. Barrington, Anthroposophic Press, 1994).

Tuchman, Maurice (ed.) *The Spiritual in Art: Abstract Painting 1890–1985* (New York, Abbeville Press, 1989).

Waite, Arthur Edward, *The Hermetic Museum, Restored and Enlarged: Most Faithfully Instructing All Disciples of the Sopho-spagyric Art how that Greatest and Truest Medicine of the Philosopher's Stone May be Found and Held* (Boston: Red Wheel/Weiser, 1999) [1893].

Waite, Arthur Edward (ed.) *Works of Thomas Vaughan: Eugenius Philalethes* (London, Theosophical Society, 1919).

Watkins, Alfred, *The Old Straight Track* (London, Abacus, 1974) [1925].

Weatherhill, Craig, *Cornovia: Ancient Sites of Cornwall and Scilly, 4000BC–1000AD* (Wellington Somerset, Halsgrove, 2011) [1985].

Wedemeyer, Christian K., *Making Sense of Tantric Buddhism: History, Semiology and Transgression in the Indian Traditions* (New York, Columbia University Press, 2013).

Weston, Jessie L., *From Ritual to Romance* (Cambridge, Cambridge University Press, 1920).

White, Rupert, *The Reenchanted Landscape: Earth Mysteries, Paganism and Art in Cornwall 1950–2000* (Cornwall, Antenna Publications, 2017).

Woodroffe, John (Arthur Avalon), *Shakti and Shâkta* (Seattle, Amazon Digital Services, 2010).

Yeats, William Butler, *Ideas of Good and Evil* (Stratford, AH Bullen Press, 1907).

Yeats, W.B., with Georgie Yeats, *A Vision: An Explanation of Life Founded upon the Writings of Giraldus and upon certain Doctrines attributed to Kusta Ben Luka* (London, T. Werner Laurie, 1925).

Young, Rob, *Electric Eden: Unearthing Britain's Visionary Music* (London, Faber & Faber, 2010).

Acknowledgments

This work has, in many ways, been gestating since the turn of the millennium, and would not have been completed without the support and contributions of many people. I wish to extend my thanks to the following people and organisations.

First to the PAUL MELLON FOUNDATION for financial support in the early stages of this project.

I have exceptional gratitude for ADRIAN GLEW and the archival staff at the TATE HYMAN KREITMAN READING ROOMS for their patience, professionalism and exceptional assistance over many years of visits to them. Especial thanks to VICTORIA JENKINS for her help in assembling the images for this book. Thanks also to SARA MATSON from TATE ST. IVES for her enthusiasm for Colquhoun and her collegiality.

I would also like to give special thanks to the many professionals I have worked with at the NATIONAL TRUST who have cared for the Colquhoun collection over the years: JEREMY PEARSON, BARBARA WOOD, JOANNA CAIRNS, and CHRIS ROWLIN, and especially JO MOORE.

I also want to acknowledge the following for their support, assistance, guidance, friendship and materials: Professor PHILIP PAYTON, Dr. GARRY TREGIDGA and my former colleagues at the Institute of Cornish Studies, University of Exeter, Dr. MELISSA HARDIE of the Hypatia Trust, PHIL BUDDEN, Professor RONALD HUTTON, CAROLINE WISE, MICHAEL STALEY, Professor SUSAN ABERTH, ED MAGGS, Dr. CHRISTINA HARRINGTON, CLIVE HARPER, TIMOTHY D'ARCH SMITH, the members of the OPEN SOURCE ORDER OF THE GOLDEN DAWN, DAVID WIEGLEB, Dr. ELLEN FRANCIK, Professor SABINA MAGLIOCCO, AMY RIHA, Professor DEBORAH SUGG RYAN, BARBARA CORMACK, JOSEPH MAX, JUDITH NOBLE, PHIL HINE, MARIA STRUTZ, RUPERT WHITE, PAM GROSSMAN, JESSE BRANSFORD, JASON SEMMENS, SASHA LLEWELLYN, THE LUCID ART FOUNDATION, and MARK ROWELL.

ACKNOWLEDGMENTS

I am grateful to Steve Patterson and Linder Sterling for sharing their love of Ithell with me and the secrets of how her hand moves in mysterious ways. Special thanks to Peter Bebergal for being the bestest writing buddy and supportive ear a girl could ask for.

I owe a huge debt of gratitude to Richard Shillitoe for support, for permission to use images from his collection, and for all the tremendous work he has done to preserve and promote Colquhoun's work and legacy.

Thank you to Robert Ansell of Fulgur Ltd. for seeing Colquhoun in the bigger picture.

Thank you to Mark Pilkington, and Jamie Sutcliffe from Strange Attractor for being excellent comrades in this work. And to TIHANA SARE for her beautiful and sympathetic book design. I also owe an enormous debt to my editor Phil Baker for smoothing out the prose and understanding the project.

My research could not have been accomplished without the companionship and generosity of Kate Tattersall and Clive Boutle, who provided care and accommodation for me in London during my visits. I genuinely could not have done this without them, and there are no thanks big enough.

To Dr. Robert Puckett, who greatly helped to facilitate the completion of this book. Thank you for your support and encouragement, for indulging my esoteric streams of consciousness, and for sharing all the magic with me.

To Rhett Aultman, who has been on this journey with me for nearly two decades: Thank you for your unwavering faith in me and in this vision, and for the incredible support that you have given me in all ways. This book is truly your labour of love as it has been mine, and it wouldn't be here without you. No words here are remotely sufficient in expressing my love and deepest gratitude.

Index

INDEX

INDEX

INDEX

INDEX

INDEX

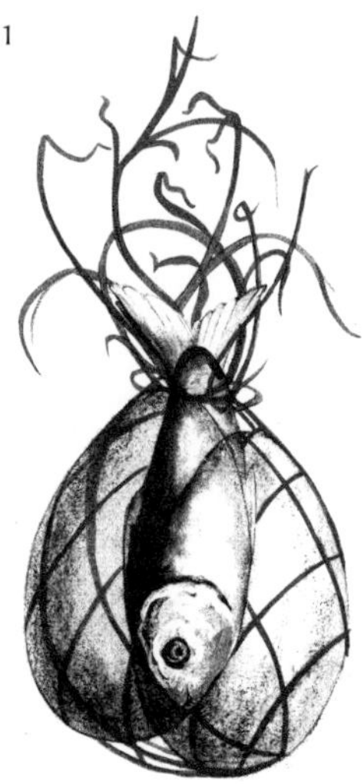

STRANGE ATTRACTOR PRESS 2020